I Remain Yours

I Remain Yours

COMMON LIVES IN
CIVIL WAR LETTERS

Christopher Hager

Harvard University Press

Cambridge, Massachusetts

London, England

2018

SECOND PRINTING

Library of Congress Cataloging-in-Publication Data

Names: Hager, Christopher, 1974– author.

Title: I remain yours : common lives in Civil War letters / Christopher Hager.

Description: Cambridge, Massachusetts : Harvard University Press, 2018. |
Includes bibliographical references and index.

Identifiers: LCCN 2017015477 | ISBN 9780674737648 (cloth)

Subjects: LCSH: United States—History—Civil War, 1861–1865—Sources. |
Letter writing—United States—History. | Soldiers—United States—Correspondence. |
Working class—United States—History—Correspondence. | United States—History—
Civil War, 1861–1865—Personal narratives.

Classification: LCC E468 .H22 2018 | DDC 973.7/8—dc23

LC record available at https://lccn.loc.gov/2017015477

For Josephine and Silvia

Contents

I Remain Yours

Introduction

ON SEPTEMBER 23, 1990, the first episode of Ken Burns's documentary *The Civil War* aired on PBS. It concluded with a letter written in 1861 by Sullivan Ballou, an army officer from Rhode Island, to his wife, Sarah. As many soldiers did on the eve of battle, Ballou had a premonition that this letter might be his last: "O Sarah, if the dead can come back to this earth, and flit unseen around those they loved, I shall always be near you—in the garish day, and the darkest night—amidst your happiest scenes and gloomiest hours—always, always; and, if the soft breeze fans your cheek, it shall be my breath; or the cool air cools your throbbing temples, it shall be my spirit passing by. Sarah, do not mourn me dead; think I am gone, and wait for me, for we shall meet again." While the actor Paul Roebling read these words, viewers saw photograph after photograph of uniformed men standing with their wives and children. After the letter had been read, the film's narrator said, "Sullivan Ballou was killed a week later at the First Battle of Bull Run," and the screen went blank.[1]

I was a high-school student at the time—too young to understand the letter's depth of feeling, appreciate conflicts of conviction, or

sympathize with a husband's longing for his wife. I certainly was old
enough, though, to notice that my father, sitting across the living room
in his usual chair, was crying. There probably has never been another
moment, leaving aside news coverage of assassinations and catastro-
phes, when as many Americans simultaneously wept. There certainly
has been no other instant in which so many were so moved by the
words of a single letter as when nearly forty million people sat before
their televisions and listened to the words of Sullivan Ballou. The next
day, public television stations were flooded with requests for copies of
the letter. Ken Burns later called it "the most beautiful letter I've ever
read," and its beauty has earned it a place as the most famous and best
appreciated Civil War letter.[2]

Sullivan Ballou was exceptional. Educated at Andover and Brown,
a well-to-do attorney who entered the Union army as a major, he
was a likely candidate to write a graceful and memorable letter. He
had practice. Since the dawn of English settlement in North America,
men of Ballou's station in life had been accustomed to writing letters
on a nearly daily basis, for reasons both personal and professional. But
Ballou's eloquence gave him no monopoly on the will to communicate feelings of longing and devotion. Larkin Kendrick, a twenty-
four-year-old farmer, born and raised where the North Carolina
Piedmont rises toward the Blue Ridge Mountains, was serving in the
Confederate army during the first year of the war when he wrote
these words to his wife, Mary Catherine:

> I often think of you and my beloved little children I of ten maid
> the wonder when the son was a setting behin the western Horising
> if it was a shedding its brite Rays on my lovely home I often look
> at the moon and the countless stares and wonder if my belove
> ones is a behold the same seen my Dear companion I never Shal
> forgit you for my love to is as costant as the Wheales of time the
> tim is a huring us on to a neve ending eturnty I hope if we never

meat on earth we may meat where the Sound of the Drum and war whoop is heard no moar.

Sullivan Ballou's education and gentility can be credited only for his spelling, not the lyrical and emotional reach of his words. That comes from some other place, to which poor farmers like Larkin Kendrick had equal access.[3]

THE FIRST MODERN history of Civil War literature, Edmund Wilson's *Patriotic Gore* (1962), began with the sour declaration that "the period of the American Civil War was not one in which belles lettres flourished." Other scholars of his era concurred—one called it an "unwritten war"—and even Walt Whitman, who lived through it, predicted that "the real war will never get in the books." Today a flourishing field of academic study demonstrates just how rich and deep Civil War literary culture was, and it has become customary to remember Wilson's book for its note of disapproval. He went on to say, though, that the Civil War "did produce a remarkable literature which mostly consists of speeches and pamphlets, private letters and diaries, personal memoirs and journalistic reports." Has there ever been a historical event, Wilson marveled, "in which so many people were so articulate?"[4]

He did not mean Larkin Kendrick. Although *Patriotic Gore* is devoted to a literature of the everyday more than to "belles lettres," it still revolves around the work of published authors, wealthy diarists, generals, and statesmen—not poor farmers who had never gone to school. It may seem difficult to muddle through Kendrick's poor spelling and see him as "articulate," but this book is devoted precisely to letters like his—to a Civil War literature authored by ordinary Americans who used letters to hold their families together during a time of great trial.

Part of what makes the Civil War such a remarkable moment in American history is indeed that "so many people were so articulate."

The personal letters that millions of Civil War soldiers and their families wrote to each other between 1861 and 1865 number somewhere close to half a billion. Although it is impossible to be precise, all available estimates point to the same order of magnitude. A Northern relief worker recorded the volume of mail into and out of Union army camps as averaging 180,000 letters per day. Multiplied out for four years of war, that translates into well over 250 million—for the North alone. A New York chaplain tallied 3,855 letters he mailed for his regiment in the single month of April 1863. If his regiment was typical, it suggests soldiers in the Army of the Potomac alone, about one-sixth of federal forces, produced a million outbound letters per month. There is no reliable way to calculate the number of letters soldiers received from civilians, but it would be nearly as large. Any reasonable calculation yields a figure of several hundred million, in a country that had a population slightly over thirty million people and a literacy rate, though among the highest in the world at the time, markedly lower than it is today.[5]

This is to say nothing of official correspondence, telegrams, and the many letters civilians were sending during the war years to addressees other than soldiers. That kind of letter writing had gone on before. In the letters exchanged by common soldiers and their families, the Civil War had sparked something new. As the conflict grew into a great demographic convulsion, with thousands and then millions of men enlisting in armies—many of them traveling farther from home than they had ever gone—the written letter became the essential medium of most Americans' emotional lives.

The Postal Act of 1845 made sending letters significantly cheaper, and the volume of letters carried by the U.S. Post Office Department grew steadily from fewer than two letters per capita per year in 1840 to more than five in 1860. Letter writing undeniably was growing more popular, yet these single-digit figures blend together some very prolific, highly literate people—mostly city dwellers—at one end of a spectrum and, at the other end, a great many people who had never written a letter in their lives. Civil War soldiers wrote, on average, upwards of seventy letters each during the course of their enlistments (which, for some men, lasted all four years of the war, but for many lasted only a year or two or even only a few months). In other words, soldiers—many of whom were little educated and sometimes barely literate—produced at least triple the number, if not ten times the number, of letters the average American had been writing before the war. Their wives and parents, who often matched their husbands and sons letter for letter, were doing about the same. These soldiers and their families *were* "the average American" before the war.[6]

The outbreak of the Civil War thus turned millions of ordinary people into users of a medium with which they had little experience. Even if they had written letters before (and many of them had not), they rarely had done so to communicate with spouses, parents, and children—people who, until a male family member enlisted, dwelled together and could communicate in person on a daily basis. Millions of Americans in every part of the country—New England laborers, western homesteaders, small-time southern farmers—began conducting their most intimate relationships through writing.[7]

These unlettered men and women provide a new perspective on the defining episode in our nation's history. They also show the central role letter writing itself played in that experience, shaping and reshaping the emotional bonds that sustained or drained the men and women of the wartime nation. Filled less with drama than with the ebb and flow of seasons, illnesses, and the simple passage of time, their letters show little of what normally seems historically significant—leaders, battles, politics—but much of the common soldier and his family in the grip of war. They show how separation, and the acts of reading and writing born of separation, transformed their lives. In turn, these novice writers transformed letters. They took a form of expression to which they were strangers—an established genre that long had been the domain of the upper and middle classes—and adapted it to the needs of common people in the tumult of war. They created one of the most eclectic and compelling literatures of the Civil War.

GRANT TAYLOR, a rebel private from Alabama, came home on a furlough at the end of summer in 1862. When it was time for him to rejoin his regiment, his wife, Malinda, and their son, Leonard, took him from their farm to the rail hub in Demopolis. Once back with the army, Grant wrote home: "Malinda, when you left me yesterday I stood and watched you till the buggy did not look larger than a dog. And Oh how lonesome and far from home I felt. It seemed for awhile as if the light had all died out in my heart." Malinda replied:

> The day I left you I knew that you was looking after us. Leonard cried for several Miles before we got out of sight of you. He would say poore Pa is standing there yet. I thought I would venture to look back. I looked back just as you turned to go back. Your beeing at home seems like a dream to me. Grant, I dont think I can feel any wors when you are dead than I did when I got home and opend the doors and saw your coat and hat and the rest of you things that you had wore while you was at home.[8]

Together, Grant and Malinda define the moment letter writing is born. Physical hands unclasped, bodies removed beyond the distance human eyes and voices can cover, a relationship enters the realm of imagination, of "seeming." It is what they *seem* to experience that unites them the instant their connection departs the plane of earth for sheets of paper: Grant's dying light, Malinda's dream, the shadow of Grant in his coat and hat. For these poor Alabamians, exchanging letters meant exploring parts of themselves to which written expression opened a door.

Most Civil War letters do not at first resemble works of literature. They are rough compositions, poorly spelled and sometimes even barely legible, often formulaic and bereft of details one would typically consider juicy. Historians who work with the letters of rank-and-file soldiers regularly attest to how repetitive and hollow they often seem. (Some editors of collections dismiss the common run of letters as "family gossip and unimaginative, routine comments" and have gone as far as to remove what they see as the boring parts.)[9] Innumerable letters, both from the battlefield and the home front, open with virtually the identical sentence. "I ritin you A few lines to let no that I am well at presant time hoping when these few lines come to hand they will find [you] enjoying the same blessing." "My Darling Wife I take the prisant oppirtunity of writing to you to let you now that I am well and hope this fue lins will find you enjoying the same blessing of God." Or again, "Dear husband I Seat my Self this eavning to let you know that we are all well hopeing when these few lines comes to hand that they may find you enjoying the Same blessing."[10]

But the reason many Civil War letters are so conventional is not that these men and their families—living through what they knew to be a historic passage in their own lives and the life of their nation—had nothing to say. Nor is it simply that they were not fluent writers, limited in the range of what they could express. It is that letters were like that and had been for decades—a ritualized form, developed over generations by better educated people, dominated by an array of time-worn protocols. What ordinary Americans had at their disposal when the war separated them was a communications technology they did not invent, did not choose, had never had much say in shaping, and knew to be bound by explicit and implicit rules they did not fully understand.[11]

They had to make do with it, and the *making do* gives Civil War letters their literary quality. *Formulaic*, after all, shares its Latin root with *formal*, and the latter word means not only *not casual* but also, simply, having a shape—in the way some kinds of writing have a shape, like sonnets and five-act tragedies. Such forms are traditional, worked out over long periods of time through (partial) imitation. Wartime families' obeisance to epistolary forms was far from complete. They wrote a lot that was formulaic, but they also did striking, unusual things with letters—things highly educated people were adept or proper enough to avoid. Their experiments and accidents, their struggles with everything from cursive letters to figurative language, reveal how these men and women wrestled with a form maladapted to their present purposes—a polite genre, many of whose conventions were, in fact, pretty stale, now called to serve intimate relations during the upheaval of war.[12]

Ordinary Americans' Civil War writing has received little attention from this angle. The letters certainly have not been neglected. Acclaimed as a distinctly illuminating set of historical sources—since, unlike soldiers' correspondence in later American wars, they were uncensored by military authorities—they figure in many of the most influential works of Civil War history. Drawing on vast reading in tens of thousands of letters, historians have reconstructed soldiers' lives, their motivations, and what they thought about crucial issues like slavery.[13] Put toward such ends, letters function mainly as a large database—a repository of choice quotations a researcher copies down while poring over thousands of documents in search of evidence about a given historical topic. But there is more to the letters than the information they contain. Stray quotations may disclose the sentiments that dwell, sometimes only an instant, in people's minds, but they cannot capture the unfolding story, whose traces are scattered across months or years of letters, in which evolving thoughts and feelings, both personal and political, are interwoven.[14]

Researchers in the archives of the Civil War sometimes find it frustrating that many soldiers' letters express little about military events.

More than one historian has noticed that the less educated and well-off a soldier was, the less likely he was to write about the principles he was fighting for, his thoughts on politics, and the like.[15] Rank-and-file soldiers and their families used a lot of ink writing about their health, the weather, and what milk or butter cost. They repeated themselves, not emptily or absentmindedly, but because they never had complete confidence any given letter would reach its destination, and because the source of their feelings wasn't going away: *I wish you would come home, I wish I could come home, I can't come home.*

Thousands upon thousands of misspelled words along these lines may seem boring insofar as they are unhelpful in answering the questions modern historians have most often asked about the Civil War. (They also, in their original handwritten form, are harder to read than those whose authors were better educated.) But misspelling, rough penmanship, and formulaic composition don't necessarily mark letters as expressively deficient—only different from what we, highly literate readers of books, think we might have done ourselves. Nor is the restrained and conventional quality of such letters especially hard to understand. Military events were matters some soldiers did not want to relive or did not want to relate to loved ones who might become worried and fearful.

Understanding what a soldier meant when he wrote something in a letter may require more than knowing the state he was from, his rank in the army, and what year of the war it was. It may require knowing whether he was in danger of going into battle soon, or thought he was; whether he had been in battle recently, or had been sick or hospitalized; what financial condition his family was in at the time; whether he had been able to send money to them recently, or was asking them to send money to him; what the tenor of the last letter from his wife or parents had been. It also requires paying attention to *how* he wrote, and the kind of writer he was. The literary quality of Civil War letters escapes the kind of attention that plucks quotations from individual letters and marshals them in service of a historical interpretation. Formal evolutions, adaptive ways of making the best of a situation and a medium—these accumulated slowly, over months of correspondence, in tension with the stressed and changing circumstances of life in wartime.[16]

In reading these letters as acts of writing—composed with intention yet harboring complex, sometimes partly submerged meanings—this book extends my decade-long endeavor (including a previous book on enslaved and newly freed African Americans) to understand the writings of relatively uneducated people as literary texts. By adopting a capacious definition of literature that embraces the richness of image, figure, and narrative in all written expression, and by fusing methods of reading inspired by history, composition studies, and literary scholarship, this larger project works toward something otherwise scarcely possible: the intellectual and emotional history of poorly educated people.[17]

I Remain Yours, taking up a single, dramatic moment in the history of epistolary writing, offers an emotional history of the Civil War. Theorists and historians of human emotion are mindful that expressions of feeling, written or otherwise, do not provide a complete picture of emotional life. People feel much that they keep to themselves. But wartime letters, if read closely and in context, sometimes show more than what their writers openly avow. They reveal abiding states of relation to other people and processes of adjustment to profound transformation. During the Civil War, the emotional lives of soldiers and their families were stretched like threads across hundreds of miles. As in all wars, practically nothing was more important to these people than the fact of their separation. Some crucial part of their experience of the war transpired neither at the battlefront nor on the home front but in a kind of *no place* aloft, along an invisible path traversed only by envelopes. Seeking that nowhere-place—which exists now, as it existed then, only in writing—we can sense what the Civil War felt like to the common soldier and his family.[18]

AN INDIANA REGIMENT on the move across northern Mississippi needed to set up camp, and it came upon a schoolhouse. Probably the roof and four walls were its principal attractions, but at least one man in the ranks, David Johnson, saw an opportunity to use a proper desk to compose a letter home. Although he commented to his sister on the novel circumstance of "sitting in a school house riting on a desk," he did not say whether this reminded him of his own school days or, perhaps, struck him as an ironic contrast with his lack of schooling in the past. It could not have felt much like being in class—there was no teacher, only the twenty Confederate prisoners Johnson was guarding ("if they dont mind us we will give them the boot")—but the scene highlights the fact that this war was giving Johnson as much writing practice as he probably had gotten in years.[19]

Like many men in both armies, and Southerners especially, Tilmon Baggarly of North Carolina found letter paper hard to come by. Somewhere in northern Virginia, he managed to acquire a copybook for aspiring clerks and businessmen. It included several pages on which students could practice their penmanship; across the tops of otherwise blank sheets ran sample text in perfect Spencerian script. "A good Penman and competent Accountant has always at command an occupation by which to earn a living and make himself respected," one page read. Others laid out models for bank notes and other business documents. Tilmon tore out these pages and used them for letters to his wife, Margaret. "Mag this paper i bought in a book," he explained. "This writing abov is on evry page i will not tar it of i will let it stay for copys an for you to see." He was never going to be an accountant and probably did not want to be, but he needed paper, and he seemed to recognize that having the preprinted script "for copys" couldn't hurt his own irregular writing.[20]

Because it put a premium on letter writing among people who previously wrote very little, the Civil War sparked ad hoc literacy education on a vast scale. The dramatic increase in correspondence among ordinary people created what some scholars call an extracurriculum in writing.[21] More ardently than if a teacher had compelled them, people practiced writing letters. They did it over and over again, bumping up against the limits of their literacy and trying to clamber over them. They experimented with different modes of expression. They read the letters they received and followed (or tried to depart from) their example. They saw and heard people all around—men in the same tents and around the same campfires, neighbor women at home—receiving, reading, and reacting to letters. From all this they were learning.

In addition to an emotional history, *I Remain Yours* is the story of ordinary Americans' informal education during the Civil War. Many had to acquire basic literacy. Once able to write, they needed to learn the protocols and expectations, the limits and possibilities, of the genre known as the letter. Once proficient in epistolary customs, they had to cope with the uncertain chances of postal transit across great distances and through war zones. And they had to call on their still-forming aptitudes as writers to do increasingly complex and difficult work—to comprehend, respond to, and communicate to their loved ones some of the most singular and trying incidents of their lives. The central figures in this book include Northerners and Southerners, both of the Atlantic seaboard and the western interior, but mostly they are white farming families of modest means. Their sectional differences do not figure as prominently as their similarities of class, education, and literacy.[22]

The chapters of this book follow these writers' collective progress from learning to write ("Letters") to using writing to report their sights and sensations ("Impressions"); from maintaining family and community across space and time ("Bonds") to meeting the challenges that tested those bonds ("Strains"); from reckoning with ultimate tribulation ("Breaks") to achieving, finally, the kinds of intimacy that written letters sometimes can forge better than anything else ("Unions"). Throughout, the incidents of war and the yearning for connection with a loved one pushed ordinary Americans to stretch themselves as writers, to expand what their letters could do.[23]

Their education was necessarily collaborative. It happened when people sat together and coached one another or took down dictation; it happened when people described letters to one another or read them aloud; and it happened in the call and response of long-term epistolary conversations. Sometimes that call and response was direct and literal, as when Henry J. H. Thompson of Connecticut would reply to his wife, Lucretia, in the blank spaces of her letters, echoing and reinterpreting in red ink what she had written to him in black.[24]

More often, writers' development and influence on each other manifested themselves in slower, less dramatic ways—in the differences between what a barely literate soldier wrote with his own hand and what he dictated to someone else; what an illiterate farm wife dictated to one male relative and what she dictated to another; what an enlisted man wrote to his wife when he was not receiving her replies, and when he was. It is discernible in the shifting tides of language, tone, and affect within a long correspondence. Picking up on those subtleties necessitates one of this book's distinctive features: its focus, wherever possible, on groups of letters that feature both sides of a correspondence—an unfolding conversation between a soldier and, most often, a wife or a mother. To a large extent the history of the Civil War has been told either from men's perspectives or women's, focused either on the battlefront or the home front. *I Remain Yours* follows the letters that moved back and forth between those spaces and considers soldiers' letters in the context of their home lives. Great battles enshrined in memory were fought by men worried about their children's measles, frustrated that the money they sent home to their mothers had not arrived, wondering whether they ought to run away

Lucretia Thompson to Henry Thompson, 4 Nov. 1863, and Henry to Lucretia, 8 Nov. 1863 (detail)

and help their wives harvest crops. Letter writing as a "dialogue with home" reveals the ways men's and women's Civil Wars met, intertwined, and shaped each other.[25]

Some of the most transformative effects of literacy and letter writing happened in intimate exchanges between men and women. One crucible of an uneducated person's entry into the realm of letters was the act of writing to an authority figure—putting one's crude penmanship and imperfect syntax on display before a well-educated stranger. But sending a letter to a governor or the president was usually a one-time event (and a desperate one).[26] In the letters passing regularly, often weekly, between people who had lived together until the war separated them, men and women slowly, sometimes falteringly, worked out new modes of emotional expression and a changing self-image. This is especially true because of the Civil War's broader impact on men's and women's social roles. In some ways the war reinforced longstanding ideas about gender—men were the armed protectors of women who stayed home—but in more ways it upended those ideas. The content of letters recorded such changes. Soldiers' most intimate correspondents—wives, mothers, daughters, sisters—may have been the very ones to whom they wanted to project manhood, yet these were the same people in whom they were likely to confide (if ever they did) about misadventures in cooking, longing for home, fears of battle, and shame that they were unable to work their own farms. Women's letters, meanwhile, often described their newfound roles as heads of households—harvesting crops, tending livestock, buying and selling farm goods, negotiating credit. Historically, women had been taught to write (if they had) in largely sentimental contexts; men learned writing for business. Now, those roles were commingled, at times almost reversed. Some women, such as Lucretia Thompson, provided the models their husbands followed.[27]

In the letters these many men and women exchanged are charted the emotional tides of wartime daily life. Through the capillaries of culture, as it were—each smaller than the arterial discourses of books, newspapers, and political speeches, but together reaching even farther—ordinary writers effected the cell-level transfers that created the meaning of the Civil War. For millions of Americans who did not read many novels or subscribe to the magazines being published in Boston and New York, letters were their window on the world. And it was through letters that they projected themselves and their ideas into that world.[28]

MUCH OF *I Remain Yours* is devoted to letters by multiple members of a single family with a single surname. To avoid confusion, I refer to people using their first names. To avoid creating hierarchies, I follow this practice even in many cases where it would be customary to refer to people using their surnames. With very few exceptions, I have not edited these writers' letters—not inserted proper spellings in brackets, for example, or added punctuation. I recognize that it is difficult to parse a lot of the letters and excerpts you will encounter in these pages. *I Remain Yours* is devoted to interpreting and understanding what these letters were trying to say, and I ask you who read this book to make your own way, even if slowly, through the words and phrases I have quoted. I know it is not easy, but I also know you can do it. Thousands of husbands, wives, parents, and children did it avidly, and they were less capable readers than you.

❧ I ❧

Letters

And the Jews marveled, saying, How knoweth this man letters, having never
learned?

—John 7:15

T HE THREE most common meanings of "letters" are like tiers of
a pyramid—first the twenty-six that make up the alphabet, then the
written messages people send to one another, and finally the estate of
those who are learned (as in "arts and letters" or "belles lettres").
Elementary, intermediate, advanced, they ascend from earliest childhood—carved on wooden blocks, paired with pictures of apples,
balls, cats, and dogs—to the highest echelons of education, where
robed figures incant the honorifics from diplomas. The whole span of
human language and knowledge, from basic literacy to practical communication to rarified intellect, balances on the narrow perch of this
word. So it has been for as long as the English language has existed.
The *Oxford English Dictionary* dates all these definitions to before the
thirteenth century, as early as almost any modern English words can
be traced. Even in classical Latin, *litterae* harbored all three meanings.
As in any triad, it's the middle definition that touches both others. Letters—the kind people send to each other—can be primitive or ele-
gant and everything in between. A child's message in crayon and a
distinguished author's lengthy epistle may stand as far apart as A and Z,

but they share a name. The middle is the meeting ground, the link between high and low, learned and barely literate.

Frederick Hooker's lineage tells an iconic story of America itself. Seven generations back, Thomas Hooker, a Cambridge-educated English Puritan, had sailed across the Atlantic in 1633. Not long after arriving in Massachusetts Bay Colony, he led a group of settlers west through the wilderness to the Connecticut River and founded a place called Hartford, earning him for posterity the name "Father of Connecticut." It was Hooker who preached a sermon in 1638 that declared "the foundation of authority is laid in the free consent of the people," which inspired the Fundamental Orders of Connecticut—what some regard as the first written constitution in the Western world. Thomas's son Samuel went back to Massachusetts to attend Harvard, then returned to his native colony and became the minister of a new town, west over a ridge from Hartford, called Farmington, where Frederick Hooker would be born about two centuries later.[1]

Thomas Hooker's descendants fanned out across the new nation. Noadiah Hooker helped bring the United States into being, fighting in the Revolutionary War and rising to the rank of colonel. Mary Hooker married James Pierpont, founder of Yale University, and from that union would issue, a few generations later, John Pierpont Morgan, who would shape the future of American finance. John Hooker married Harriet Beecher Stowe's half sister, became an antislavery activist, and helped secure the freedom of James W. C. Pennington, the escaped slave who became one of the antebellum North's best-known black leaders. Henry Clay Hooker went west and started what became the largest ranch in the Arizona Territory.

Back in Farmington, Hookers remained the town's leading citizens. Edward Hooker, son of the Revolutionary War colonel, went to Yale, where he met and married a niece of Roger Sherman, one of the drafters of the Declaration of Independence. He returned to Farmington and started the town's first college preparatory school. Other

Hookers spread beyond the town's neat center. Edward's older brother James, more eccentric, had gone to sea and sailed on voyages to China. Even he returned to Farmington, eventually, and late in life married a much younger woman. At almost seventy years old, he fathered a pair of twin boys. One lived only four months. Less than two weeks after the infant died, James himself did. Four days later, distinguished Uncle Edward passed away, too.[2] Frederick was the twin who survived.

Despite his illustrious pedigree and his welter of highly learned ancestors, Frederick Hooker, when he left home to fight in the Civil War at age nineteen, did not know how to write. His first letters home, from Fort Trumbull on the coast of Long Island Sound, were dictated to a fellow soldier, who was barely literate himself: "have and optarneaty to write you i thought would write to you to let you know where i be i have enlisted in to 2th CV heavy Artillery for three years."[3] By the end of his second month in the army, Frederick had learned to handle a pen. Although still not equal to the challenge of cursive script, he managed to compose a letter—mostly in block capitals, many of them backwards. As if to substitute for the longer description of his situation he couldn't yet provide, he drew a small illustrated map of Fort Ellsworth, in Alexandria, Virginia, where he had lately arrived.

His mother, Jeannette Sweet Hooker, was elated. She took the letter, wrote a note of her own in the space he left blank, and sent it on to his sister to show what he had done.

Dear nancy i am So glad fred wrote him Self ant you. you may not find it all out but i can read evry word of it i think you will be able to corispond with him with out his gettin Som one els to write for him Sinc you went to bristol i have had a letter from pensylva nia with a new years presant in it iwill tell you all about when you come good night
    from your mother

Frederick Hooker
to "der Mother," 23
Mar. 1864 (verso)

WRITE AS SOON AS
YOU CAN THIS.

Dear nancy

Dear nancy now I glad first wrote
him self out give you may not find
it all out but I can read write
word of it think you will be able
to con spend with him with out
his getting some one else to write for
him Give you ought to be still
been had a letter from him to love
me with a new years present
on it I will tell you all about when
you com good night
          from your mother

"SEND ME 2 DOLLARS.
IN OR GIVE ME BACK 2.
IF YOU CAN FOR TO
DO IN F WAZHING 2.
I SHAL HAVE ABOUT
50 DOLLARS COMING
NEXT PAY JANUARY IF IN ANY
EXCUSE ALL MISTAKES.

WRITE SOON WILL I

LETT ME KNOW W ALL
ABOUT BRIDGET.
PEOPLE & NETTIE.
ALL 20 IN ——

ROAD TO ALAXDA

I am so glad Fred wrote himself, ain't you? To readers well versed in American literature, the words "written by himself" call first to mind the many escaped slaves, such as Frederick Douglass, whose published autobiographies carried this assurance on their title pages. Against a widespread presumption that African American slaves were illiterate—either because southern slaveholders kept them so, or because of their supposed intellectual inferiority—the phrase "written by himself" (or herself) sent out a challenge and a proof. Some fugitives authored slave narratives by dictating to someone else, but many others, Douglass among them, were literate, wrote their stories with their own hands, and wanted their books to announce that fact.[4]

Fred Hooker had endured none of the agonies of slavery, and learning to write did not bear the burden of proving his humanity, but he nevertheless would have had powerful reasons to want to write himself. As had the more famous Frederick whose *Narrative* came out the year he was born, the young descendant of Puritan colonists approached the realm of letters from the outside. Evidently not brought up to writing, he found himself a neo-literate adult, trying to master a skill most people his age already had. People like Fred stood on epistolary culture's margins as the Civil War began raging.

Fred had tried to become a sailor, but in his first letter home—one of the ones he did not write himself—he reported to his mother, "i Could not enlist in the navy at any advantage." He may have aspired to follow the path of the seafaring father he had never known, or the more immediate example of his older cousin. (Uncle Edward's oldest son and namesake had joined the navy at the start of the war and, by 1862, was a lieutenant commanding a division in the Potomac Flotilla.)[5] But Fred may have failed to pass muster with the navy. Even if he had been the stronger of the twins in infancy, he probably was not the healthiest nineteen-year-old: it took three medical examinations before he was accepted into the army, which was not especially choosy in 1864.[6] Saying he could not join the navy "at any advantage" sounds like a euphemistic cover for something. The army did offer more generous bounties, but many men still saw the navy as the more desirable branch of service, having decided (rightly, casualty figures ultimately would show) that it was safer.[7]

If Fred lacked the inclination to take after his father, he may not have wanted to say as much to his mother. If the navy rejected him, he may not have wanted to admit that to the companion who was writing this down. And maybe it's all true, as simple as what he said: he "Could not enlist in the navy at any advantage" and he just decided for himself that the army was a better deal. We do not know, because all he wrote—or, rather, all he asked someone else to write—was that single line. Fred had never done anything like this before—explaining himself to his mother through the medium of another person's written words—and he produced a short first letter: he had enlisted, he would send home his bounty when he got it, he was pretty well though he had a cold. "Keep good Courage for i am all wrigt do not feel bad because i am in service some bristal boys are hear with me." (Bristol is the town next to Farmington.) "Now if you will to write to me tell me all about things."

By the following week, his mother had obliged, and it had become real: Fred had sent a piece of paper out into the distance, and his mother's words had come back in reply. There was something a little wondrous about it. Fred's second letter—taken down, it appears, by the same person who penned the first—began by declaring, "i recived a lettr with much pleasur as it writting so plain that i found out ever word of it." This was a pleasure many people took for granted. For better-educated Americans, letters in which you could not find out every word were more notable, by their deficiency, than "plain" ones.[8]

Even Fred was on his way to literate complacency. A month later, though still relying on someone else to do his writing, he had gained some experience as a letter reader, and after receiving another letter from his mother, he replied and told her, "when you write again have Nancy write the letter." He made no sign of complaint, but there can be little mistaking his meaning. Jeannette had fair penmanship, as we can see ourselves, but her spelling was erratic enough that a barely literate teenager might struggle to read her words. Later in the same letter, Fred commented, "you said some thing about Samuel hills in the last letter i Could not a really what it meant when you write again tell ^{me} about it." Having had his own troubles making out Jeannette's letter, Fred may have asked someone else to help him read it, as was common in the army. Did the more literate man remark that Jeannette's writing wasn't very good? If so, Fred would have been neither the first nor the last embarrassed teenager to try keeping his mother out of view of his peers after that. In any event, Fred would shortly find out just how hard Jeannette's literary labors were—the same letter closed, "i have a friend in the Co. with me write my letter for me i am goin to learn"—and he would never thereafter insinuate that his mother's writing fell short.[9]

Relying on someone else—an amanuensis, scribe, or ghostwriter—made literal and obvious some of the challenges facing an uneducated person trying to become a letter writer. If not being able to write very well limits what you can say, asking someone else to do it for you opens up the possibility of saying anything you want, more clearly than you could yourself. At the same time, it forecloses that possibility: you may not wish to share with your scribe everything you want to put in your letter, and any added clarity or grace would not be your own. For illiterate and marginally literate people, letters dangled the promise of intimacy with a distant loved one, yet getting a letter written—and, on the other end, read—could dash precisely that promise. Fred was beginning to discern the subtle ways in which depending on others to decipher and compose letters could unsettle the very relationships those letters were supposed to sustain.

LARKIN AND MARY CATHERINE KENDRICK of North Carolina generally wrote their own letters to each other, and Larkin seemed neither critical of Catherine's writing, initially, nor self-conscious about his own. He had even told her, in the letter that romantically declared his love "as constant as the Wheales of time," that she could "let as many as you pleas Sea this." (Having made that invitation shortly before composing the long, stirring passage about the sun and moon and stars shining on his beloved wife and children, he may have been, in addition to expressing his love to his wife, showing off a little for the neighbors.) On one occasion, a year later while he was hospitalized in Richmond, Larkin did employ an amanuensis. Then, amid the comparative ease of lying abed and speaking to a person at his side, he remarked to Catherine: "I want you to get some one to write for you that will write plainer as the last letter I received was writen so bad I could hardly make it out." Charley Futch, another North Carolinian, had even less patience for his brother's penmanship than Larkin had for Catherine's: "John I want you to write me more plainer than you have bin a writing for the letters that capt williams brought to me I carried them though the 3d regement and they was not a one that could read them so I can not answer them letters and I carried them to the 40th regement and they was not a man that could read the date of the month."[10]

If Fred Hooker felt a little ashamed of depending on other people to do his writing, he owed the feeling in part to growing up in a state where less than 2 percent of the population was illiterate.[11] Larkin Kendrick, from a state with an illiteracy rate almost four times Connecticut's, may have seen less stigma in it. But that doesn't mean poor Southerners lacked desire to become letter writers. Occasionally, using an amanuensis could get a person into real trouble. William Cline was initially befuddled by an angry letter from his wife, Mary, until he realized a trick had been played on him. "The boys had rote nasty leter for mey," he explained (they had written to Mary, in William's voice, about a visit to a brothel). "After dis i will rite my one leters," William assured her, as he tried to heal the misunderstanding; "i rote dis leter my self."[12]

Thomas and Martha Warrick, farmers in central Alabama, could barely read and write, but they kept up a brisk correspondence during the war. Thomas sent Martha almost a hundred letters during the three years of his service. Although only a handful of Martha's letters survive, she wrote regularly, too—and in her own hand, at least some of the time. Thomas, in the Thirty-Fourth Alabama Infantry, was surrounded by available scribes. His letters appear in the hands of several different people, some barely literate themselves, some apparently well educated. Little bothered, it seems, by having to speak to his wife through an intermediary, Thomas may even have wished Martha would do the same. Within the first few months of his enlistment, he made the same complaint Larkin Kendrick had: "My wife I waunt you to write your letters a litel plainer for I had not a like to a maid out half of your words theare is som that I havt maid out yet nor I cant."[13] But Martha, off in rural Coosa County, was not surrounded with willing amanuenses, and she did not like the semipublic nature of her exchanges with her husband.

She believed their correspondence was restricted by Thomas's intermediaries. She appeared to grow frustrated with her husband's tendency to encode sensitive subjects when he dictated. On one occasion, he told her, "I herde a bad tale on one of our old nabers that yust to live clost by when we lived on littel Rock there by the sholes I waunt you to send me word if it is so or not." Two weeks later, he had to repeat essentially the same request after getting Martha's flummoxed reply. This time he seemed to realize there was something farcical about trying to exchange whispered gossip across two hundred miles via letters dictated to third parties: "you wannted me to send you word who that was that I wrote to you it was a man that lived there clost by the Rock sholes if you dont no hoo it was I will step on over som morning beefore brakfast and then I will tell you all about it."[14]

Thomas was beginning to share Martha's frustration: "you sed if I could reed my letters that you would write a heep more that you dont write I wish that I could read and write my own letters and I would write a heap that I dont I cant think of all that I doo waunt to write when I have a letter rote I have to have it rote in a hurry and I cant think of half that I doo waunt to write." What conversation ensued after Thomas dictated this passage to his more literate comrade? Did his scribe offer to slow down? Did the two men talk about their different experiences of composing letters, about what letters meant to them and their wives, or about the relative importance of confidentiality and neat penmanship?[15]

Though the exact scenes are lost, countless such conversations helped form ideas about epistolary culture. Little inconveniences and big ambitions spurred people on the margins of literacy to practice their writing. Affluent Southerners even thought, a little condescendingly, that increased literacy would be a happy side effect of secession. A South Carolina rice planter's wife recorded in her diary that the president of a nearby college "thinks the war will be a great benefit to the country, enlargement of mind to very ignorant, contracted, country people. The families of soldiers now take news papers, and if they can't read themselves they get people to read to them, and some of them have learned to read themselves. One woman in his neighborhood whose husband, a hard working man and gone off to the wars, had learnt to write & read writing since her husband left her, and he had, too, learned to read & write that he might write to her, she could read his letters, but no other writing."[16]

Thomas Warrick, who probably did not think of himself as an "ignorant, contracted, country" person, seemed to intuit there was something more to literacy than gossiping with his wife in plain language. The act of writing, whatever its utility, also would alter his thinking. Were he able to write with his own hand, he believed, "I would write a heap that I dont." When dictating, he found, "I cant think of all that I doo waunt to write." The slower and more inward process of composing his own letter would generate new thoughts. Still, he did not seem deeply troubled by such missed opportunities. He could, with easy conviviality, confide to both his wife and his amanuensis that he didn't put into his letters everything he thought. The curtain of illiteracy fell heavier over others.

SAREPTA WARD WAS born in the Saluda Mountains of western North Carolina the same year that Frederick Hooker was born in Connecticut. She was barely sixteen when she married twenty-four-year-old Daniel Revis on the eve of the Civil War. By the summer of the following year, when Daniel enlisted in North Carolina's Sixty-Fourth Regiment and left home, they had a baby boy named Slocum and Sarepta was pregnant a second time. She could not write, but most of their extended family lived nearby and many of her male relatives were literate, if barely. A cousin on her mother's side of the family, John Morgan, wrote Sarepta's first letter to Daniel:

> N. C. Henderson county October the 12 1862
>
> we air all well at presant and I hop thes few lines may find you well I wold be gld to see you and I hop you will cum home to me as sun as you can and Judy is with me John as well sone be cuting teath and he is cralling all over the place and we are gitting along very well with the horse ~~very well~~ and hour hogs are dwoing very well that was spaid but won and hit is dead and I want you to rite back all the war nuse we heard that all the officers is called off to gethe and we hop that it is to try to mak a comprimise so I have nohing more at presant to danel Revis Srepty Revis[17]

Presumably Daniel required no explanation of who was writing this down. Nevertheless John made it explicit ten days later. Upon writing a second letter for Sarepta, John turned the paper over and added his own note to Daniel:

John Morgain 1862 Oct 22

I will right you all a few lines to let you no that i am coming
to your company in about 13 days and everybody in the hold
wearld is cuming wimen and children all and then we will make
a mash of the war

John's enlistment would give Daniel the company of an in-law, and
an enthusiastic, pep-talking one at that (if we interpret making "a mash
of the war" to mean winning it). But it would also mean Sarepta had
to find a new scribe.[18]

It's not easy to gauge how comfortable Sarepta was speaking to her
husband through the intermediary of her cousin. On one hand, the two
letters John wrote for her are quite short (a single side of a single small
sheet of paper), but that may owe as much to John's limitations as a
penman as to Sarepta's reserve. She did allow John a glimpse into the
more private side of her marriage: in the second letter, she asked him
to tell Daniel, "I wood be glad to sea you a cuming home and I will
hug your nack good for you and giv you one good kiss." Perhaps the
strongest indication of Sarepta's trust in John is that he was the first
person she asked. After he was gone, she had to move down a list.[19]

Her next amanuensis was her older brother, Hezekiah C. Ward, who
went by Clint. Clint wrote at least six letters for Sarepta, in finer penmanship than John's and characterized by a somewhat firmer embrace
of epistolary conventions. John had ended letters to Daniel abruptly,
and Sarepta apparently did not direct him otherwise. But once Clint
began writing for her, customary valedictories appeared: "sow re-
maines yours respectfuley un tell death." If John Morgan acted more
or less passively as Sarepta's secretary, Clint seems to have exercised
some of the authority of an older brother, either suggesting what she
should write or simply supplying it at his own discretion. When Clint
wrote over his own signature, he began letters predictably: "My Dear
Brother I take my pen in hand to let you know that I am not yet I hope

these few lines may finde you and Burt Well I have nothing Strange to rite to you at presant," and "My Dear Brother I tak my pen in hand to let you no that I am not very well but I hope theas few lines ma finde you well and doing well I have nothing strange to rite to you at presant." When he wrote for—or, it may be, *as*—Sarepta, it was much the same: "My Dear loving Hus ban I take the presant time to in form you that I am well at presant and I hope theas few lines ma finde you in good health and doing well I have nothing strainge to rite to you at presant," and "My Dear loveing Hus ban I take the presant time to inform you that I am well at presant and I do hope thaes few lines ma finde you well and doing well I have nothing strainge to rite to you at presant."[20]

Most of these niceties could be found reproduced in thousands upon thousands of letters. "Nothing strange" was a less common phrase than, say, "nothing of interest," but it was not unheard of, and all the rest was thoroughly conventional.[21] If these lines are no trademark of Clint's voice, even less are they Sarepta's. She doubtless had too little familiarity with letters to spout their stock phrases even if she had wanted to. She may not even have known "she" was "saying" these particular words to her husband. She and her brother may have agreed, or perhaps Clint simply told her, that certain parts of the business of letter writing were the job of a literate person and a man.

Letter writing by proxy had happened for years, anywhere illiterate people could call on the aid of literate ones, and this was widely known. During a congressional debate on postal reform, future speaker of the House Schuyler Colfax urged consideration of local postmasters' "laborious task of writing letters for poor persons in their vicinity who are not able to write themselves." During the Civil War, scenes of writing such as Sarepta's exploded. Urged on by separation from their families, people like Fred Hooker and Sarepta Revis, who previously had no one to write to or had been too shy to ask for help doing it, sought out amanuenses. For young men like Fred, gathered into army units with hundreds of men, differently educated and from diverse class backgrounds, amanuenses were easier to come by. A New Yorker named Simon Hulbert, who kept a log of his epistolary output, sent 164 letters of his own in 1863 and also wrote 37 letters "for other men." Army hospitals were hotbeds of dictation. The illiterate as well as the dying and badly wounded needed help to send a letter home. Louisa May Alcott and Walt Whitman, both of whom worked as nurses, are probably the most famous amanuenses of the war. "I write this by means of a friend who is now sitting by my side," a soldier named Nelson Jabo told his wife through the pen of the poet.[22]

Some encounters across borders of class and literacy also spanned borders of race, and those scenes of writing revealed pronounced gaps of authority and authorship. An unmarried white soldier from Massachusetts, working in an army recruiting office in the South, wrote so many letters on behalf of freedwomen to their husbands in the Union army that he expected to become "adept in writing love letters, when I have occasion to do so on my own account." Elizabeth Hyde Botume, a middle-class white New Englander, went south in 1864 as a missionary teacher for former slaves. In her memoir, she recalled being prevailed upon constantly by freed people to write letters to lost family members. One time, a freedwoman came to Elizabeth wanting to send a letter to her husband. She gave her husband's name and location, mentioned the names of several relatives who also wished to send their greetings, and said she wanted to tell her husband "to say his praise." Then she paused, and Elizabeth asked, "What else?" The woman replied, "Why, you know, ma'am." Elizabeth concluded, "Evidently to her mind there was but one outline for letters, which I was expected to fill up. . . . They always thought that those who could 'put down handwriting' must know everything else." This may have been only Elizabeth's interpretation of the situation, not freed people's actual attitude. Even so, it reflects a widely shared belief that writing a letter involved forms of knowledge above and beyond alphabetic literacy.[23]

These were unequal relationships to begin with—a black woman and a white one, a teenager and her older brother. Letter writing could intensify those dynamics of power, invert them for a time, and make them more complicated. It could put the dominant person in a position resembling service, while the other, voiceless in public life, now was invited to hold forth. It could be a moment of education. Alonzo Reed, an African American soldier in the 102nd U.S. Colored Infantry, got someone to write a letter for him to his mother in Michigan, then took the sheet, read over what the person he called "my hand riter" had set down, and decided to try adding a little in his own hand. No doubt following the model of his amanuensis's lines—"give my love to Jim that I am well at present and i want to rite to me if he pleases"—Alonzo penned a further message to folks he perhaps had forgotten: "tel my ant tat i send my love to her and sester and mrs gray and mr gray tel my brother tat i wand hem to rite to as soon." Although Alonzo's unpracticed hand turned out cursive script quite different from that of the scribe, he copied the more literate person's rendering of his first name, "Alonzo," almost exactly.[24]

The person dictating, even if learning something by the transaction, even if freed to have her words put down in writing, remained bound by assumptions about literate and illiterate people's authority (as in Elizabeth's reminiscence) and by the exactions of custom (as with Sarepta and Clint). Despite romantic associations of writing with expressiveness, the hyperconventional quality of nineteenth-century letters could subdue authorship as we usually think of it—doubly so in cases like these. Clint held the pen and wrote not what Sarepta wished to say but what millions of people have always said, for years, almost robotically. Sarepta may as well have been filling out a form—actually, having it filled out for her.

In fact, common people's literacy can be said to have originated in the filling out of forms. The written word overspread England's North American colonies faster than education did. Literacy was parceled out

for the next time
That I get my
pay i Will send you
Some of it give my
love to Jim and
Jim that i am
Well at Present and
i Want to write to him
if he pleases and i Will
answer as soon as
no more at present
i remain your
Dear Son
Alonzo

Reed Co 102
U.S.C.J.
U.S.C.J.

Dec hors act gff the
Let me dont tell
i send my love to her
and sister and mother and
my pay to my Brother
to Want them to let it
down as beche home and
i want some postom and it
Proper i hoste my letter
to Close it is my hand
Hter and

Charlinton S C

from your son
Alonzo Reed t.
a H. Inne's Reed next
102 Us 6 t Co "B" 8

based on class, race, and gender throughout the colonial period and even, in many parts of the new United States, well into the nineteenth century. Affluent white men were taught to read and write in childhood, but few other people were. In Puritan New England, a commitment to individual relationships with God made it a priority to teach all members of the community, including women, to read the Bible, but even there the teaching of *writing* was primarily for young men—particularly those being groomed for Harvard, Yale, and the ministry.[25] Yet as the colonies grew, the ordinary business of legal and economic life—for everyone, from a Harvard-educated Samuel Hooker to an illiterate Frederick—began to happen in writing.

In an increasingly cosmopolitan place with, on balance, a middling literacy rate, there was a need for greater documentation than many people could compose and inscribe on their own. That need was met by a nascent bureaucracy's printing of standardized forms. These included, in one scholar's inventory, "writs of attachment, deeds of transfer, apprentice indentures, customs receipts, surveyors' certificates, tax assessment forms, land grants, powers of attorney, military supply requisitions, returns, executors' warrants, vouchers, bills of exchange, bonds, debentures, election decrees, jury summonses, petitions for military discharge, complaints for suits in equity, recognizance appeals, commissions civil and military, post-rider oaths, special warrants, bills obligatory, mortgages for slaves, bills of lading, oaths of allegiance, and more." As early as 1700, colonies were beginning to require the use of printed forms for most official business, and by the time of the American Revolution forms were ubiquitous. Designed to demand little more of their user than to enter his name and maybe a few numbers, they became a feature of everyday life even for people who, unable to sign their own names, authenticated documents by "making their mark," or inscribing a simple X. (The English jurist William Blackstone called such people "our illiterate vulgar.")[26]

Popular literacy proceeded along this track—hammered out through encounters with *forms* of authority in multiple senses: official printed forms, the powers of political and commercial life—at least until the common-school movement in the antebellum North. (Public education and universal literacy were slower coming to the South.) Meanwhile, the evolution of the written letter had been proceeding along a different track, largely among social elites. These tracks came together in the Civil War. Fred Hooker may have been Thomas's direct descendant, but in his relationship to reading and writing he, like Sarepta Revis, belonged to the lineage of struggling colonial farmers and artisans who remained on the margins of literate culture until the Civil War brought them nearer the center.

IF PRINTED FORMS had been one of state authority's first ways of reaching out to embrace the illiterate, letters—indeed, writing itself—began largely as the way state authority operated internally. Long before the modern era, the novel technology of fixing language in clay or on paper met the demands of administering governments.[27] The technology's communicative potential—the ability of writing to move language across distance—became vital in expanding civilizations and early empires. All the way from the Italian Renaissance through early modern England and into the colonial United States, what would come to be called letters were modeled more or less explicitly on ancient Roman rhetorical principles and the letters of Cicero.[28]

Letters broadened in their uses from kingly pronouncements to private communications, but they remained the domain of highly educated people—because literacy itself was likewise restricted and because the norms of letter writing were tightly intertwined with conceptions of class and social station. That is, how you were supposed to write a letter depended on who you were. Addressing someone "beneath" you on the social ladder was considered a very different activity, rhetorically and substantively, from addressing someone "above" you—forbidding terrain for those below. Even though literacy expanded dramatically during the eighteenth and nineteenth centuries, newly literate people did not find it easy to take up letter writing, so intricate and obscure were its unwritten rules. There ought to be a rulebook, someone doubtless said aloud at some point, and entrepreneurs in one of the economy's hottest industries seized the opportunity.

Publishers of letter-writing manuals responded to the social and economic aspirations of a rising middle class—the first wave of relatively ordinary folks who might hope to penetrate the aristocratic domain of letters. In England and the colonies, the late eighteenth century witnessed something unprecedented in world history and revolutionary for written culture: a large group of people, lifted by nascent capitalism out of peasantry, acquiring both literacy and disposable income. With the proceeds of their flourishing trades or their new jobs in the increasingly industrial economy of the nineteenth century, they bought a lot of books. Rapidly, they created a market for new kinds of literature—some, like magazines and novels, that never went out of style, and some that were more peculiar to their historical moment. Letter-writing manuals became tremendously popular in England in the early eighteenth century and ubiquitous in America from the colonial period to the Civil War.[29]

Eighteenth-century manuals fostered much of what made letters formulaic for decades to come, and they enforced those formulas by implicit or explicit threats about respectability and chances for social mobility. Early in the century, epistolary writing was mostly for men of business, and manuals catered to people of humble origin trying to enter that realm. Writing a letter in the proper fashion could smooth a young man's path into a profession, the middle class, even modest wealth, while sloppy or inappropriate letters could dash those hopes. In 1740, the English novelist Samuel Richardson broadened the letter-manual genre to include private life as well as business. He published a collection of 173 fictitious letters as models for how to write on a vast array of delicate occasions—seeking or dispensing advice, asking or being asked for money, courting or being courted. Sometimes Richardson composed whole sequences of letters that (like the epistolary novels he was writing at the same time) formed narratives about vice and virtue. He hoped these models would serve "for Rules to THINK and ACT by, as well as Forms to WRITE after."[30] Following the prescribed forms of letters, in other words, did not just make your *writing* respectable, it made *you* respectable.

In both public and private spheres, the stakes were high. A person learning to write letters faced the fearsome prospect of being judged unrefined or out of line, if not dismissed altogether. Writing to one's supposed superiors was especially hazardous, but even the task of writing to a friend or loved one involved navigating ideas about proper form. Perils of power and identity in social life were not peculiar to letter writing, but presenting oneself on paper seemed to intensify them. Throughout the era, manuals, conduct books, even cookbooks widely quoted an ominous sentiment from the English philosopher John Locke: "The writing of letters enters so much into all the occasions of life, that no gentleman can avoid showing himself in compositions of this kind. Occurrences will daily force him to make this use of his pen, which lays open his breeding, and sense, and his abilities, to a severer examination than any oral discourse."[31]

Versions of this warning were everywhere in letter-writing manuals. The first English manual printed in the colonies, *The Young Secretary's Guide*, appeared in at least twenty editions during the early 1700s, and it offered this among other warnings: "In directing your Letters you must be very wary, for a little mistake may give disgust and spoil all, especially with those of the higher Rank." Another best-selling manual included a list of epistolary practices that differed based on whether you were writing to "your superiors" or to "your equals or inferiors." When writing to those above you, you needed to use "quarto fine gilt paper," inscribe the address in precise fashion on the outside, and studiously avoid contractions, post-scripts, and other familiarities within. But when writing to those far-ther down the social ladder, you were "at liberty to act as you think proper." Some authorities even held that the amount of space you left at the end of your letter, before signing your name, ought to re-flect your distance in the social hierarchy from the person you were addressing.[32]

The rigidity of this approach to letter writing flourished in England's class-stratified society, and it did not disappear across the Atlantic. Although publishers in the newly independent United States tried to tailor letter-writing manuals to the democratic sensibility of their local market, the "new" manuals somewhat resembled the portrait at Rip Van Winkle's village inn—King George painted over to repre-sent George Washington. In America, no one needed to know how to address an earl or the younger son of a marquis, but allusions to social "superiors" persisted in letter-writing manuals into the mid-nineteenth century. Some publishers simply replaced lists of proper forms of address for the aristocracy with ones for public officials—which people in the U.S. government should be addressed as "His Excellency," which as "the Honorable," which as "Esquire," and so forth.[33] The residual primness of British letter manuals mingled with the enterprising former colonies' emphasis on efficiency, with the re-sult that many guidebooks purveyed an even more bluntly standard-ized approach to letters—almost like the filling out of a form. One writing guide for students offered "skeletons" which young people could "fill up"—the same phrase Elizabeth Hyde Botume used to describe what freed people wanted her to do with their letters.

Dear Sister,

I take this opportunity to write you a few lines.

1. Mention the state of your health, and that of your friends.

2. Of your school and how you like it—of your studies—the progress you make in them—how you like each, and which the best—and why.

3. Use of these branches—and which the most useful.

4. Particulars.[34]

The "particulars" were the hard part. It isn't surprising that a great many little-educated writers, Clint Ward among them, began to apologize for having "nothing strange to write" the very moment they had finished mentioning the state of their health.

That thousands upon thousands of intimate letters—or, letters trying to be intimate—had an unmistakable pro forma quality does not necessarily signify that American letter writers were reading guidebooks with sheep-like obedience. Rhetorical and structural protocols spread in another way, too, less coordinated yet highly effective: people learned to write letters from the letters they received.[35] The conventions of letter writing were always ready at hand. Just as letter writing itself had trickled down from kings and clerics to bureaucrats and small-time merchants, the "rules" trickled down from published authorities, through everyday usage, to the farmhouse tables where people like Clint Ward wrote letters for people like Sarepta Revis.

CLINT WAS ABOUT the same age as Sarepta's husband, Daniel Revis, and he held a distinctive place in their lives. Clint's wife was Ellen Revis. The two men had married each other's younger sisters, and the four of them were siblings-in-law twice over. It isn't hard to imagine that the dynamics of these intertwined families were complicated. There is no way of knowing exactly why Sarepta and Daniel preferred not to have their communications intermediated by Clint, but clearly they did not: Sarepta first went to her cousin John, and Daniel, in what appears to have been his first letter home, said "tel John morgan to rite for you." By the time that letter reached Sarepta, though, she could not follow Daniel's advice even if she wanted to. John had left for the army.

The first letter from Sarepta written in Clint's hand was longer and newsier than those John had penned. Maybe Sarepta was more garrulous around her brother, or maybe Clint simply swelled the letter, not only with stock phrases like "take the present time" and "nothing strange" but also with his own reports of life back on the farm. As hard as it is to distinguish Sarepta's own words from what Clint may have advised her to say, or added on his own authority, the letter did include one thing Clint would surely not have written down had Sarepta not told him to: "if icould see you i coul tell you maney thinges that i cant tell you now."[36]

This comment seemed to announce Sarepta's resolve not to grant Clint full access to her private life, even at the expense of keeping in contact with her husband.[37] By uttering the sentence at all, though, she displayed a level of confidence in her brother. Evidently he was not greatly offended. The barrier that Clint interposed seems to have been merely irksome, at least at first. The increased formalities in Sarepta's letters following John's departure may not signify that Clint was being overbearing. He may have been trying very hard to help. He may have been copying, or trying to impress, his slightly older double brother-in-law. Daniel himself signed off his generally faltering letters in formal language: "I remain your affectioanat hus ban untill death," and "I re main your af fexinate husband unti ldet." Sarepta may have liked these tender sentiments, clichéd though they were (to others—perhaps not to her). She may have asked Clint to reciprocate for her. Or Clint— because he had read a letter-writing manual once, or because he had other models from his experience in mind, or because he was taking a cue from Daniel—just wished to help his sister produce "good" letters.[38]

Uneducated people hewed to timeworn ideas about what made a good letter neither senselessly nor for lack of imagination, but for lack

of instruction otherwise and for fear of the consequences. Subject to
rules handed down by authorities of various stripes and reinforced by
the millions of people writing letters, the intricate and prodigious culture of letter writing—with its tendency, as John Locke perceived, to
expose a person's "breeding, and sense, and his abilities" to scrutiny—
hardly encouraged the calm indulgence of expressive tendencies. No
less famous an American than Andrew Jackson learned the truth of
Locke's caution when, in 1828, the John Quincy Adams campaign got
hold of one of his letters and used it to brand Jackson too ignorant
to be president: "Proof positive is afforded, that the man who aspires
to the chief magistracy is incapable of writing a commonly decent
letter."[39] For ordinary Americans, sending off a letter could understandably be a matter of some anxiety. The language of the authorities was at times as frightening as a fire-and-brimstone sermon. According to one manual, the quality of a letter was a "just reflection upon
any Man," and the "Shame of doing it ill" was so profound that "every
Endeavor" must be made to become "more perfect in this Art." One
of the mainstays of nineteenth-century American publishing, *The New
Universal Letter-Writer*, issued this warning: "We ought not to write
anything of which we may hereafter be ashamed. Well-written letters
are as often burnt, or destroyed, as slovenly epistles are, by accident or
design, preserved, to rise up in judgment against us hereafter."[40]

Shame, disgrace, and zombie-like letters that "rise up" to mortify
(as Andrew Jackson's actually had)—with these afoot, it seems less
remarkable that so many people wrote so similarly than that so many
people ventured to write at all. Running afoul of a published book's
guidelines is a thing one might not mind (or even know one had done),
but the prospect of having your letter viewed in light this harsh could
not have been very emboldening. Evidence abounds that letter readers
could indeed be exacting in their assessments, whether in the high-
flown terms of grace and refinement or the practical ones of simply
not being able to decipher everything. The Civil War not only impelled

many barely literate people to write letters despite their limitations, it also had a way of exposing those people's literary efforts. In the chaos of battle, caches of letters could fall into the hands of curious enemies. An 1862 issue of *Vanity Fair* commented on Southerners' letters seized by Union soldiers: "That these documents, letters to the soldiers, are almost always wretchedly written, hopelessly spelt, and ungrammatical enough to make Lindley Murray turn over in his grave—that this is so, does not astonish us, knowing as we do, the sort of educational system prevailing throughout the South."[41]

People like Clint Ward and Jeannette Hooker didn't read *Vanity Fair*, but such assiduous critiques permeated ordinary life nonetheless. When Fred told Jeannette, however gently, that she should have Nancy write for her, he was sending one of the innumerable messages uneducated people constantly heard, even from loved ones, about their deficiencies. The standards people had for letters—and their judgments of people who didn't live up to them—were not often voiced in letters themselves. A young Michigan soldier wrote to his parents, "Frank Baker the Trobel is that I dont write to him is his letters are not worth redding if he dos write a gain I shal not answer it"—giving no indication of exactly what it was that made Frank's letters worthy of neither reading nor answering. Substantive judgments circulated and made their impressions in ways we cannot directly perceive today, for complaints about someone's poor writing would have been expressed most often in spoken language, or even nonverbal signs of disgust or exasperation. A child looks up from her play while her parent unfolds a letter, reads it (or tries to read it), and says something disparaging about it. A young man of modest literacy says to his friend, "Listen to this!" and reads aloud, with mocking tone, a garbled passage from a letter he has just received. Even if we lack hard evidence for such scenes, their occurrence is easy to infer from their appearance in fiction of the time—a cosmopolitan factory girl, for instance, giggling over the infelicities of a composition from her rural cousin.[42]

The single most telling indication that letter writers anticipated and feared such judgments is that they incessantly apologized for the quality of their writing. Some variant of the phrase "please excuse bad writing" was nearly as ubiquitous as "I take this opportunity to write you a few lines" and "I remain yours." Like those, this convention pre-dated the Civil War. (The earliest occurrence I have found is a letter to Thomas Jefferson from a pleading Maryland ship's captain who had been imprisoned as a smuggler in France: "Please to excuse bad writing and errors as I am so distracted.") By the middle of the nineteenth century, it had ossified into as stale and reflexive a gesture as the others, sometimes even merging with them: "you must excuse Bad writing and spelling we are all well to day and hopeing when these few badly written lines come to hand they may find you all enjoying the same blessing." Most often, less well-educated people appended such apologies to letters to their "superiors" (as the letter-writing manuals had it), but during the Civil War they became a mainstay of letters between family members, too.[43]

A twenty-two-year-old South Carolinian named Abram Hayne Young saw nothing wrong with saying, "Sister pleas excuse this bad wrote letter," but he still knew it was "bad wrote." (He wasn't talking about his penmanship, which the editor of his privately held letters characterizes as "beautiful, rather Spencerian script.")[44] Martha Warrick's brother, evidently worried that his labors over a sheet of paper had been for naught, closed a letter to her by saying, "I dont no how you can read this or not hit is bad dun." Fred Rogers, a young man from Maine, found the sight of his own penmanship a little dispiriting: "I suppose you have some trouble to read my writing," he told his mother, "but you must get used to it for I cannot write any better not now and I think I never can learn to do any better."[45]

Many men and women were facing precisely what John Locke, over a century earlier, had said would befall gentlemen: their letters would expose them to "severer examination." In an era when it was customary to read letters aloud, or even pass them around among friends and neighbors, it was not uncommon for letters to include injunctions against publicity, even explicit requests to burn letters. Sometimes this was because of the confidential nature of the contents, but such requests were just as often linked to self-deprecating remarks about the quality of the writing. Richard and Ellen Goldwaite of New York each asked the other, on occasion, to burn letters that they were "ashamed" to have anyone else see because of their "poor writing." Confederate volunteer Henry Barrow wrote to a friend, "you will please Excuse bad Spelling and writing please dont have this Exposed." A woman who signed only the name Olivia likewise asked that her "badly writton & uncornnected letter" be burned upon receipt.[46]

Soldiers wanted folks back home to know that the deficiencies in their writing should be understood as effects of their physical conditions. Army camps were far from ideal settings for concentration or careful penmanship. Enlisted men could rarely write uninterrupted or in solitude, and virtually never at a desk. Countless soldiers narrated almost comical scenes of writing. "You must excuse bad writing," wrote a Georgian, "as I am lying down and Johnnie is asleep with his head resting on me, and also I have been up two nights now and have been marching all of one night and day." A Vermonter wrote, "I have never said any thing about my bad writing but you take A board and go out in the door yard sit down on the chips put the board on your knees curl up like A sick monkey in A sour apple tree and then write and you will not find falt with my writing."[47]

A Union private from Rossville, Indiana, William Allen Clark, wrote home almost weekly for the whole of his nearly three-year enlistment. He took enough pride in his literacy that he tried to act as a tutor in absentia for one of his younger brothers: "You mustent forget to commence all proper names with a capital letter. Sentences the same, and always make a little black spot at the end of a sentence." It likely pained him, then, that he had to write his regular dispatches to his

parents under conditions so disadvantageous that he rarely sent anything he considered a good specimen of his writing: "Please excus my
writing with a pencil. The paper is so thin I cant write on it with ink."
"Excuse poor writing, for my Desk is a newspaper." "You must excuse poor writing. My fingers are so cold I can hardly hold my pen."
By the final year of the war, marching in William Tecumseh Sherman's
army, Allen was reduced to mixing blackberry juice and gunpowder
for ink and fashioning his own pens: "I am writing with a quill pen of
my own make. Aint I an apt Scholar?"[48]

It seemed to amuse Clark to fashion himself "an apt Scholar" while
he lived hand to mouth on the scorched Georgia countryside. But many
others found that writing's circumstances made them somehow not
themselves. Their solemn, often frustrated apologies suggested that
their letters were inadequate reflections of who they were. The notion
prevailed in antebellum America that one's handwriting, especially in
a letter, attested to one's integrity. How fine a "hand" one wrote—that
is, the quality of one's penmanship—showed strength of character.[49]
Handwriting was also, in its physicality, a substitute for actual presence. Countless times, letter writers described their pleasure upon
opening an envelope, seeing the distinctive "hand" of a loved one, and
holding in their own hands something only once removed from the
touch of skin. "There is something in the exchange of letters," a New
York journalist wrote to his wife in the 1860s, "that ranks next to the
greeting of palm to palm. When I receive one of your letters the sheet
seems to contain more than you were writing; it is something which
has been touched by your hand, which has caught a pulse of your
feeling, and which represents more than the words can possibly say."
In the context of such familiar hopes, it would have been disappointing
to send home, as George Worden did with his first letter to his wife,
something written "on a board on my knees."[50]

In poorly educated families, people who knew each other quite well
formed new impressions, not always favorable, of each other as writers.

"Tell lisa that I recieved hur letter," a North Carolina soldier wrote home, "but I hant never got scollar a nuff to make it all out yet it was so badly rote." Many people announced that they were writing their very first letters—sometimes with the sort of pride Jeannette Hooker felt on Fred's behalf, but rather more often to excuse themselves for their greenness. A girl somewhere in the South, writing to her uncle and signing herself "Your Dear nece Cora," declared, "This is my first letter, so you must excuse all mistakes I have neber gone to school yet, but ma says she will send me to school, when the war over." An Indiana woman named Lucinda Silk wrote, "you must look over my por riten for inever rot eny till about ayer ago." Her undated letter appears to be from 1863 or 1864, meaning she began writing letters in 1862 or 1863—once the war had shown itself to be a protracted affair, and probably once someone close to her had enlisted.[51]

Perry Leonard, too young to join the Union army, wrote to his older brother John, himself only seventeen, a few weeks after John mustered in to the 125th Illinois Volunteers: "Dear Brother, I for the first time in my life take the present opportunity of writing to you." What Perry meant by "writing" was in fact dictating to his father, Gene Leonard, who signed the letter and added: "N. B. this is all Perry's own composition." Even if Perry, like Sarepta Revis, could not write himself, he and Gene apparently thought "composing" a letter was itself a specialized skill of which not everyone was capable, for Perry's letter included this report on the family's youngest brother: "Wally often cryes because he cant Writes to you."[52]

Poor Wally, like everyone else, just wanted a place in the vast circle of letter writers that had sprung up with the war. For all the inhibitions young or barely literate people felt as they contemplated the hard and unfamiliar work of putting pen to paper, it must have been irresistible. Even those not consumed with longing and worry for a husband or son in the army would have witnessed, and maybe envied, the increasingly common spectacle of wives and parents exulting over the

arrival of letters from the front. Sending letters was, as it would remain in future wars, a prime way of showing support for the troops.
An eighteen year old named Amanda sat down in snowy Minnesota
on Christmas Eve in 1862 to write to an Iowa cousin, away in the army,
whom she had never met: "Dear Cousin as I am not personly acquainted ~with you, I do not know ~what to write, that yould interest
you. Please answer this as soon as you can, and ~we will try to get acquainted although we are far from each others."[53]

WHEN JEANNETTE HOOKER received a letter from Fred in his own
hand, their family circle was joined. In telling Nancy, "i think you will
be able to corispond with him with out his gettin Som one els to write
for him," she conjured the promise of direct contact. Fred likely strived
after that very ideal. Writing through an amanuensis seemed sufficient,
evidently, while Fred was sixty miles away at Fort Trumbull and could
plausibly make a brief visit home.[54] His first effort to write in his own
hand dates exactly from his regiment's departure for the front, reaching
out across the 350 miles between his Connecticut home and Fort Ellsworth in Virginia. But as Fred quickly began to discover, once he was
on the inside of literacy, even if no *person* restrained or mediated his
communication with his family, the medium of writing itself still would.

On that first self-written missive, in his primitive block letters, Fred
inscribed "excuse all mistakes." He had not asked his amanuenses to
write anything similar, nor had they (though they made many mistakes)
felt obliged to apologize for themselves. It wasn't *their* mother they
were writing to. Along with the elation of sending first letters came
letter writing's culture of propriety and judgment, as well as the simple
hard work of reading and composing. Fred Hooker probably had no
idea before this that his mother's penmanship wasn't the best. He may
never have tried to read it; little or none of what she wrote would have
been directed to him. Jeannette doubtless was Fred's first and possibly
his only teacher, for children of almost any station in antebellum New

England received their first lessons in the alphabet from their mothers.[55] But she may have been unschooled herself and lacked confidence in her writing. She made a first effort to write "Dear nancy" in the blank space of Fred's letter, judged it unsatisfactory, and tried again. Nineteen-year-old Fred, marching off to war, was having at least some of the following realizations: that literacy is not something you either possess or lack, but rather a skill that can be developed to varying degrees; that his mother's had developed only partially, and that this might explain his own illiteracy; and that, firmly resolved though he was to write his own letters home, the project faced challenges from both sides. Would Jeannette be able to read Fred's poor writing? Would he be able to read hers?

He expressed worry about this in almost every letter he sent home during his first month in Virginia. The second time he wrote unassisted, he remarked, "per haps you canot read my wrighting But i will print some i sent you a letter last wendesday of my one writing." His next letter began "dear mother haveing time to day i thougt i would practice wrighting a little & Let you know how i am geting a Long." A few days later: "excuse such Bad wrighting i mean to write a little & print a little so with Both you can read some) oF it tell me when you get this whither you can read any oF this or not iF you cant i wiLL PRiNT HEARAFTER." Two days after that: "dear mother i think you will git tierd oF haveing me write so oFten i am well i hope you all the same But the oBject in writeing so often is to learn how to write."[56]

Fred's regular expressions of worry and apology, mingled with his vows to improve, open a window on the experience of early literacy. "This is poor wrighting," he wrote at one point, "but you must know i am a new Beginer." "Please excuse bad writing" was a cliché, but its meaning and force changed during the Civil War. There were a lot of "new beginners," and writing was mediating many family relationships for the first time. In addition, most first-time letter writers, because of the material and social conditions of the war, were undergoing changes in themselves—in their self-perception and their place in the world. Farmers were becoming soldiers in a volunteer army. Teenaged boys were leaping forward into something they perceived as manhood. Women were running farms and managing households on their own. All these changes, simultaneous with becoming a person who wrote and received letters, increased the symbolic load letters might carry. Apologies, as formulaic as they at least partly were (although the specific excuses ran the gamut), reveal a great deal about the affective situation of such writers.[57]

Thus did apologies for "bad writing" often morph into meditations on writers' inward states, on their alienation from home or from their former, or better, selves: "Pleas excuse the bad lines and I will try to do better next time"; "excuse all mistakes you know I write so seldom"; "excuse bad spelling and form For I feel so bad." A nineteen-year-old Virginian named George Parker found the material conditions of letter writing straining enough that they might seem to change the very workings of his mind: "Ma i reckon when you reed this you will think i am gone diranged but itis dark an i have no candle an am writng by star light on my knee you may guess How it is I have to keep writing to keep from forgetting i cant see how to read it." (George evidently means it is so dark that if he stops moving his pencil even for a moment he will lose his place on the page and be unable to recall what he was writing.) When Joseph Sherman Diltz sent his first letter home from western Virginia, barely a month after enlisting in the Sixty-Sixth Ohio Infantry, he implored his wife, "Mary you must excuse my bad riting I have not a good Chance to rite lik I had at home." Whatever there was at home that Joseph thought made him a better writer—a proper desk, a manual, or a spelling book—did not ease Mary's anxiety about presenting herself in writing: "Dear Joseph i am at a loss to no what to rite for i cant think of eny thing worth riteing i would like to rite something to you worth reading if i could but i hope you will excuse mi letters."[58]

Fred Hooker likewise found himself changed by his entry into the army and into letter writing. His new view of things—his mother's imperfect literacy, his own struggle to write legibly and be understood—informed his developing self-image. In practical terms, it left him constantly unsure whether he ought to write in cursive—which was more proper, but at which he was decidedly not good—or print. In turn, his identity as a writer became intertwined with his sense of his purpose as a soldier:

> perhaps you cant read this if you cant let me know & i will try to write plainer keep good courage old woman & nancy i hope For the Best this is poor wrighting But may Be You can read it but you must know i am a new Beginer it Probbly will be the making of me to come to the ware so let every body that wants to come to the ware dont discourage them for there ant any thing so very hard in it the real thing is that they ar homesick

Many a young man thought to himself, it probably will be the making of me to come to the war, but perhaps only for an illiterate one would that sentiment flow from his self-description as a "new beginner" at letter writing.[59] For Fred Hooker, the growing pains of entering manhood were entangled with those of becoming a writer. He continued:

> i WRITE THIS TOdAY & Am Kind oF looKiNg For a letter today it is noon no Letters today But i will keep writeing & what shall i say o plenty we drill 1 HOUR BeFore BreakFast & when we get Break fast we have a good apetite . . . But we heard that we wer going to move away But we dont know as we Be iF we do We shant know it untiLL we have orders to pack knap SACS &

(3) days rations keep good courage old / woman & dONT
FEEL BAd FOR my Long aBsence For iF nting happens youl
see me again Some dAy But iT wont make mutch diFERANCE
WHETHER i am to home or not For YOU CAN get yalon as
well wiTHOUT me AS WELL AS / YOU CAN WIT me now
i am waiting to get another letter from you[60]

Approaching his writing almost with the martial discipline of drill, he
seems resolved to write up until the very moment he receives a letter
from home: "Am Kind oF looKiNg For a letter today it is noon no Letters today But i will keep writeing." He needed "practice," as he had
said in his letter ten days before, and he needed to keep up his side of
the correspondence. *What shall I say? Oh, plenty!* Writing, like drilling,
was both a duty and a form of self-improvement. In turn, being a soldier gave him something to write about.

Fred was energetic about both his transformative projects—military
service, of which he says "there ant any thing so very hard in it," and
letter writing, which he must try to do "plainer" for the good of the
"old woman." Yet every time his cursive deteriorated to the point he
expected Jeannette would be unable to read it, he reverted to printing.
As if with accumulating frustration or disappointment with himself,
he arrived near the bottom of a page despondent: it makes no difference
whether I live or die. You can get along as well without me as you can
with me. I am just waiting for a letter. To go risk his life, as he knew
he must ready himself to do whenever the order came to pack knapsacks and three days' rations, was of no avail. Getting a letter was.

As winter approached, Daniel and Sarepta Revis had graver
troubles than their letters could reckon with. The mail had been unreliable. Daniel wrote home on November 26, "I hav not had aleter from
you sinc Johnmorgan brought it"—presumably, when John joined the
regiment more than three weeks earlier. They were stuck speaking to

each other through an intermediary, and even the letters passing through Clint had little of the feeling of conversation, since neither husband nor wife had anything they could respond to that wasn't weeks out of date. When, at last, they had, it was almost beyond them to know how. On December 7, Daniel replied to a letter from Sarepta, presumably penned by Clint, that does not survive:

> Dier wife I take my pen in hand to let you no that I am well at presant and hoping thies few lines may find you wel I hav just received your leter in forming mee that our sweet lit tle slocum is dead which giv mee grate troble . . . Serrpty dont griev for him for it wont do no good he is gon to rest bles his sweet lit tle soal he is gon to heaven to sweet Jesus whar he wil never suf fer no more hecan not come to us but we can go to him sereptia I want you to prepair to meet me and little slocum in heaven I thought wheni left home I wold see you and little slocum again but I shal never see lit ttle slocum no more hier and I may never se you hier any more but stil I hope I wil but if it was gods wil that I shold not I hope I wil meet you in heaven whair we shall havto part no more I hav praid for you ever since I left home and all our folks and I want you all to pray for mee and I wil not forget you[61]

It is a letter to which one would like to have a reply. Sarepta—illiterate, grieving, and probably having just endured her second labor and delivery—could not oblige. The next letter Daniel got from home came from Clint. It was addressed "My Dear Brother," and the heart of it, between the pro forma beginning and end, read, "if I could git a discharge I would stay with sarepta and tend to the things till you would come home." After filling the front of the paper, Clint signed his own name, "H. C. Ward," turned the sheet over and wrote six lonely lines at the top of an otherwise blank page: "My Dear Hus ban take the presant time to let you now that I am weell but the baby is not well but I hope these few lines may finde you well."[62]

This terse missive in Clint's hand, without even the pretense of a signature, is difficult to interpret as an actual letter from Sarepta. Either she was too weak and depressed to direct Clint to write anything more than this, or she was so flattened that she could send no message at all, and Clint took it upon himself to fabricate a letter for Daniel's benefit. It would have been cold comfort, this curt reply to a heartfelt letter of mourning, delivering no news except the dispiriting report that their second baby suffered some unnamed affliction.[63]

If Clint was trying to aid his suffering brother-in-law, he probably only made matters worse. The next time Daniel wrote—having heard nothing but these six cold, ghostwritten lines from Sarepta, if he had heard anything at all—he simply did not know what to say:

> Dier wife I take the presant opertunity to let you no that I am well at presant hoping thies few lines may find you well and doing well I found John hier at the straw bery plains 15 miles from knoxville but I expect to liev hier to nite to go down to knoxville but I do not no how long we wil stay hier I will rite to you and let you no they say we wil go to the big creek gap I want you to rite to me and let me no how you air geting along I hav not time to rite much at presant I found my cows I hope we will get to come home before long I want you to to take good cier of your self til I come home I hant time to rite much at presant so I must bring my let ter to a close by saying that I remain your affectiat husband until death[64]

Many a Civil War soldier's letter has struck modern readers as uninteresting, formulaic, hollow. Individual letters, taken in isolation, may be exactly that. Understood, though, as phases in a relationship, their very hollowness may become as significant as any strident declaration or vivid description of battle. A writer who can eulogize his infant son in a letter—who elsewhere writes to his wife, "Wide rivers runs be twixt us and high mountains rise betwixt urs and many miles seprate urs but I hav not fer got you yet nor never will while my hed stays hot"—does not write a listless letter for lack of literacy or imagination. Listlessness is the emotional state his letter bespeaks. Well, let me know how you are getting along. I have not time to write much. Oh, I found my cows. Well, I haven't time to write much.[65]

Responding to the little he had heard from his wife, perhaps none of which he could even attribute to her, unsure who he was even talking to, Daniel may not have lacked for something to say. He may have been overflowing with things he did not wish to say to his brother-in-law, or had not yet figured out how to say with his hand and a pen.

2

Impressions

The stars are the apexes of what wonderful triangles! What distant and different beings in the various mansions of the universe are contemplating the same one at the same moment!

—Henry David Thoreau

FRED DALLY was somewhere in the South Atlantic, bound from New York to San Francisco, when he began writing a letter to his mother back home. Not long out of port, early in a four-month voyage, he was getting used to new things. Writing at sea wasn't easy, for one. Already he was running out of paper and envelopes, having "damaged so many by spilling the ink so many times over them." From below the equator, the heavens themselves looked different. Thinking his mother would be interested to see some of the Southern Hemisphere's distinctive starscapes, Dally headed his letter with careful pen-and-ink drawings of two constellations—Crux, or the Southern Cross, and Hydrus—as well as the Magellan Clouds.

He commenced his letter on June 25, 1862, and continued adding to it, a little each day, until the passing of a New York–bound ship gave him an opportunity to send it home. Just before handing it off, anticipating that his mother might try to reach him out in California, Dally scrawled a note of instruction in pencil at the top of the letter's first page, right across the Magellan Clouds: "do not send them through the troubled states."[1]

Though afloat on the other side of the globe, Dally knew what was transpiring back on the American mainland. Perhaps that was why he left. If he thought the rolling billows and the Pacific coast were safer places than the Army of the Potomac, he was right. On the day he greeted his mother and inscribed the Southern Cross, New Yorkers in McClellan's army were down near Richmond, taking fire from men under a flag that borrowed the same constellation's name. It was the first of the bloody battles of the Seven Days. Those New Yorkers had not gone as far south as Fred Dally, but they had gone quite far enough to find their world turned upside down. Once men could write, one of their first challenges was to convey the impressions their departures from home made on them—the look of new places, the shocks of war.

DANIEL REVIS WAS about a hundred miles away from Sarepta in Knoxville, Tennessee, when he learned that their first-born son, Slocum, had died. He was still just outside that city when he wrote his taciturn letter of January 12, 1863. Now almost three months gone, he seemed resigned to prolonged separation from his wife with minimal communication between them. Still, he closed his letter in tones of subdued optimism: "I hope we will get to come home before long I want you to to take good cier of your self til I come home." A few days later, he would indeed begin to march back in Sarepta's direction—up the Blue Ridge and across the border into his home state. He was among two hundred Confederate soldiers detached from the Sixty-Fourth North Carolina Infantry and sent to hunt Unionist guerrillas in a tiny mountain hamlet called Shelton Laurel. Now less than fifty miles from home as the crow flies, Daniel nevertheless found himself in an alien environment. "I hav bin about agood deal but i havnot met with such aplace before," he would write home from this place a few weeks later. To an outsider, these mountains might appear little different from those around Daniel's home two counties over, but to him—who witnessed things there he probably had never imagined—it was another world.[2]

For decades, the march of English-language epistolary history had followed patterns of human migration. British colonists sent letters to authorities and mercantile interests across the Atlantic. Explorers of the American interior sent dispatches to coastal cities. Youngest sons of New England families homesteading on the Western Reserve, women on the Oregon Trail, forty-niners in California: all of them wrote home. Unsurprisingly, it became a hallmark of the genre to report impressions of new and strange places to people who remained behind. "The Sceanery of The Country is very Romantic," wrote Harriet Henderson in 1863, recently arrived in Utah as the war raged east of her. "Every thing is on a Very Gigantic Scale, especialy the Mountains." Louisa Cook described Nebraska as "one vast ocean of land" when she crossed it in the summer of 1862. Once over the Rocky Mountains, hungry and cut off from news, she wrote that she was "seeing the elephant"—the same phrase soldiers would use to describe their first time in combat.[3]

The more people migrated, the more letter writing became a part of their lives. Only with the coming of the war, though, did nearly everyone, even the most deeply rooted and poorly educated, become a correspondent.[4] Men traveling with their regiments to the theaters of war were seeing, often for the first time, the geographical expanse of the nation about which they were now fighting. Their families back home yearned to see distant places, too, through the medium of the soldiers' letters. Ralph Waldo Emerson observed that the war "added to every house & heart a vast enlargement. In every house & shop, an American map has been unrolled, & daily studied." Soldiers fleshed out those maps by describing their new surroundings, even sending home little bits of them. Northern men seeing the exotic South for the first time wrote wide-eyed descriptions for their families. Dolph Damuth of Wisconsin wrote home from the lower Mississippi River, "This is the most beautiful place I ever saw. Such fruit trees of all kinds peaches are a quarter grown Apples are as large as Robbins eggs the

Gardans are full of flowers of all kinds. I will send you a rose and an other kind. They will likly be wilted but you can see a rose that grew away down South in Dixie." From coastal South Carolina, Henry Burnell wrote home to his father in still-frozen Maine in March of 1862, "the orange trees are all in blossom & the peach trees also; they have had some green peas so they tell me; that beats Maine. . . . I am going to send you some orange blossoms." George Patten, an Iowan on the Red River in Louisiana, tucked a bit of Spanish moss into a letter to his mother. Henry Thompson sent Lucretia a boll of cotton. From Maryland, Elijah Barker wrote to his sister and brother-in-law in Indiana, "you will find inclosed some seeds that came off of a evergreen tree I want you toplant them I think They will gro in that country it is a butiful tree and bears A red berey the name is holley." George Ewing sent his parents persimmon seeds from northern Virginia.[5]

Although Northerners saw more of the South than Southerners did of the North, the latter, too, were impressed by what they saw of enemy territory. Iowa Royster, a North Carolinian in Lee's army, wrote home from Chambersburg, Pennsylvania, a few days before the Battle of Gettysburg: "It is the most beautiful country you ever saw. the neatest farms, large white barns fine houses, good fences—The whole country is covered with the finest crops of wheat. Such wheat is not seen in our country." But such appreciation of the picturesque rarely overcame sectional antipathy. Iowa closed his letter rejoicing over the destruction the Army of Northern Virginia soon would sow in Pennsylvania: "All the fences that are burnt now are Yankee fences. They'll be willing for us to stay out of the Union hereafter. We've come back to the Union, but not as they expected." It was a bitter sentiment from someone whose parents could be taken for Unionists, given what they named their children: five boys were christened Vermont Connecticut, Iowa Michigan, Arkansas Delaware, Wisconsin Illinois, and Oregon Minnesota, and the three girls were Louisiana Maryland, Virginia Carolina, and Georgia Indiana.[6]

Many small farmers and mountain folk had scarcely ever left home and did not have to go far to see startling sights. Benjamin Barrett, who lived just down the mountains from Daniel and Sarepta Revis, across the border in Pickens County, South Carolina, had never seen the ocean until the Confederate army sent him to his own state's coastline at the start of the war: "hit is with plesure to take mi pen in hand to Let yo No that i am well at this time An hope that these fue lines ma find yo all well. i have a many a strange thing to right to you. i have Sene a many strang thing Since i sene you. Sea is a strange looking water Cause the tide rize ann falls evry twenty four ours." But exotic scenery was not a deep well of material. It would run dry long before most newcomers to letter writing became fully accustomed to the new medium. Even someone like Daniel Revis, who had never "met with such aplace" as two counties over from his home, could prove notably laconic about what he was seeing and doing.[7]

Daniel and his company had been dispatched to Shelton Laurel to avenge a salt heist. A band of guerrillas had recently raided the town of Marshall, county seat of Madison County. They plundered the homes of well-to-do townspeople, taking money, clothes, blankets, and most of all salt. Of the many wartime shortages Southerners faced, salt was among the most worrisome, especially in the mountains, where its absence portended abject starvation. Winter was slaughtering time, and without salt a family's stores of meat would be ruined in a matter of weeks. Some saw crisis approaching on the horizon. Early in the fall of 1862, John Jefcoat, an inland South Carolina farmer stationed on the coast, wrote home to his wife: "Rachel you must be cearfull with your Salt I have bin all over charleston to day looking after Salt liver pool Salt is such as you have is worth $75 dollars a Sack and hard to git at that." By January, with hogs ready to butcher, people were desperate. "The people are generally in great distress about salt," wrote a Mississippian the same week as the Marshall raid. The following January, Martha Poteet, also from the Carolina mountains, told her husband, "I went to the cross Roads last Saturday and got two dollars worth salt and Sunday Night some body stoled about half of it." Another Southern woman told her son "Salt Salt Salt is the cry." (Imagine their reactions if they could have read Harriet Henderson's impressions of Utah the same year: "Nearly Every Summer there is a incrustation of salt formd on the Banks of the salt lake which supply us with any amount of salt.")[8]

Most of the salt raiders of Madison County had never wanted this war. They owned no slaves, grew no cotton, and stood to gain little or nothing by secession. Many had enlisted in the Sixty-Fourth North Carolina Infantry under duress and, as soon as they could, deserted and returned to the mountains. Confederates who styled themselves the inheritors of the American Revolution dubbed such men "Tories." For them and their families, all the rebellion had brought was disruption, privation, and fear, and when they went to steal salt, they targeted the homes of the leading rebels in their neighborhood: Colonel Lawrence Allen, the commander of the Sixty-Fourth regiment, and John Peek, the captain of one of its fourteen companies. John was home on leave, and they shot him. They terrified the colonel's wife and children, two of whom had scarlet fever and were near death.

The colonel and his lieutenants orchestrated swift and shocking retribution. Under their orders, Daniel Revis and the two hundred men with him flushed the guerrillas out of the woods near Shelton Laurel. Going house to house, they seized the men they found. Where they found none, they tortured wives and mothers, demanding to know where the men were hiding. They tied nooses around women's necks, ran the ropes over tree limbs, jerked them off the ground, and let them down: Where is he? They did it repeatedly. One of these women was eighty-five years old. Others they whipped with hickory switches. When one woman refused to tell where her husband was, they tied her to a tree, set her infant child down on the ground where she could not reach it, and threatened to leave both of them there. It was January, and snow was on the ground. She did not tell.

Daniel's company rounded up thirteen men and boys and marched them a few miles out of Shelton Laurel, allegedly taking them to Knoxville to be tried. Although it is impossible to know exactly what happened, Lieutenant Colonel James Keith is believed to have ordered the prisoners to kneel and his soldiers to shoot them. He threatened his own soldiers with death when they hesitated to carry out the executions. The youngest prisoner, thirteen-year-old David Shelton, watched as his father and older brothers were shot to death. He pleaded for his life but, like all of them, was killed.[9]

When Daniel Revis next wrote to Sarepta, a few weeks later, he said: "you must excuse me for not riting no more thani hav for i hav had no paper til now we keep hunting tories we ketch one ons ina while."[10]

EMERSON CALLED THE Civil War "a new glass through which to see things." Its excitements and its trials made it so—the devotions as well as the atrocities it inspired. Ordinary people saw themselves and the world around them in wholly new lights. Men who had never been far from their birthplaces traveled hundreds of miles and confronted the carnage of battle. Women who had never been expected or encouraged to venture beyond certain "proper" spheres of responsibility now hauled wagons and managed finances, in addition to the cooking and child-rearing they had always done.[11]

For the many people whose daily lives had never involved much reading and writing, the war was a "new glass" in part because they transferred their wartime experiences onto paper. Sending and receiving letters was itself a new and affecting experience. The challenges of navigating the class-bound cultures of literacy and form were exacerbated by the circumstances of the war. What they witnessed and what they suffered, the feats they performed and the agonies they endured: they had to assimilate these startling new turns for themselves and, at the same time, figure out how to articulate them in words a loved one could understand and appreciate. If they could not—if their inward transformations went uncommunicated—they risked estrangement from the very people to whom letters were supposed to connect them. Some, like Fred Hooker, struggled to write legibly at all. Others, like Daniel Revis, could string words together well enough but met with realities that overtaxed—or, in their view, did not belong in—their writing.

It is impossible to say why Daniel, his eyes scorched by Shelton Laurel, said nothing more to Sarepta about it than "we ketch a tory once in a while." One may imagine that, lacking the fluency for more than a letter's conventional pleasantries, it never occurred to him even to attempt writing about matters of such gravity and complexity—although he had been willing to try when Slocum died. He may have thought the doings of soldiers were men's business—but he thought nothing, evidently, of informing Sarepta he was "hunting tories." Details of the brutal vengeance on Unionist mountain families may have been more than he wanted to divulge to Clint, Sarepta's amanuensis, whom Daniel expected would read the letter to her. They may have been more than he wanted to divulge to Sarepta, even had he been able to do so confidentially. All three of them voiced ambivalence about the war at one time or another (Daniel: "I hop that pease will be mad be fore long"; Clint: "thare is no jestus in this old war"; Sarepta: "I do wishe this old war would stop"). Daniel may have wanted to hide his role in events at Shelton Laurel from everyone, forever, in craven fear of the consequences for himself, or in guilt and shame that he was involved, or for reasons we cannot surmise. He may have been ordered never to speak of it.[12]

It is likewise impossible to locate Daniel himself in his words, to form any interpretation of his thoughts and feelings that rises above conjecture. There is something sinister about his terse account—a callous indifference in using "ketch" for what might better be named "murder" or "terrorize"—and something haunting about "ons ina while." There is no evidence on record that Daniel's company captured any more Unionists in the weeks between the massacre and his letter to Sarepta—certainly nothing on the order of what had happened at Shelton Laurel. Did the massacre make so faint an impression on him as to blend into the ordinary flow of what happens once in a while? Or was Daniel's reticence the quiet sobriety of the soldier who prefers not to speak of what he saw in combat? Was he traumatized? Had he thought of "sweet little slocum . . . gon to heaven" when he was told Colonel Allen's children died of their illnesses just after the Marshall raid? Did he, like his leader, seek misplaced vengeance? Had he seen the Shelton Laurel woman tied to a tree, out of reach of her shivering baby?

It is an unremarkable letter ("I hav not much war nuse to rit"; "I hav nothing very interesting to rite at presant"), or would be without its dateline: "shelton loral" in "Materson co." Even once pinned to that place, the letter becomes again a disappointment, for it penetrates none of the fog surrounding events at Shelton Laurel. It yields up only more fog, now gathered around Daniel's mind. We cannot recapture what he—cold and dirty, writing on scarce paper to his illiterate wife— thought about the massacre. But his example reminds us that what makes a "dull" moment in a common soldier's letter may not be its emptiness of meaning but its over-fullness.[13]

If Daniel could not or would not give Sarepta the "particulars" or "interesting news" a good letter was supposed to have—if his letter amounted, in the end, to a form: "so I must bring my leter to a close by saying that I remain yur afectinat husband until deth"—he was hardly alone in this. Much of the time, rank-and-file soldiers and their families sent letters simply because they knew their loved ones would be disappointed if they did not; because they wanted to give each other proof they were still alive; because they wanted the sense of connection letters promised, even if they did not know how to unlock that promise. Unsure what feelings a letter might be capable of conveying or how to make one convey them, too shocked or overwhelmed by what war had shown them to begin to describe it, many writers made scant discernible effort to communicate matters of substance, instead fumbling through litanies of stale convention.

What people like Daniel and Sarepta were trying to turn to their purpose was a form optimized for disseminating news, relaying official information, and transacting business. In such contexts, it had been useful for letters to follow predictable patterns. Consistency of formats, structures, and styles is an inestimable good for business but not for the sustenance of emotional bonds between people. Still, many people did find ways to adapt the letter form to their ends. War made impressions on them, and they in turn made impressions on letters.[14]

THORNTON CLARK, IN all likelihood, had never been south of the Ohio River before the Civil War. Born a little east of Cincinnati, he migrated in his youth to Indiana. There he married Nancy Phipps in 1851, and by the time the war broke out a decade later they had four children. Alice was eight when Thornton enlisted, Jacob five, Jane three, and Annie an infant. A farmer who also did some carpentry, Thornton may have been motivated by patriotism, an army bounty and regular pay for his family, or both. He enlisted in 1862 just before his thirty-sixth birthday, in the wake of Abraham Lincoln's summertime call for three hundred thousand men.[15]

That executive order inspired the New York abolitionist James Sloan Gibbons to write a poem called "We Are Coming, Father Abraham, Three Hundred Thousand More." The poem inspired a popular song, and it fittingly cast the second great wave of Union enlistment as an affair of the Northern heartland. In the anthem of the first year at war, Julia Ward Howe's "Battle Hymn of the Republic," the Civil War was a righteous crusade—the result of God unleashing "the fateful lightning of his terrible swift sword"—and Northerners were called to martyrdom: "As [Christ] died to make men holy, let us die to make men free." Gibbons's poem (like the other big enlistment song of summer 1862, George Frederick Root's "Battle Cry of Freedom") was earthier. "Three Hundred Thousand More" did not cast God as the main character but rather a mass of working families facing three-year deployments:

> We are coming, Father Abraham, three hundred thousand more,
> From Mississippi's winding stream and from New England's shore
> We leave our ploughs and workshops, our wives and children dear,
> With hearts too full for utterance, with but a silent tear;
> . . . .
> If you look all up your valleys, where the growing harvests shine,
> You may see our sturdy farmer boys, fast forming into line;
> And children from their mothers' knees, are pulling at the weeds,
> And learning how to reap and sow against their country's needs;
> And a farewell group stands weeping at every cottage door:
> We are coming, Father Abraham, three hundred thousand more![16]

Thornton Clark was one of the three hundred thousand—almost half a million, it would turn out, by year's end—who left their "ploughs and workshops," their "wives and children dear." The response to Lincoln's call was not strong at first, but in early August the War Department threatened that, if states did not reach their quotas by the middle of the month, a draft would be instituted. Enlistment drives reached fever pitch all across the North. By the end of the summer, recruiting offices in Albany, New York, were staying open on Sundays. The governor of Massachusetts ordered all businesses to close early every day during the last week of August to make time for enlistment activities. In the Midwest, where a Confederate drive into Kentucky was threatening to bring the war straight into Indiana and Ohio, men rapidly filled up their states' quotas. Thornton signed up on August 26.[17]

The farmer boys leaving their families "weeping at every cottage door" made for stirring imagery. Even if these were romanticized scenes, they captured an important aspect of the war's meaning for people in what was then called the West—the Old Northwest Territory and the Upper Mississippi valley, states such as Michigan, Indiana, Iowa—where slavery had never existed and abolitionism had not thrived. If the West at first felt distant from a conflict begun by secessionists in South Carolina, blamed on abolitionists in New England, and waged between capitals at Washington and Richmond, it came in time to seem absolutely central.

Western farmers had an unquestionable stake in the conflict between union and disunion. The West's agricultural economy would wither if it could not send its bounty to market on a freely navigable Mississippi River. The Republican Party's commitment to "free soil, free labor, and free men" had evolved from Thomas Jefferson's vision of a republic of yeoman farmers. That vision had been focused on precisely this great tract of land, which Jefferson pushed to keep free of slavery when it was organized under the Northwest Ordinance of 1787. The region's economic prospects made him so desperate to have the Mississippi that he made the Louisiana Purchase in 1803 despite believing he was acting unconstitutionally. By improving small plots of land and reaping the abundance of the great interior, the millions of people who pushed west across the Alleghenies embodied what many Americans believed distinguished their nation from Europe. It was this pattern of settlement in the Old Northwest—in contrast to what happened in the Southwest, where large planters made fortunes in cotton by exploiting slave labor and an emerging system of finance—that Republicans valorized in their campaign against the territorial expansion of slavery in the 1850s. It was what helped make one of the region's native sons, Abraham Lincoln, a standard-bearer for the party. Now, the Mississippi River was, in military as well as economic terms, what William Tecumseh Sherman called "the spinal column of America"—so vital that the Ohioan general wrote in late 1863, "To secure the safety of the navigation of the Mississippi River I would slay millions. On that point I am not only insane, but mad."[18]

This is not to say that westerners were unanimously fervent about the war. In fact, few places in the North were as deeply divided at the start. Lincoln carried these states in the 1860 election but by smaller margins than in New England. Indiana's Republican governor, Oliver P. Morton, wrote to Lincoln early in the war to explain the political constraints he found himself under owing to Indiana's "larger proportion of inhabitants of Southern birth or parentage—many of these, of course, with Southern proclivities—than any other free state." The Ohio River valley—the north bank, that is, across from Kentucky—was the birthplace of "Copperheads," both the term and the phenomenon. The *Cincinnati Gazette* first applied this derisive term for northern opponents of the war to Indiana Democrats.[19]

By the summer of 1862, the possible consequences for the West of long-term disunion had grown more worrisome. Not coincidentally, it was during this summer that the word "Copperhead" came into use—when being opposed to the war started to warrant a special pejorative in many westerners' eyes. Recent events had dashed Northern hopes of a glorious, heaven-ordained suppression of the rebellion. The Battle of Shiloh in April shocked the nation with casualty counts that exceeded anything in American history to that time. Throughout the spring, Stonewall Jackson and his men were outmaneuvering and roundly embarrassing Union forces in the Shenandoah valley. While George McClellan was leading the Army of the Potomac up the Virginia Peninsula on a campaign to capture Richmond, Confederate cavalry under J. E. B. Stuart rode clear around the Union force. And McClellan's drive was frustrated by the Seven Days' Battles, even bloodier than

Shiloh. His army withdrew from Richmond's doorstep just as Lincoln was issuing his call for reinforcements.

And so they went forth, the three hundred thousand. There were few abolitionists among them, and they were not sufficiently fired by patriotism to have enlisted the year before. But they were, more or less, volunteers—not the conscripts, substitutes, and bounty jumpers who would come later. If they were not consciously fighting for the political and economic destiny of their nation and their region, they probably did think they were fighting for a microcosm of them. Perhaps not many poor western farmers engaged in exactly the political prognostication of the Massachusetts officer who believed civil war, if forestalled, would only afflict the next generation: "I know if this war is not fought through and settled as it should be," Joseph Collingwood wrote to his wife, "that our boys will have to be soldiers and pass through what I have." But they understood that their own families' futures were implicated in the war. The Northern states that sent the most soldiers to the war, as a percentage of their military-age male population, were Illinois, Indiana, and Ohio. In Indiana, even with its many "inhabitants of Southern birth or parentage," almost three-quarters of men between eighteen and forty-five joined the Union army.[20]

When they left home, their families did not simply stand and weep. Their industrious wives and weed-pulling children were helping to prosecute the war. And as the men fanned out across a land they had perhaps never known except through maps, their letters—trying to convey the new sights before their eyes back to those within cottage doors—became crucibles of their understanding of the war, of themselves, and of their families.

WHEN THORNTON CLARK arrived in Spencer County, Indiana, as a young man, he was settling in Abraham Lincoln's old neighborhood. The year Thornton was born, the Lincoln family was living in a thickly

wooded valley amid the hills of southwest Indiana, much of which
would be farmland by the time Thornton and Nancy Clark started
their family about five miles north of the sixteenth president's boy-
hood home. In Abe Lincoln's youth, Indiana was a brand-new state.
A hundred-odd miles to the north, the city of Indianapolis had recently been designated the state capital. By 1860, Spencer County's
population had increased nearly tenfold from what it was when Lincoln lived there, and Indianapolis, though a fraction of the size of
Cincinnati and Chicago, was the seventh largest city in the former
Northwest Territory. Most of the state's recruits traveled first to that
city. For them, as for farmers throughout the West, enlistment's first
great transition, even before departure for the theaters of war, was
the spectacle of humanity massed in urban centers and vast military
encampments.

Many of the men converging on Indianapolis were ardent young
volunteers. Isaac Mark Abbot was only a boy—eighteen years old
when he enlisted in the summer of 1862. Thornton could practically
have been his father. For an unmarried man, first days in the army
could feel like a grand adventure, and Isaac wrote home to his parents
from "Camp Joe Reynolds" in high spirits: "It is with pleasure that I
take my pencil in hand to scratch a few lines to you to let you know
how I am making it Soldiering. . . . I don't have any duty to perform
except to dispose of my share of the grub and I have discharged that
duty promptly so far." From the very beginning, his novel surroundings widened his eyes: "I wish you could be right where I am for a little
while just to see the sights I am in the busiest fort of the city and I bet
a thousand people have passed me on the pavement since I commenced
my Letter."[21]

Thornton arrived in the same camp less than two weeks later. The
adventure was markedly less fun for him than Isaac found it to be.
Written on a sheet of patriotic stationery, emblazoned in blue with a
waving flag and the motto "The Union Forever," Thornton's first

letter home conveyed enthusiasm in its outward appearance. Internally, it did not.

> Dear Companion
>
>   I take this opportunity to inform you that I am well and have been ever sience I left home except my eyes I got sinders in them on the cars as we came from terrahut to Indianapolis but they are nearly well a gain I was examined to day they had me to strip off naked but they would not let me off so I have to go in to the service but I dont want you to grieve abut me and think that you will never see me again but I want you to content your self the very best you can under the circumstances and I want you to go to a throne of grace as often as you can and ask our father to spare my life and health that we may be per mitted to see each others faces on this earth and enjoy eachothes society in peace I want you to take as good care of your self and Children as you can we have not drawed our uniform nor pay yet but expect to draw to morrow and then I will send my money home as soon as I can give this to Alice and tell her to be a good girl I got it in a bunch of paper I want you to write to me as soon as you get this and let me know how you all are as I dont know how soon we will be ordered a way from here direct your letters to Indianapolis Camp Jo Rheynolds Ind your affectionate and loveing Husband untill death Thornton Clark

The letter proceeds in the ordinary way: "I take the opportunity," a report of his health (fine, except for the eyes), followed by a dive into particulars. And it is quite a dive. Although he uses no punctuation, there are easily discernible starts and ends to sentences as he commences doing what letters are supposed to do—relating what's new and interesting. "They are nearly well again." "I was examined today." "They had me to strip off naked." Then, Thornton's solid syntax melts into a fluid race of thoughts, coursing over *but*s, *so*s, and *and*s for almost a hundred words until he reaches anything like a period.[22]

It was the nakedness, it seems, at which his letter forked, the customary report of the news giving way to a spontaneous reflection on what is happening to him and how it veers from his expectations. "*But* they would not let me off," the cascade begins, as if this harshest possible examination of his physical self—his older body set against those of eighteen-year-olds—obviously, Thornton seems to think, should have ended his military career. He must have intimated to Nancy, upon his departure, that this would be all—that he would go as far as Indianapolis, be judged unfit, and get sent home. Otherwise, why report to her, as if she did not already expect it, "I have to go in the service"? Quickly turning again, he adds "*but* I dont want you to grieve about me and think that you will never see me again." It has taken only a few dozen words to travel from irritated eyes to the prospect of death. Though presented as the worry he anticipates Nancy will have, it may be Thornton's own fear which speaks now, and the sentence's final turn—one more *but* to press upward from disappointment and anxiety into hope and reassurance—may console him as much as it seeks to console her. "But I want you to content your self the very best you can under the circumstances and I want you to go to a throne of grace as often as you can and ask our father to spare my life and health that we may be per mitted to see each others faces on this earth and enjoy eachothes society in peace."

Many soldiers, especially the more devout, wrote out nearly identical intercessions, bidding their wives and parents "go to a throne of grace," seek the "help in time of need" that the fourth chapter of Hebrews promises, and repeat the prayers of their husbands and sons for a physical reunion in a time of peace. But Thornton Clark had a peculiarly striking tendency to make his letters to Nancy a devotional form, a way of casting his eyes upward—cinder burned though they were, less interested than Isaac Mark Abbott's in scanning the throngs of thousands and trying to relay those sights home. The maturer man's eyes would widen to other things, and he would have to stretch the letter form to capture them.

For soldiers who were more literate than Fred Hooker but, like him, found enlistment a time of expanded horizons, it did not take long to realize that many of letters' conventions were an ill fit. Most significantly, letters were supposed to report "the news." Newspapers themselves branched off from epistolary forms in sixteenth-century England, when what was known as the private "news letter"—an authoritative source's account of important events—became public, anonymous, and commercial. Before long, newspapers had shed most outward signs of their epistolary origins (only the habit of referring to reporters as correspondents remains today), but letter writers continued to feel the imperative to be "newsy." Thus did countless letter writers, once they reached the point in a formulaic structure at which they knew they were supposed to supply "particulars," instead offered apologies for having nothing much of interest to write at present.[23]

People on both sides of wartime correspondence appeared sheepish about their inability to "fill up" a letter with news. They often took the shape and size of the paper itself as the measure of a satisfactory letter. Leaving blank space on the page showed that it was no physical constraint of the medium which kept the writer from saying more, and a letter writing manual counseled, "never send off a half sheet, for it looks niggardly." Writers sometimes apologized when they did this (Franklin Alford to his enlisted son Warren: "I shall have to close this letter for the want of time hopeing you will pardon me for not filling my sheet") or got upbraided by their loved ones (the numerous soldiers who explained why their past letters had been so short were obviously responding to explicit or assumed complaints). As the war went on and paper grew scarce, leaving space blank also seemed wasteful, unless it was a practice a couple had worked out together. Henry Thompson commonly wrote on Lucretia's letters and mailed them back to her, so she occasionally left part of a page unused and gave the instruction, "you must fill up the Blank." Betsy Blaisdell frequently wrote on only the first half of a folded sheet so that her husband, Hiram, hard up for paper, could tear off and use the blank part: "you can take half of this sheet and write on it."[24]

Apologizing for having too little news was an old tradition. Letter writers of the late-Renaissance English countryside, especially when they wrote to London, expressed regret that they could not narrate many interesting events. But soldiers in the U.S. Civil War felt unusual pressure to write newsy letters. They themselves, of course, wanted their families to "tell them all the news," but they at least were familiar with the sights and routines of life at home. Their loved ones were practically desperate to learn the distant and unknown realities of army life and the war. Yet, in a frustrating irony, news was precisely what soldiers most lacked. They spent long periods of time encamped, waiting, not knowing where they might go next, or when, and not understanding what role they were playing in the larger war effort. Useful public information was almost their greatest deficiency, after fresh food and sanitary facilities. Milton Barrett of upcountry South Carolina explained all this forthrightly: "hit is all ways expected of those at home when tha git a letter from a solger in serves to hear all that is a going on in the armey but hit is a mis stake. a sholger nows but litle moar what is a goin on than you do only in his own ridge ment or when he receves orders to march and than he dont know whether hit is for a fight or to change en campements til he sees the enmey."[25]

Americans of the Civil War era dwelled in an age of emergent mass media, when much important news traveled by telegraph. They felt even more outmatched by the press than aristocratic writers more than a century earlier, who likewise had been frustrated to find printed newspapers bursting on the scene and eclipsing the news-reporting function of epistolary culture. Even soldiers from sparsely populated western regions knew that by the time their letters from the front reached home their families' local papers would doubtless have explained everything they themselves could report. "I dont know any thing more that will Be interresting to yu," wrote Elijah Barker; "as for war nuse you can see more in the papers then I have got time or space to write." Soldiers' frustration with their lack of news obtained across rank and class. George McClellan's letters to his wife have become famous windows into the early operations of the Army of the Potomac, but most military men, even of officer rank, had too little access to "war news" to satisfy their loved ones' curiosity. One Union colonel wrote, "I actualy can not tell you half as much as you know yourself. After we begin to move I may be better posted and shall not fail to give you any and all such information as may intrest you, but you can read more in one day in the papers than I *now* could give you in a week."[26]

Folks at home often mailed newspapers to their men in the army, and soldiers voiced great appreciation for these glimpses of home. But poring over these printed pages surely reminded the men that they possessed nowhere near this much information, and that most of them also could not measure up to that standard of verbal facility. Even men who were in a position to offer eyewitness testimony on a historic event, like a major battle, begged off reporting the details because they felt themselves and their language inadequate to the task. Joseph Hollis wrote to his younger brother after the Battle of Chancellorsville, "I suppose you have seen an account of it in the papers but it is beyond discription the roar of artillery and musketry is beyond anything you can imagine." When a South Carolinian wrote to his sons, "You hav no doubt read the particulars in the papers, but the horror & fright cannot be described on paper," he tacitly characterized what was "in the papers" as essentially false—a futile effort to put "on paper" what never could go there. Larkin Kendrick began a letter to Mary Catherine by confessing, "i have nothing Straneg to wright to yo at this time," yet went on to tell her—without explanation or comment—that he had briefly been held as a prisoner of war behind Union lines.[27]

Again and again, "particulars"—precisely what should fill a letter's body, make it original and distinct from its prescribed frame—were unavailable, had been superseded by the newspapers, or were simply inexpressible. It could seem unclear to many writers just what their letters were supposed to do, or how they could possibly convey realities of war for which they had no words. Everyone loved receiving letters and knew how happily their own letters were received, but what should or could they say?

CIVIL WAR LETTERS are hailed as especially revealing historical sources because the army did not censor them (as it would in later conflicts), but plenty of other forces constrained what people wrote, especially poor and uneducated people. Many soldiers, trying to give "the news" when they possessed little vital information, ended up producing labored, wooden, mechanical letters. They and their homefolk alike often felt incapable of what counted as good writing and forbore from anything that might worry their loved ones. Because few of them spent much time on political reflections, historians have debated how ideologically motivated people were in fighting this war. But the most plausible explanation is not that these men and women lacked political thoughts; they may simply have thought that was not what their loved ones wanted to read.[28] What was left? They talked about a lot that we might find trivial—the food, the weather, minor illness, local prices for salt, bacon, and flour—and that, if not trivial to them, no doubt did fall short of forging the emotional connections they craved. What was genuinely *new*, and not available in the papers, was personal—new experiences, new feelings—and they had to discover by experiment how writing and the letter form might capture those.[29]

In one sense, it scarcely mattered what went into letters. Isaac Mann wanted them from his wife so desperately he didn't care what they said. Marching toward Cheat Mountain in western Virginia, the Ohio private wrote to his father-in-law: "I hav not had aletter from susan since i left home i am afraid that she is sick or some of the children I want you to write to me as soon as you git this letter . . . I you could send me anew paper or too i bough me some stamps at marsh field & thay all stuck to gether & spoiled the drums are beating & i close forgiv my bad writ_{ing} & spelling . . . rit me a long letter & tell me all the news." Fully a month later, a regimental mail delivery brought a newspaper with his name on it. As Isaac told Susan, "[I] thought it was from your father but when i come to open it i found too little peases of paper in it my dear wife i was glad to hear from you & to hear that you was all well i am so glad to git letters from hom." The two little pieces of paper Susan enclosed have not survived. They perhaps said little, for she evidently was not very literate. But Isaac so treasured them that, in his reply, he implored his wife, "i want you to rite big letters if you cannot think of any thing to rit make a b c s and when you get tired tired of that mak black marks."[30]

This could be the warmest and most generous expression in epistolary history. Isaac was releasing Susan from everything: from the formulae prescribed by letter-writing manuals, from the standards of good writing and spelling, from literate people's expectations, from the imperative to "tell all the news," from all deliberation about how to represent oneself to a distant loved one. To him, writing out the alphabet, even sending a paper covered in "black marks," would be entirely satisfactory.

And why not? With ABCs written out in the hand he would recognize as hers, Susan could send Isaac almost all the messages he most wanted: I am still living, I have not forgotten you, I remain yours. The maxim that 90 percent of human communication is nonverbal ostensibly pertains only to in-person interactions, where body language, facial expressions, and tones of voice carry meaning. A paper-based medium appears to work with words alone, yet only a moment's consideration reveals numerous ways a letter "speaks" beyond language: through its handwriting, its length, the blankness or fullness of the paper, and every imaginable nonverbal feature that might be inscribed thereon, not to mention the accidental circumstances and timing of its arrival—like Susan's scraps, in a wondrous surprise, slipping from the folds of the newspaper when Isaac returned from guard duty.

Isaac's suggestion—a zero degree of letter writing, with centuries of accumulated protocol swept away—defines the end of a continuum. At one extreme is the idealized formula, evolved slowly over generations; at the other is a page of black marks. Scarcely anyone operated at the extremes (there is no evidence Susan took Isaac up on his invitation, nor is there any letter anywhere wholly devoid of some individual stamp), but Civil War letter writers collectively were engaged in renegotiating the balance. People who were not highly literate to begin with had little to lose by experimenting.[31]

One option was to slip the medium altogether, if not in exactly the way Isaac Mann imagined. Soldiers trying to communicate something about their new surroundings frequently resorted to drawing. They created maps of their encampments, sketched layouts of their sleeping arrangements, and drew tents, cooking facilities, and the winter quarters they took pride in building. On April Fool's Day, Fred Hooker made a crude caricature of a big-nosed figure wearing a hat and carrying a saber; he labeled it "Jeff," presumably for Jefferson Davis. Children sometimes drew pictures on their mother's letters to their father.[32] A great variety of preprinted stationery offered both soldiers and their families another kind of expressive supplement to what they themselves could write. Letter paper with patriotic images and mottoes—flags, portraits of generals, and the like—was purveyed widely among men in both armies, and on the home front, at the outset of the war.[33] Also common were sentimental images with snippets of verse. Isaac Mann's letter to his wife bore a full-color engraving of a soldier holding his bayonet in one hand and, with his other arm, embracing a young woman pressing a handkerchief to her eyes. The image was captioned "The Girl I Left Behind Me," and next to it in fine print ran a stanza not from the popular song of that name but from another one, "The Soldier's Tear":

> He turn'd and left the spot—Oh do not deem him weak—
> For dauntless was the soldier's heart, though tears were on his cheek;
> Go, watch the foremost ranks in danger's dark career.
> Be sure the hand most daring there has wiped away a tear.[34]

Lafayette Alford wrote a letter to his mother on paper bearing the image of an early Union hero, Elmer Ellsworth. In May 1861, Ellsworth personally removed the Confederate flag from an Alexandria, Virginia, hotel and then was shot and killed by the rebel hotel owner. The last letter Ellsworth wrote before his death had appeared in the press, and an excerpt of it now was reproduced on memorial stationery. "I thought these lines would express my Sentiments," wrote Lafayette. "These words were expressed by Colonel Elsworth in his last letter to his parents."[35]

For most people, drawings and special stationery were helpful but insufficient. The feelings associated with unprecedented experiences and historic events, if they were to travel across distance, for the most part would have to go in a person's own words. For this purpose, the inherited forms of letter writing, however ungainly, were at least the starting point; under a little pressure, they proved malleable. Caleb Henry Phillips, a private from Massachusetts, wrote his only surviving letter to his wife, Caroline, from the same Union camp in Indianapolis where Thornton Clark began his service (Camp Joe Reynolds, now dubbed Camp Morton). Like countless uninitiated letter writers, Caleb did a few things wrong: he dated his letter without a year, and he didn't use the paper in the appropriate way. But the latter deviation from custom opened the way to a mode of expression previously inaccessible to him.

Nineteenth-century Americans generally wrote letters on folios of stationery—large sheets of ruled paper, folded down the center to form a little book with four pages. Writers began on the first page (the front of the folio); then opened it, laid it unfolded or folded it back, and wrote on pages 2 and 3; and finally closed it and finished their letter on the back, the fourth page.[36] Unfamiliar with these mores, Caleb Phillips opened his folio, skipping the front page, and on the inner two pages did the best he could to write a proper letter to his wife:

Indianapolis Sept 9th

Dear ^{Wife} i now sit down to write to let you know that i am well i want to let you know that you are a going to get your bounty money the other was lost the other is on the way now do you get all of my letters i should like to know if you do i have sent one to Herbert for him to let you have Some money and i want you to let me know if he has i write two and three letters a week and get none what is the i see Maley to day and he said that we should Come home before our time was out and i hope we shall dont you are you all well at home i tell you this is a lazy life they all are sick of it i hardly know what to write Harrison is well so is tomy and so is Edward he let me have this paper to Write on Send me four needles full of thread if you Can Carraline how is your health is it good or poor let me know now do you get enough to eat What is Herbert doing is he at With Jonathan Willis or no is John Ames going to move of has he sold out yet has Mother got home yet how is her health this is all Caleb H Phillips[37]

This is the letter Caleb was supposed to write, in at least two senses. Not having received a letter from Caroline lately, he had nothing to reply to and perhaps felt little inspired to write (and he had to prevail upon Edward to give him the paper). But he was obliged to stay in touch this way; he probably had made a promise. Furthermore, it did what letters were supposed to do: make inquiries after health and people in the neighborhood, provide news, check on the delivery and nondelivery of letters (with a touch of complaint). All this was standard, and not very personal. Caleb folded the paper closed, presumably, and prepared to mail it.

The back, or outside, of the folio was blank, perhaps because he had never thought to use it, or because he was saving it in case he found one more occasion to write before mail went out, or because, a little grouchy, he declined to write more and didn't mind what Caroline thought about it. The outer pages remained blank and in Caleb's possession when something happened to change his mood and reorient his approach to writing. He received a letter from Caroline—possibly the first since he had been in this place.[38] Thus awakened, he took up his pen again and, on the outside of the folio, wrote something entirely different from the conventional letter on the inside:

the mail has Just Come and i got a letter it got here the 9 of Sept i am glad to hear from you do Write more letters to me When yyou get this answer it i Could not pay the postage on it

d dear .Wife my health is good

this is from Caleb Henry Phillips to Carroline A Phillips

my things are all good

my good W Wife

i tell you

i have forgot nothing

you have been to good to me Write more

send me a pen

> in in a letter
> i have got all of your letters in my knapsack
> and my knife fork and spoon i dont use them i use them that i
> brought from home i must stop now i have got to drill

Caleb's short bursts, spaced out on the page as he apparently stops and
starts, show him working outside the rules of the genre, writing not in
the mold of a schoolroom composition but in tandem with other activities: pausing to reread Caroline's letter, certainly, and perhaps
simply to sit, stare into space, and really think, as he may not have before, about what he wants his writing to do. Associative and conversational, this afterthought letter answers the questions Caroline must
have asked (how is your health? how are your things? do you need
socks?) and also, it seems, gives free rein to strains of feeling that made
no appearance in his initial missive. Caroline may have expressed
worry, as many spouses did, that Caleb had forgotten or would forget
her, and his response has the slow rhythm of seriousness: "my good W
Wife"—he erred in forming one loop of the W on his first try and
started over—"i tell you / i have forgot nothing / you have been to
good to me." This may not be the most eloquent expression of love,
but it is easy to imagine that, coming from the man who wrote the first
rather wooden letter, it would strike Caroline's eyes with force.

By the end, Caleb has made his way toward an original idea about
how to represent himself in writing—roughly the same idea, incidentally, another writer had about another war a century later. Caleb could
make his inward experience visible, to borrow Tim O'Brien's phrase,
in the things he carried: "i have got all of your letters in my knapsack / and my knife fork and spoon i dont use them i use them that i
brought from home." Saying he has kept her previous letters is likely
no answer to a question; this was Caleb's spontaneous effort to assure
Caroline that he could be apart from her and attached to her at once—
joined as in one of Thoreau's "wonderful triangles" by the "countless

the mail has been
and i got a letter it got
here the 9 of sept to am
glad to here from you
to write your letter to
me where you get this
answer it & i [wated] and
for the postage on it

i am Wife my health
is good

this is from Caleb Henry
Phillips to Caroline et
Phillips
my things are all good

my good of Wife
i tell you
i have forgot nothing
you have been too good to
me Write soon

send me a pen
in in a letter

i have got all of your
letters in my
knapsack

and my knife fork and
spoon i dont use them
i [use] them that i [brought]
from home i must stop
now i not got to chill

stares" Larkin Kendrick hoped he and his "belove ones" together beheld. In the doubled forks and spoons, Caleb struck upon a literary
image: his military-issue utensils and "them that i brought from home"
lie mingled in his knapsack, like the soldier and the husband in one
body—neither discarded, the latter preferred.[39]

OF ALL THE novelties of his time in the army, what Thornton Clark
tried hardest to communicate to Nancy was a kind of inner awakening,
intellectual and religious, that his time away from home made possible.
Where Isaac Abbott wrote to his parents "I wish you could be right
where I am for a little while just to see the sights," Thornton wanted
Nancy less to see the sights he saw than to feel what his spirit felt. Not
surprisingly, such efforts brought him up against his limits as a writer.
Trying to describe a "tolerable smart" woman he heard lecturing on
temperance in camp, he pulled up short: "I have not time in this to tell
you the hallf." Reporting a kindness he received, he stumbled through
a malformed sentence apparently about either the inexpressibility of
what he felt or his inadequacy as a writer: "if I was only able to write
I could tell you a heap think through."[40]

When Thornton left Indianapolis on October 13, 1862, he was going
to join a regiment, the Forty-Second Indiana, that had just seen its first
serious fighting in the Battle of Perryville and lost almost a third of its
number. It may have been no great disappointment, therefore, that he
did not get very far into the South. No sooner had he crossed the Ohio
River than he fell ill. He was allowed to stay with a Unionist family in
Louisville who offered to care for him. Three days later, his company
departed for the front, but Thornton, though improving, was not
deemed well enough to go. This left him for a period of more than three
weeks in the unusual position of an enlisted man leading the life of a
private citizen. Mostly recovered but waiting to be sent on to the regiment, he enjoyed the hospitality of his newfound "kind friends," the

Bulkley family, and freely explored one of the largest cities in the West.[41]

Will H. Bulkley was in his early forties, a little older than Thornton, and more worldly. Born in Connecticut, he now operated a bookshop in downtown Louisville and was that city's agent for the American Tract Society, a leading publisher and distributer of Christian literature. The elder man, likely pleased to find Thornton as devout as himself, introduced him into some of the city's churches. What became a day-long religious observance was the subject of the longest letter Thornton had yet written to Nancy—one of only two, out of almost fifty he wrote during the course of the war, for which he took an additional sheet of paper. "I want to see you and the Children the worst kind," Thornton wrote, "but it is useless to talk and grieve about things that cant be so I will content myself with telling you about how I spent last Sabbath in the morning I arose and got my self ready for breakfast and as soon as breakfast was over Brother Bulkley and my self started off for Sabbath School."[42]

After years of home routine, Thornton was abroad in the world. The Bulkleys lived a few miles from the river, and as Thornton and Will walked downhill, they traversed midcentury American Protestantism. Thornton narrated this journey more methodically than he probably had ever described anything in writing before.

> we had not gone far before Brother Bulkley found one of his boys out on the commons a playing with some bad boys so he asked me to excuse him for awhile untill he took his Boy back home so I sat dow on an old stump and too out my Bible and read a Chapter or two while he was gone but he soon joined me again and we proceeded on our journey to wards tow the first place that we stopt was at the presbyterian sabath School it was quite an interesting seen for me it is divided into three divisions an infant class

a Bible Class and a general division where spelling and reading
is learned we stayed there a short time and then we left for the
Methodist School there we found about one hundred and fifty
Scollars divided a bout the same as the other here we stayed untill the School brok when Brother Bulkley gave a short lecture
and then we had singing and then it and then we left there and
called at the colored School this was the most interesting one of
all here we see all ages from five to fifty here Brother Bulkley left
me he had to return home to give a sick Soldier some meda-
cine so I was left here With the Blacks the superintendant is a
white man and secesh at that he came forward and invited me
to the Stand with him to talk to the Children there was a hundred and fifty three presant and that beat every one of the others[43]

Thornton writes with a steady fluidity that belies the stepwise nature
of his movements, shifting from scene to scene and punctuated by his
repeated separations from his host. Will leaves his side first to take his
son home, then to address the Methodist children, then to visit a sick
soldier. In the successive moments that Thornton is left by himself,
he proceeds incrementally through forms of religious practice: first a
solitary reader of his Bible, then part of the 150 congregated for Will's
lecture, and finally as the impromptu coleader of an African American
Sunday school. A religious and worldly education in one long walk,
Thornton's day takes him through environments that must have been
at once familiar (because Christian) and strange (because in Louisville,
more crowded than he was used to, denominationally and, in one case,
racially different). And he was not yet finished.

The letter approaches an astonishing moment: "I was left here With
the Blacks." An off-duty Union soldier, alone with one white secessionist ("secesh"), is invited to stand facing a room filled with more
African Americans than he has probably ever seen (the black population of Spencer County, Indiana, in 1860 was exactly two).[44] It is little

wonder that, for Thornton, this Sabbath school, probably not only in its head count, "beat every one of the others." Did he speak? What did he say? What was he thinking? Did the faces of the free black children of Kentucky put him in mind of the war he was nominally fighting? Somewhat maddeningly, Thornton's narrative moves on from that moment without a further word about it. He had almost used up his paper but still hadn't finished his account of a single Sunday, so he moved on: "so after School was out I left there for the Presbyterian Church were I expected to join my friend Bulkley again but disappointed for he did not get back so I took my seat."[45]

As Thornton the character takes his seat near the end of a peripatetic day, Thornton the writer slows the rhythm of his spirited narrative. Nearing the bottom of the page, he may have determined he would spend another sheet of paper on this letter. He could afford to slow down. He could attempt to communicate to Nancy something of what occurred during the reflective moment in that church pew, alone and at peace after hours of eye-widening church hopping: "all wes as quiate as a death room nothing disturbed the stllness but the quea king of the door on its hinges." In the middle of the next sentence, he takes up the new sheet of paper: "but kuick there comes a sound as though it sprung from some enchanted fairy place at first it comes in a still small voce but hark now it breaks forth full strains and a portion of the congregation breaks forth in musical strains with the instrument ~~now they all~~ after that is through we have prayers and then a sermon I suppos that it suited them that was used to woshaping god by mascheinary but it put me much in mind of reading abut fairies when I was a boy nothing more at presant but remain your loving husband until death."[46]

Apparently the staid manner of the Presbyterian minister did not appeal to Thornton; he supposed it suited those who were used to worshiping god by machinery. He and Nancy worshiped with the United Brethren (whose antislavery teachings may have influenced his relatively early enlistment), and they likely were used to a more revivalist atmosphere in their small crossroads church that had cost $400 to build.[47] But if Thornton was not much moved by the preaching at probably the largest church service he had ever attended, he was by its music: "a sound as though it sprung from some enchanted fairy place," a sensation so transporting that he sat through a sermon to which he barely listened, meditating the while on "reading abut fairies when I was a boy." Though surrounded by the bustle and diversity of a big city, Thornton was diving inward. Military service so far resembled a kind of devotional retreat. Away from his wife and children, indulging in a form of ecumenical tourism, he could reconnect with his boyhood, his mind could sail out into the ether, and then he could sit down and try to share it all with Nancy in writing.

About two weeks later, Will Bulkley introduced him to "Brother Chidlow." This Ohio preacher and Sanitary Commission agent was passing through Louisville on his way to Indiana. He apparently had known Nancy in her youth, as well as the family of Jacob Scammahorn, the Brethren preacher with whom Nancy had migrated to Indiana. "We had a long talk," Thornton wrote to Nancy. "He says that he remembers you and he is very well acquainted with Scammahorns folks so it was almost like meeting an old friend." The three men—Chidlow, Thornton, and Will Bulkley—ventured out together to an army hospital, "where we visited the various wards of the sick," and where Thornton listened to Chidlow the missionary: "it is no trouble for him to talk to the sick and wounded it seems to me that all he has to do is to open his mouth and the words of life just flows out he gave them a short exortation on the importance of liveing a Christian and putting their trust in God in the army as well as at home and after a short but fervent preyer to almight God in behalf of our Country and for the poor sufering soldiers in the Hospitals."[48]

In a certain light, this outing could not have been very encouraging for Thornton. He would have been in this hospital himself had Will

Bulkley not taken him in. Among the hundreds of sick soldiers he looked upon, there must have been some lingering casualties from Perryville, reminders of what might await him when he rejoined his regiment. At the same time, he was enjoying an unlooked-for sense of connection with Nancy, feeling the intimacy of an "old friend" coursing through his brand-new acquaintance with someone who knew her. And Thornton, who recently had stood at the front of a black Sunday school, listened with awe to a more seasoned exhorter. As if inspirited by Chidlow's speech to the sick troops, Thornton tried his hand at this kind of rhetoric—on paper, for Nancy. After concluding his narrative of the hospital visit, he took an extra sheet of paper for the second and last time in all his Civil War letters, and he penned a prayer more florid than anything he wrote elsewhere: "so pray for me that my life may be spared to return home again in peace and may the Blessings of the good Lord who is the giver of evry good and perfect gift be and rest with you to sustain and support you in this your trying hours of affliction and if through the providence of God we should not meet each other here on earth we may be permitted meet in Heaven a bove where there is no more pating but where we will be permited to enjoy each other socciety for ever and eve while eternity rolles its amples around."[49] By now, two months from home, Thornton has found in letter writing a venue for inventing a voice. That voice—a pastiche of his own words, Brother Chidlow's, and those of others he has heard in Louisville, of phrases retained from prayers, hymns, and fairy stories he read in his youth—directs itself lovingly to Nancy.

But even she, now, is a Nancy of his own fashioning—his companion of more than a decade, to be sure, but, as a reading audience for what he was writing, an unknown. For Thornton had yet to receive a single letter from her. She had been writing to him regularly, but all her letters were addressed to the Forty-Second Indiana Regiment, from which Thornton had been separated for almost a month. His sojourn in Louisville had been a sojourn from epistolary contact and his

letters, in effect, a serial autobiography, a venture down a solitary reflective path, unmindful that Nancy—caring for four children on her
own with no regular income—may not have been as jubilant about
reading all this as he was about sharing it.

As Thornton traveled 150 miles south by train on November 13,
1862, to join his company on the Tennessee border, he was hurtling
toward his unread letters from Nancy. Abruptly, he would confront
the reality of what besides his own spiritual awakening his absence
from home meant. He also was descending into the pit of war. In Louisville, he had been barely a hundred miles upriver from his home.
Older than average, struck by illness before he even got to the front,
he did not promise fair to be a durable soldier. A differently inclined
army surgeon at a different moment in the war might have sent him
home. His relations, had they been wealthy and politically connected,
might have secured his discharge. He might have deserted and returned
to Nancy, in some dishonor but largely unnoticed, to raise his children
in the lessons of his brief expedition. If he had given his country no
real service, he had come to understand it better—a little more of its
size and shape, of the fullness of its citizens, white and black, and of
their God. But he continued south.

❧ 3 ❧
Bonds

As they passed by me I could but think of the many hearts centered around each man—and multiply from one, the anxiety of wives, mothers, and sisters.

—Helen M. Noye, assistant nurse,
Naval Academy Hospital, Annapolis, 1863

To a male resident of Camden, New Jersey, contemplating joining the Union army in the summer of 1862, a wife was worth $144. "Married Men, $366 Bounty!" screamed the top line of the three-foot-tall recruiting broadside. The second line, squeezed just above a fierce-eyed eagle, read "Single Men, $222!" In the tacit logic of army bounties, a married man was especially good to have in the ranks—he had his family to fight for—but also harder to keep there—he had their welfare to worry about and his future with them to lose. As a Mississippi private wrote home, "if I had know famley this war would not pester me at all I would take a pleasure in it as it is it hard for me to be seperated from you all." Families, too, were both strengthened and more vulnerable. With fathers and brothers out in the field, they had this extension into the world, this conduit of new impressions and connections, and they rose to meet the challenges of life on their own—wives to do the work of two people, children to grow up faster. Still, those wives and children were deprived of a husband's and father's presence and support. Many lived in near-constant fear for his life.[1]

Marriage and family bonds, imperiled by distance, had to be sustained by letters. Emotional ties had to be adapted, reinvented, and sometimes clumsily approximated through the work of writing. With its many conventions, letter writing could seem a poor replacement for idiosyncratic habits of expression that prevailed at home—glances, touches, private jokes, small rituals of affection. The magnitude of the war effort, with millions of families turning to letters at once, made these very personal acts of writing also a form of cultural participation. Years earlier the famous Unitarian preacher William Ellery Channing had said the post office "binds the whole country in a chain of sympathies." That may have been true for many in 1829 but not for the "whole country." By the middle of the Civil War, letter writing manuals catered to the much broader community, both "educated and uneducated," who now really were bound together through the post. A publisher of dime novels popular among soldiers put out a "Dime Letter-Writer," more reassuring in tone than its predecessor manuals, that promised "any person of ordinary intelligence" could learn to write letters: "life and spirit *will* make a good, impressive epistle, even if the rhetorical and grammatical proprieties are largely wanting." In letters aiming to "bring together the divided members of the household," the book assured writers, "the *heart* can afford to be perfectly itself; the mind may be exerted less, the feelings allowed more complete sway." A New York publisher might purport to welcome the ordinary men and women of the wartime nation into a sentimental culture of family correspondence and a lenient educational regime. In fact, those men and women themselves had pushed ajar the doors the manual held open—by their prolific letter writing, their experiments with the form, and their alertness to the epistolary bonds visible all around them.[2]

THORNTON CLARK HAD slipped almost into another dimension—cut off from Nancy's letters and sending her, rather than replies, dispatches from a spiritual education—but, back home, his absence was all that had changed. His letters arrived reliably, for he knew perfectly well how to address them. While his convalescence in Louisville brought him moments of solitude with his Bible under a tree or reveries of fairy music, Nancy remained surrounded as ever by the bustle of a large family and the business of a small western community. The Clarks owed money to Charley Jones and Jim Brown. Levi Kemp owed the Clarks. Someone named Brooner, to Nancy's evident distress, had garnished part of the army pay Thornton sent home. "Brother Hammond" might be able to lend them something. Their oldest child, Alice, going on nine, was learning to write and might soon be able to send Thornton letters of her own. For Thornton in Louisville, writing from an epistolary cul-de-sac, letters had been exercises in self-reflection, experiments with voices, vessels in which to mix the source material of his expanding world and produce an artifact of himself to give Nancy. On the receiving end, his letters were rather different. They became a part of social life.[3]

Starting a few months after Thornton's enlistment, Nancy began tacking his letters up somewhere. Each one written after October 1862 has pin-holes poked through the upper left corner. Perhaps she put them up in a secluded part of the house, keeping them safe for her own rereading—high enough to elude the grasping hands of the younger children, though maybe within the reach of Alice, who probably could read them by now, or at least would want to try. More likely, Thornton's letters, hanging by their corners like off-kilter diamonds, attracted a wider readership. The letter with by far the most pinholes, taken down and put back up more than a dozen times, is the one that describes Thornton's outing with Brother Chidlow, the man whom Nancy and the Clarks' family friends, the Scammahorns, had known back in Ohio—in other words, the letter in which the several Ohio-born settlers at Dale, Indiana, would have taken the greatest interest.

Nancy might well have wanted to share it with them, notwith-standing the possible embarrassment when they noticed the line Thornton squeezed, upside down, into a blank space at the top of the letter before he mailed it: "I have not received any letter from you yet." If she frequently felt she had to explain herself to a neighbor—she had written to her husband, numerous times—she may have found it a fair trade for what this letter, shared around, could foster. Suffering an iso-lation from her husband worsened by her own letters' going astray—to say nothing of the burdens of single-handedly managing their home, their farm, and their four children—Nancy needed the people around her more than ever. Tacking up Thornton's letters, she could make her home the nerve center of a small community.[4]

Even what seems like one of the most intimate forms of written expression—letters between husbands and wives or sons and parents—frequently served more collective purposes. They were the vital tools with which mothers kept children mindful of their absent fathers and older brothers. They were entangled in extended family relationships, like those among Daniel and Sarepta Revis and Clint and Ellen Ward. Each one from the battlefront brought news of a regiment in which the neighbors' absent men also were serving, and the home folks com-pared notes. One man wrote to his wife, "I am all the time thinking every word I write that others are going to hear it read." A New England woman walked around town with a letter from the front pinned to her dress.[5]

Scholars of printed books speak of a "communications circuit" in which authors, publishers, booksellers, and readers all are linked. Handwritten letters do not often figure in such theories because they did not circulate publicly, yet the culture of letter writing does repre-sent a vast and powerful circuit of communications. Even if not me-chanically reproduced like books, letters in the aggregate were as ubiq-uitous as anything in print. They reached everywhere, and most people, especially the least educated, read them as fervently as anything else.[6] Circulation through space was not just letters' essential function; it was a central part of their cultural meaning—the import they held and the terms in which they were imagined. Moving first from point A to point B via a railway mail car or a man on horseback, letters then ran in tighter circuits through a family or a neighborhood— read aloud, passed hand to hand, or forwarded on to point C. The movement at the heart of letter writing held the emotional allure of putting a person in two places at once, and it bolstered people's sense of belonging to families and communities beyond their immediate surroundings.[7]

THE CIVIL WAR made families aware they were joined in larger networks. People had for decades marveled at the reach of the postal service, but the war made letter writing unusually visible, even tangible, for the simple reason that mail was often part of the conflict's collateral damage. Anyone opening a newspaper anywhere in the country could read about mail wagons captured by enemy forces, mailbags rifled, and letters picked up on battlefields. What Americans wrote to each other now was more exposed than it had ever been. Epistolary culture as an extracurriculum in writing was in high gear. People could learn how to write letters not only from the ones they received but from plentiful samples of other people's mail. Surrounded by models good and bad, ordinary Americans could rapidly assimilate the mores of the personal letter and adapt the genre to their own situations.

Since the foreshock of the war in 1859, violence had been rendering private letters public, revealing the lives Americans were living across great spans of distance and circumstance. Dangerfield Newby, a former slave among John Brown's raiders, was the first man killed in the fighting at Harpers Ferry. Three letters were taken from his pocket and published among the supporting documents in the Virginia governor's report on the "Harpers Ferry Invasion." Thus could the whole

Virginia General Assembly read what an enslaved woman named Harriet had written to her husband:

> Dear Dangerfield you Can not amagine how much I want to see
> you Com as soon as you can for nothing would give more plea-
> sure than to see you it is the grates Comfort I have is thinking of
> the promist time when you will be here oh that bless hour when
> I shall see you once more my baby commenced to Crall to day it
> is very dellicate nothing more at present but remain your affec-
> tionate wife. Harriet Newby[8]

The war created abundant opportunities for reading other people's mail, and the hostility between warring sections drove off inhibitions about doing so. It became a great pastime of Northerners to read what they called "secesh letters" and of Southerners to read "Yankee letters." For military officers, captured mail could offer intelligence about the opposing army and its plans. For newspaper editors—to whom many combatants sent contraband mail, and who published much of it—letters by enemy soldiers and civilians provided fodder for partisan commentaries. For people of all walks of life throughout the country, captured letters were a matter of tremendous curiosity.[9]

They were appearing with great frequency in the papers, and they even were arriving in people's mailboxes. Many soldiers took the letters they found on battlefields and in abandoned camps, or when they seized whole bags of mail in transit, and sent them home for their loved ones to read. One Northern woman recorded in her diary: "Mary has another letter from Joe enclosing several Secesh letters taken from battle field of 7 Pines, the kind we see in the papers. We have been much amused in reading them. When the 2d Mich. drove the rebels through the woods, the rebels threw away every thing they had & Joe took these letters from a knapsack." Union soldiers themselves recorded in diaries, with the same matter-of-factness as reports on food, health, and the weather, "sent home five secesh letters," or "sent home the picture I found and some secesh letters &c." Even future president Rutherford B. Hayes, then a lieutenant colonel in the Twenty-Third Ohio, included in a letter home to his wife "some Secesh letters." A Georgia soldier in Cobb's Legion wrote to his sister: "I got three pictures out of a dead Yankee's knapsack and I am going to send you one. . . . The pictures are wraped up in a letter from the person whose image they are. . . . She signed her name A D. Spears and she lived in Main somewhere." The dead Yankee was on the field at Gettysburg, about halfway between Georgia and Maine.[10]

Many people, North and South alike, read captured letters as tea leaves that might tell the outcome of the war. Newspaper editors reveled in evidence of low morale on the other side. A Richmond newspaper printed a large batch of Yankee letters "picked up on the battle-field at Chancellorsville," and a Georgia paper reprinted selections from them because they "disclose a growing disgust for the war" in the North. An Atlanta editor going through letters in a recently captured U.S. mailbag was particularly interested in one Missouri correspondent who opined that Union conscription would send six men into the Confederate army for every drafted federal. A Northern correspondent reported in 1863, "The secesh letters shown to me by some of the boys, are full of complaints and lamentations about the hard times, stating that flour cost about $150 a barrel, bacon and pork from 75 cents to $1 a pound, and so on. They all cry for peace and bread; and I am sure the most formidable enemy to rebeldom is General Starvation."[11]

In private as well as in the papers, captured letters were interpreted to show the enemy's general debasement—their corrupt values or their poor education. Relatives of the wealthy South Carolinian Mary Chesnut brought letters home to her, and she informed her diary: "Yankee epistles found in camp show how illiterate they can be, with all their boasted schools. Fredericksburg is spelled 'Fretrexbug,' medicine, 'met-son,' 'to my *sweat* brother,' &c&c." Meanwhile, a young officer from Connecticut named William Thompson Lusk also found that "penmanship, spelling and composition showed that the greatest need of the South, is an army of Northern Schoolmasters." Southern ladies, he remarked wryly, "are so modest that they write of themselves with a little *i*." Scrutiny of enemies' literacy sometimes rippled outward into condemnations of their moral character. Writing to his hometown newspaper, a soldier with the Eleventh Wisconsin Infantry reported (rather dubiously) that out of more than seventy rebel letters he had read "there was not one love letter, there was scarcely an affectionate expression in one of them, every writer seemed to be wholly engrossed with thoughts of himself." Richmond papers attacked specific moral failings they glimpsed—"Among the thousands of Yankee letters picked up on the recent battle-field the gist and burden of the majority has been money"—as well as Northern civilization generally: "On the battle-field a great number of letters were found to the dead soldiers from their friends at the North . . . . Most of them were exclusively vulgar and disgusting, and were well calculated to produce the impression that Northern society is hideously deformed."[12]

As much as captured letters were exploited for political purposes, they excited a conspicuous interest in what was normally furthest from the public eye: women, families, and emotional life. Letters written by women, and love letters especially, were usually singled out as the most interesting form of enemy correspondence. In Missouri in 1862, the capture of a rebel spy—more particularly, the great sack of mail he was transporting—produced a field day for Unionist newspapers in St. Louis. Many of the letters held "important information to the Confederacy," but those did not create the sensation the more intimate women's letters did. The *Missouri Republican* devoted twice as many column inches to reprinting letters "written by females—wives to their husbands, sisters to their brothers, gushing maidens to their lovers"—

as to those containing war intelligence. Another paper ran its selection of captured letters under the headline "Rare Revelations. Inside View of the Fashionable Secesh of St. Louis." The editor called the three letters he printed, all from women, "the richest exposé of the season."[13]

Readers on both sides had an apparently insatiable appetite for the saccharine letters of "gushing maidens." A Confederate chaplain, surveying the aftermath of the Battle of Stones River, saw among the "dead Yankees, who lie by scores," several Confederate soldiers pillaging knapsacks; there was one who, he said, "I fear will kill himself with laughter over a Yankee love-letter he is reading." When the Northern nurse Elvira Powers published a memoir of her labors in a Union hospital, she included transcriptions—and mocking commentaries on the "orthography and punctuation"—of three "rebel love letters" that had been captured in Virginia and sent by a Union adjutant to his sister, who shared them with Powers.[14] Love letters published in newspapers almost always appeared beneath some remark of subtle derision. So widely circulated were captured letters by women—so recognizable, by the middle of the war, to virtually everyone—that they could spawn parodies:

> The following specimen of Yankee literature was picked up on the battle field near Murfreesboro by a Confederate soldier, and sent to the Columbus Sun. We publish it *et verbatim, et literatim, et spellatim, et punctuatim:*
>
> 1000 eight hundred and 60 tew my Dear Thomas I embrace this opportunity to let you knough as how I had a spell of aiger and I does hope these fue lines may find yew enjoying the same gods blessin why dont yew only rite a sweate line to tell suferin kathrun all about her sweate Thomas, Oh my sweate Thomas my turtle dove my pidging, my deer deer Thomas how my pore sole is longing for to hear yer sweate voyce. I think I heer him singing jordan is a hard road to travel as he comes from his plow now

Oh my deer Thomas come home and lets gets married, so no at present but remain your lovin

Kathrun an T.

P S. part sekkund . . . my pen is bad my inck is pale my luv to yew shall never fale for Thomas is my own true luv my pidging duck and turtle dove so no more at present.

Ps Noty Beany—muther is almost ded and Timothy says he dont keer for anything. so no more at present from yer lovin

k. A. T. used to did so wonce more yer wife as it is to bee send 2 kisses and sez fare well. yours till deth do us part. k. A. T.

final Ps. I had most forgot to tell that Jake has cum home from California, and is poorer than he went poor Jake he says as how Californa is all a hoax so no more at present from yer dotin K. A. T.

It bears numerous marks of fakery, including some that had been and would be staples of epistolary jokes for years—like relegating a dying mother to a postscript, or seeming to wish someone, by the mangled syntax of a stale convention, the *blessing* of a *spell of the ague*—as well as incongruously evoking the outdated cliché that the Gold Rush was "all a hoax" and using regional dialect more Southern than Yankee ("that are" for *that there*). But amid its implausible strains for comic effect lies unmistakable evidence that, especially for marginally literate people, the conventions of the intimate letter were largely held in common. Everyone knew roughly what other people's letters sounded like, and they modeled their own accordingly—sometimes, probably, laboring to avoid what they had seen held up for mockery. The private letter was a public form, and the wartime vogue for contraband mail made it even more so.[15]

Sensationalism, derision, political sniping: these were the purposes to which intimate letters were put in public, and these, therefore, are the reactions best preserved in the historical record. Lost to us are Civil

War Americans' whispered or wholly inward reactions when they read the letters of strangers. The impact of this genre of wartime reading material—private letters that never reached their rightful audiences but wound up as souvenirs or in the pages of newspapers—is mostly impossible to know. Those that may have humanized "Yankees" and "secesh" are not ones on which people wrote commentaries. Occasionally, a candid response slips through. William Lusk wrote home to his mother the night before an engagement, "we can hardly fail of success," but then caught himself recognizing an affinity with his enemy: "It is dangerous though to make predictions, so often have I read similar sentences in 'Secesh' letters written just previous to a defeat." Mary Chesnut, as merciless as she could be about Yankees' spelling, admitted: "One might shed a few tears over some of [a Northern soldier's] letters. Women—wives and mothers—are the same everywhere." When Oliver Wendell Holmes Sr., the famous poet, learned his son had been shot at Antietam, he rushed to Maryland. Traversing the battlefield, he picked up a letter sent from the same North Carolina county where Larkin Kendrick lived. It was addressed to "J. Wright" from his wife and had been written for her by an amanuensis named Vaughn. When Holmes published in the *Atlantic Monthly* an essay about this search for his wounded son, he quoted a snippet from the letter about "nancy's folks" and their crop of corn. "I wonder," Holmes mused, "if, by one of those strange chances of which I have seen so many this number or leaf of the 'Atlantic' will not sooner or later find its way to Cleveland County, North Carolina, and E. Wright, widow of James Wright . . . get from these sentences the last glimpse of husband and friend as he threw up his arms and fell in the bloody cornfield of Antietam?"[16]

Most of the enemy letters soldiers mailed home from battlefields arrived in their families' mailboxes without comment, and some appeared in newspapers that way, leaving us to conjecture what thousands of readers thought about them. The following one was introduced—

in a Republican paper that certainly had no interest in provoking sympathy with rebels—with only the quiet remark that it might "furnish an inside view of the life" Confederate soldiers were leading:

June 20th 1862

Dear Wife it is with much pleasure thats embrace the opportunity of writing to you once more to let you know that I am well and hope when these few lines comes to hand will find you and the children all the same I have had my helth very well and all of the boys is well at this time I have writen some six or eight letters to you and have received but one in return for them, whither you have got them or not I can not tell but I hope you have I should like to see you and the children very much indeed and be with you all in peace once more. I think if we all live it wont be long before we shall see each others face once more Oh, but the time would when our land would be in peace once more and all of the people of the meny State cold return to there dear homes and fier sides with there dere friends and companions who are now at home in grief woe pouring out there trobled soale in unuterable prayers for the dear ones of there hearts.

Tell milly that Ambrose is well and hearty and would like to see very much and all of the children but under the preasant sircumstances it is out of his power to see them. Tell Martha also that William is well too and sends his well wishes to her and all of the children and all enquiring friends &c Ransom and Yuba sendes there best respects and well wishes to you all and all enquiring Girls &c tell granmother and Aunt viney for me that when I get back I am coming to see them and I want them to have something good to eat for thay know I am a great one for good things to eat tell mother I would like to be there to eate some of her Strawberrys and rasberys pies but I fear they will all be gone unless she cands some of them away. Ann you must not be uneasy about me and bear it all with as much fortitude as you can untell we see each other if we are ever permitted to do so on this earth if we are not I hope we will be so fortunate as to mete in heaven where parting is no more there is no war, no sorrow, nor eny sighing there oh that will be joyful to meet to part no more. So I will close for the pressant so nothing more only remain yours,

D. A. Wilkinson to A. M. Wilkinson[17]

Not everyone had one of their letters end up in a newspaper, but it could not have escaped many writers that they were participating in forms of expression shared incalculably widely. Each pinhole in one of Thornton Clark's dangling letters marked a tiny moment of publication; each told of his and Nancy's connections with other people. One of the Civil War's signal effects—and nowhere more than in letters—was to heighten, and often to transform, Americans' consciousness about their ties to people close to them in feeling, far from them in space. Amid an impromptu education in writing, they might reimagine their roles as spouses, parents, children, and members of communities ranging in size from a neighborhood to a nation.

ONE OF THE era's many epistolary conventions reflects Americans' basic understanding of letter writing as a network of emotional ties. Sometimes by habit and sometimes by design, writers closed by sending their "respects" or their "love" to "all enquiring friends." Knowing their letters were likely to be read aloud or passed around—recall the opening pages of *Little Women*, in which Meg, Jo, Beth, and Amy gather to hear Mrs. March read a letter newly received from their father, "far away, where the fighting was"—they often took care to mention by name everyone they thought would see what they had written. A nod to "all enquiring friends" safely covered anyone they might have missed. Josiah Athey of southern Alabama wrote to his

cousin, "tell ant Jane and Cosen loo howdy for me tell Cosen loo to
rite to me I will close by saying give my bst respect to all inquiering
frends." Many soldiers' letters to wives, mothers, and sisters wrapped
up with barrages of brief messages, instructions, well wishes, and virtual winks and nods for sundry family members. Thomas Warrick told
Martha, "tell Markus to take good car of Diner and take all the milk
from it if he dos it will die Martha you must nurse our little hogs for
you no our interest is identical in them tell pa and mother howdy for
me giv my respects to enquiring friend tell Fanny that I am all right
saw Ab a few days ago he was well." Abram Hayne Young wrote to
his sister, "give my best respects to all enquiring friends &c and love
to pa, Ma & Martha, to you and Lilla and kiss Lilla for me, (and tell
Lilla for me to kiss my Sweete hart 'if She nowes hoo it is' for me)."
Other times, writers deployed the same convention with a tinge of
lonely self-pity: Thornton Clark once asked Nancy to "give my respects to all enquireing friends if you find any such."[18]

   "Friends" carried a broad yet deep meaning for nineteenth-century
Americans. A person referring to his "friends" might mean members
of his extended family as well as nonrelatives—anyone in the circle
of people who took an interest in him—and letter writers plainly hoped
what they wrote would broadcast their feelings outward into that
circle.[19] Yet even as writers sent their respects to "enquiring friends,"
they usually were careful to reassert the letter's private, intimate function—the feelings they wanted their words to convey to the one
person to whom it was addressed. And there was a convention for
doing this, too—a clichéd twist on that closing line, reminding the recipient not to give all the writer's love away to his friends. "Give my
love to all of the family," wrote Harvey Hightower to his sister in
Georgia, "and at the same time reserve A due portion for your self."
The phrasing appeared in many variants, with writers often specifying
that the recipient get "a double portion" of the love and regards sent
to friends. The common injunction to "reserve" or "retain" some "por-

tion for yourself" obviously played on the even older cliché, *"give my love."* If soldiers at the front imagined their wives or sisters as vessels through which affection flowed to others, they also did not want them to serve only as such. Much of what a letter carried should stop in their hands.[20]

When Isaac Mann closed a letter to Susan by saying "i send my lov to you my dear wife giv my love to all enquireing friends"—and then encircled Susan's name with a starburst of ink dots—he created an image of precisely this duality. On one hand, it calls to mind a letter striking its target and then scattering its news, its sentiments, its offered love, to the community standing in a figurative circle around Susan Mann. At the same time, Isaac may simply have wanted to highlight Susan's name—to emphasize her place above and before all enquiring friends in his life and his letter's attention.[21]

Women played both roles, confidants and conduits. Their letters, when pulled from mailbags and knapsacks, were the particular objects of newspaper editors' and private citizens' interest for both reasons. The proverbial angels of every home's hearth, women could be expected to write and receive the letters that captured the most heartfelt expressions of a separated family's wartime life. At the same time, many women had burst well out of their antebellum molds as domestic angels. Besides running households and farms, they became their families' clerks, newspaper editors, and switchboard operators. They figured out new ways of bending letter writing to their family's needs, and it was through them above all that new bonds were forged and old bonds were reinvented.[22]

Many women had the advantage (compared with soldiers) of ready access to paper, ink, and proper writing desks. They could explore and experiment—practice their letter writing, gently tutor their husbands and sons in epistolary craft, and seek novel ways of connecting through the mails. A well-to-do woman like Rebecca Pitchford Davis, matriarch of a slaveholding family on a modest North Carolina plantation,

I want father deaver to rite to me how mother deaver an jonah an fam is gitting along an giv me ther post office adress i send my lov to you my dear wife giv my love to all enquireing friends i must bring my letter to a close rite soon I saac Mann to Susan Mann

Isaac Mann to Susan Deaver Mann, 1 Jan. 1862 (detail)

could coordinate a formidable family bureaucracy. With four sons in the Confederate army—sometimes in the same location, sometimes not—Rebecca busily dispatched letters, often enclosing one just received from one brother in an envelope outbound to another.[23] The Davis home bustled like a telegraph office, with Rebecca gathering up the material for outgoing mail—"Your Pa told me not to fill up until he told me what he had to say, but when he read the three first pages, he said he believed I had said all that was necessary"—and processing the incoming. "Thursday morning after breakfast," she headed a brief note to her son Burwell. "Your letter has just this moment been handed in and read to us all, so I cannot reply to it more than simply to acknowledge receipt of it, for they are just fit to leave." She kept her brother-in-law busy as a courier to the post office in town—and sometimes doubted his reliability. "Your Uncle Sam brought your letter from town yesterday, and broke it open and read it, but he is not to blame, tho I have not given him liberty to open my letters, yet he feels so much concern for you all that he cannot fairly help it." When a letter to her son Burwell took awhile reaching him, she recollected she had "sent it to town by your Uncle Sam, and it may be in his coat pocket yet."[24]

Rebecca readily assumed the role of maternal pedagogue, guiding— and sometimes rather exactingly evaluating—her sons' compositions. She tried to encourage certain habits in Burwell. Some were compositional: "You said in your last, 'I do not think I have written all I intended, but have forgotten the balance.' I can tell you how to manage that. Whenever you think of anything you intend to write, note it down, just a word or two will suffice." Others were material: "I like very well for you to direct your letters with a pencil, so I can use the envelopes again, but when you write the letter with a pencil you can't write so much on the same paper." To the same son she wrote, "I would send you [Tom's] letters, but they are *writ* so badly that I dislike to impose such a burden on you, in addition to reading of this." Either anticipating or having received similar disapproval, another son, Weldon, wrote home once Lee's army got into Pennsylvania to apologize for a letter he had sent on the northward march: "When I wrote home from Hagerstown I only found out about fifteen minutes before dark that there would be an opportunity to send a letter next morning, so I had to write mostly in the dark, and it was so dark that I could not see the words after I had written them, which will account for the bad writing." (Neither Weldon nor Rebecca made any comparisons between his penmanship and other specimens they recently had seen: "I will send three Yankee letters I picked up on the field," Weldon wrote home after Chancellorsville, "more because they came from Yankeedom than for their contents.")[25]

Frances Parker of Virginia also closely superintended her family's mail network. The little town of Liberty, she said, never "was watched as closely for letters as at this time." Frances kept up a vigorous correspondence with her son Robert—whose younger brother averred he *would* write except that "Ma writes every thing and leaves nothing for him"—and even tried to fill gaps in other families. "Give my love to your messmates," she wrote to Robert; "tell Stephen or jo or some of them that has no wife to write to me." And in writing to that same Jo, Frances frankly advised, "Just here I will give you and all your mess a hint if you should ever want to write any thing to any individual you do not wish every one to see write that something on a separate slip from the letter—all your friends are so anxious to see every letter they hear ^{of} it is a cross if they cannot and on the ^{other} hand it would be a cross to me for one not to let friends see what few I get."[26]

Frances wanted a social network; her son and daughter-in-law craved intimacy. Robert Parker and his wife, Rebecca, or Beck, lived in a nominally separate household on the same land as his parents. When Robert left at the outset of the war, twenty-one-year-old Beck became in effect a ward of her in-laws. When Robert had his photograph taken shortly after enlisting, he enclosed two copies in a letter to his wife—"I send too likenesses the small one for sister, the other of for you or Ma"—leaving Beck and Frances, as he had by his departure, to work things out between themselves. They did not always see eye to eye. After the Battle of Bull Run, Frances wrote to her son and recalled, "I do not know why it was but I believed you were safe from harm in the battle I told Rebecca I did not feel like you was killed and wanted your shirts made and sent on by some of the recruits but I found she was not inclined to make them until we heard expressly from you."[27]

No wonder Beck kept her correspondence with her husband as private as she could, mostly separate from Frances's traffic in letters. Robert valued Beck's confidence, too. Midway through the war, she asked him to hire a substitute and leave the army, possibly because she was pregnant. He replied with his thoughts on the idea and added, "Say nothing about my writing you so as it will get out publicly if I attempt it I want to Put it through." For Beck, letter writing was solitary and inward, like her fear for her husband's life. (How could she make a shirt for a body that might no longer breathe? She evidently did not try to explain to Frances why this was more than she could endure.) Beck filled empty moments with efforts at communing with Robert, even when no trace of him beckoned. On at least one occasion, she sat down and began composing a reply to a letter she had not yet received—that may not even have existed yet—leaving a blank she could fill once her husband's long-awaited letter finally arrived: "My dear Robert. I have just received your letter of _____ and answer it without delay, assuring you of the pleasure and relief it afforded me to hear from you after such a long silence." Men in camp rarely enjoyed the luxury of rehearsals and rough drafts, but Beck was doubtless not the only woman who wrote out lines and pages of letters they never sent, experimenting in ways we cannot recover.[28]

Drafts, aborted missives, and stray notes generally get discarded. A literate and relatively comfortable woman like Beck Parker might file away even her scrap paper, and Rebecca Davis could produce and preserve a rich family archive. But women in general are underrepresented in the annals of Civil War letters. For decades, readers and scholars placed a premium on the information that flowed in a single direction: away from the battlefield. Yet what came from the front was most often written for a woman's eyes, and most often it was women who preserved soldiers' letters. Women poorer and less literate than Rebecca Davis and Beck Parker did as much to shape the culture of letter writing, but their work is harder to see.

Their letters had abundant opportunities to disappear—first, from soldiers' hands, pockets, and knapsacks. (If some lost in such ways wound up in newspapers or enemy mailboxes, most did not.) Then, even when a soldier managed to preserve the letters he received, later generations may have seen them as having less historical importance than the ones written by the soldier. If a woman's letters survived to the day a soldier's descendant brought the family cache to a library or historical society, they have been preserved but not necessarily rendered as visible as others. Research for this book turned up catalog records for manuscript collections identified only by the name of a soldier, described by a cataloguer principally with reference to the battles in which that soldier participated, and featuring no mention of materials written by any other person—yet including one or more letters by the soldier's wife.

Some women's letters were preserved systematically—by a soldier who kept them and brought them home, or periodically mailed bunches of them back for safekeeping. Other times, a woman's letter survives only because it was written on the same piece of paper as a man's—like Jeannette Hooker's message to Nancy on Fred's first handwritten letter, or the letters from Lucretia Thompson that her husband, Henry, annotated and mailed back. Margaret Simon Ross of Dripping Springs, Texas, would be entirely lost to history if her husband, Robert, had not written a letter on the back of one of hers. In December of 1863, she wrote, briefly and pleadingly, "Dear Husband I have been looking anxiously every week for a letter but only to be disappointed My Neighbors invariably get letters from your company by every Mail I dont know why I cannot hear from you . . . . Cannot you get paper that you dont write. or what is the reason." The same sheet of paper came back to her with a penciled letter on the reverse, dated January 3, 1864. Robert wrote, "Dear Wife I take this oppertuinity of writing a few Lines to you. as a Answer to your whitch I received yestrday . . . so you will see by this letter that paper is not so verry plentful."[29]

In some cases, a woman's letter was saved from oblivion by a simple accident or a stroke of grace. Ann Butler, a former slave living with her children at the Freedmen's Village contraband camp outside Washington, had written to her husband, William, in January of 1865. When William, a soldier in the Second U.S. Colored Infantry, was killed in Florida a little more than a month later, a young Jewish Confederate named Jacob Gardner found the letter. In the blank space below Ann's signature, Jacob wrote: "This letter was taken out of a Knapsack found close by a body on the Battlefield of the Natural Bridge near St Marks Fla March 6th 1865." Whatever Jacob did with it next, it ultimately found its way into the Georgia Historical Society.[30]

To find Civil War letters by women is sometimes to stumble into the contingencies by which they survived to the present day, which in turn illuminate the ways letters actually circulated and were experienced during the war. The care with which many soldiers' letters have been preserved and organized (and in some cases published) tidies up the more unruly lived experience of letter writing and reading.[31] Seeking out the wives, mothers, and sisters who anchored networks of correspondence, we discover their literary labors as tutors and curators.

SARAH CREATH, WHOSE family called her Kate, was nine years old when the Civil War started. The oldest of four children, she was probably the only one who could remember the family's westward migration from central Ohio, across the Mississippi River, to Washington, Iowa, a town of more than two thousand people. Kate's father, Owen, a thirty-three-year-old blacksmith, enlisted in the Thirteenth Iowa Infantry during the first year of the war. Her mother, Harriet, was expecting their fifth child. Kate was growing up fast. When her father settled into camp life, he wrote home, "Kate I wish you was here to wash my dishes for I have to wash them myself but it cant be so and you must be a good girl and gow to school and learn to write to me and then you can write me a letter."[32]

She was soon ready. Harriet was an able correspondent, but Kate took upon herself the responsibility of representing the children. While Harriet wrote to Owen about the family's health and finances, Kate delivered the perspective of the youngest Creaths. After the baby arrived, she wrote to her father, "liz zie is a pretty little babe." Of her toddler brother: "tommy says that he wants to see pa." And of her eight-year-old sister: "mary says that she cant write to you she thinks that she cant write good enough to write yet." Owen set these two girls to competing: "Kate I am glad you are getting sow you Can write to your Father you Dont no how much good it Done me to see how fast you was learning to write . . . . Mary I want you to write to me as well as Kate and let me see which is ahead in writing for I want you to keep up with Kate and I want you to be a good girl and mind your mother."[33]

On the Sunday evening in late February 1862 when Mary decided to take a stab at it, she performed creditably (Owen would later write back, "Mary I think you Can write as good as Kate"). Then, as if to assert her seniority, Kate, who turned ten that day, took Mary's unfilled sheet of paper and added:

> Dear Father mary has not finished her letter and I thought that I would right som to you it has been a prety day but it has turned cold this evening and ~~it snowed about to feet last week~~ it snowed abou a foot last week tommy has to bed my letter is short as ever Sarah C Creath

Kate may not have been having the greatest birthday. Her little sister had just matched her writing ability. Someone—the upstart Mary? her mother?—had just accused her of overstating the amount of snow that had fallen. She corrected the error with evident frustration and then let her penmanship—as meticulous as she could manage in her previous letters—go literally downhill. It is unclear whether she concludes

Dear Father

mary had not
finished her letter and I thought
that I would right some to you
it has been a prety day but it
has turned cold this evening and
~~it snowed about a foot last week~~
it snowed about a foot last week
tommy has to bed my letter is
short as ever Sarah C Creath

Sarah Catherine (Kate) Creath to Owen Creath, 23 Feb. 1862

by saying "my letter is short as ever"—with a tinge of regret that none of her letters ever has measured up (although each of the others that survive is longer than this one)—or saying, with the terseness of disappointment, "my letter is short" and then signing off, "as ever, Sarah C Creath." Either way, whether in a sour mood or obliged to go put her little brother to bed, she left the sheet unfilled. It was the last letter Owen would receive from her before he left the Thirteenth Iowa's encampment in Missouri and boarded a steamboat bound ultimately for Pittsburg Landing, Tennessee.[34]

A girl with a father away at war could feel exhilaratingly close to adulthood yet face discouraging reminders of her childhood—all in the same evening, as Kate may have. Even while she watched with pride as the sibling under her wing successfully wrote a letter, Kate remained mindful that her mother's authority prevailed. Across the room, Harriet was writing her own letter to Owen—about her aching neck, a relative's quinsy, the two-dollar debt a man refused to pay her ("he commenced swearing . . . so I walked off and left him for I did not care about hearing him talk in that way"); about the worry she felt when she heard (wrongly) that Owen's regiment was involved in the assault on Fort Donelson a week before; about the three of their acquaintances who had been killed or wounded there. Kate's youth may have spared her most such cares. If Harriet instructed her not to tell her father two feet of snow had fallen when really it had only been one, Kate probably did not appreciate the possibility that her mother, rapidly filling her own sheet with much that might worry Owen, did not want the family's letters to paint too dramatic a picture of hardship at home.[35]

Harriet, halfway through the letter she was writing while Mary and Kate worked together across the room, tried to muster a little something to lift her own mood and the children's: "you think I may prepare a dinner for you on the fourth of july. I think that is a long while ahead to speak for a dinner but I think it will be very pleasant to get dinner for my husband once more if I ever have that privilage." February is no easy time for an Iowa family, and the winter of 1862 was a harsh one. "We have had some of the coldest weather I ever experienced th last week," Harriet had written on February 16. "Water would freeze on the floor in two feet from the fire from morning till night and you had better think I had some trouble in keeping the children warm." Toward the end of the month, she would discover all the produce stored in their cellar had frozen—everything but the crab apples. (At least, Harriet reasoned, "we had used the most of the potatoes before they froze I only lost about a bushel.") Spirits could rise and fall with the temperature: at the height of the mid-month cold snap, Harriet got a letter from Owen declaring, "I do think the war will be over against the first of April and then we will be made to rejoise." She replied: "I am glad to know thea you are in such good spirits but I am afraid that you will be deceaived in your expectation that is about this war coming to a close so soon . . . but you always said that I allways look at the dark side of every thing." Thinking ahead to July offered an antidote. Owen, steaming into Kentucky and Tennessee by the time he received this kind invitation, was growing a bit less sanguine: "I still think that you may fry a chicken for me on the fourth of july but I expect to see a good deal between now and then."[36]

With their worried yet cautiously hopeful letters, parents like Harriet and Owen could weave blankets of words that, if they did not wholly envelop their daughters, at least dampened fear's chill. Hellen Alford, with three older brothers in the Union army and a barely literate mother, bore more responsibility for the lines of communication through her home in Alfordsville, Indiana. Hellen turned thirteen during the first winter of the war; her birthday was a month before Kate Creath's. Her father, Franklin, was an avid writer, but he—patriarch of both his family and the little town that bore his name—had much else to contend with. There was a farm to manage with three grown sons gone, and there was an elder relative to have committed to an

asylum. On March 9, Hellen wrote to her oldest brother, Warren, away
in Virginia: "Now Warren Aunt Kellams is gon Crazy again and father
brought her here and we just put her up stairs and make her stay there
father is A going to send her off tomorrow to Indianapolis . . . . father
says the reason that he did not wright he is so trubbled with Aunt Betsa
that he can not wright to tonight that he will wright in A day or to or
at least hewill try." Hellen's other brothers, Wayne and Lafayette Alford, were south of Nashville that day, on the march to join Ulysses S.
Grant's command at Pittsburg Landing.[37]

The trials of Aunt Kellams meant that responding to letters from
the front became Hellen's job. Her mother, Mary, had been working
on her writing, spurred on perhaps by the pitfalls of less direct communication. Back in the fall, something she apparently had dictated to
her husband provoked an angry reaction from Lafayette. So, in January, she toiled through a letter to her oldest son, Warren, concluding,
"I had forgotten how to wright I thaut I would try to learn agan I guess
you think it poor writing." Thus far, Mary could do only what the
children had been doing—composing letters and short notes that ac-
companied the patriarch's letters to his sons, sometimes on separate
sheets, sometimes in spaces Franklin left for them. Only Hellen could
take on Franklin's epistolary duties when he was otherwise occupied.
Those duties included more than embracing the opportunity to let her
brothers know that she was well and hoping her few lines would find
them enjoying the same blessing. She also kept information moving
through the family network.[38]

The Alfords well knew that letters reverberated throughout their
community. During the first months of the war, a member of Warren's
regiment, Clem Reily, came home on leave and wrote Warren with a
report on the tense confrontations between Unionists and Southern
sympathizers in southern Indiana. There had been "quite a fight" at
the post office last week, Clem said. A man named Lewis loudly complained that Nathan Kimball, the captain of the hometown company
in which Warren enlisted, "was treating their men worse than Ne-

groes." When Clem demanded an explanation for such an allegation, Lewis "said that he heard Lem Kelly read it out of a letter that he got from Billy." Clem denounced it as a lie, and chairs began flying.[39]

Knowing that a letter's words could ripple so far abroad—from Bill to Lem to Lewis to a post office brawl—might terrify a letter writer, but it also could be exciting. It was perhaps with such episodes in mind that Warren, an avid Unionist, wrote home a month later wondering, "how does my letters take at home and is their any get up about them." Expectations about letters' broad audiences ran in the other direction, too. Franklin Alford wrote dignified, if sometimes misspelled, disquisitions on the "Glorious old Constitution," and these sometimes carried the invitation that they be shared with other young Daviess County men in Warren's regiment. "Give my lov to all my friends who would be Interested with A perrusal of this Epistle," he wrote, "and donot stint your self."[40]

When Hellen took her seat to write to her brothers, she assumed responsibility for curating the "particulars" that circulated among "all enquiring friends." Like an editor sorting dispatches, she tracked the comings and goings of letters and decided what news to republish. On February 9, her younger brother, Thomas Greene (about Kate Creath's age), tried writing to Warren but left off after a few lines: "I am so slow I believe I will get george." George, age fifteen, had perhaps begun to imagine himself going off to war. He scribbled out a few more lines about a contentious town meeting on the subject of the war, then he stopped, too. Finally, Hellen produced what seemed to count as the official family letter for that week.

She acknowledged Warren's letter of January 25; reported the receipt of a letter from Lafayette, who was doing well; and relayed some of the local news ("there was A Mad Dog running throug the Country and bit most all the Dogs . . . he bit Bill Williams Cow"). She also reported that they had had a letter from "Dock Laverty," the town physician, who was on the surgical staff of Wayne and Lafayette's regiment. This letter—across the top of which the doctor had

written, "Read to friends if you see fit"—was a lengthy update on
military affairs in Kentucky, including a paragraph on the recent and,
in the North, celebrated killing of Confederate general Felix Zollicoffer
at the Battle of Mill Springs. Hellen seized upon this paragraph. She
had not yet reached the bottom of her own first page, but, with Doc
Laverty's letter on the table beside her, she filled up the rest of that
page and all of the next by copying out his (probably apocryphal) tale
of Zollicoffer's body being transferred out of Union lines to the rebels.
Hellen followed her model mostly verbatim—even reproducing some
colloquialisms she may not have recognized (she rendered Laverty's
"to cap the climax" as "to clap the clinx")—but she also improved
upon the doctor's spelling in several instances. It was probably thanks
to her in-progress schooling that she could fix Laverty's misuses of
"their" and "there," and probably thanks to a newspaper at hand that
she could spell "Zollicoffer" instead of the doctor's "Zoligoffer."[41]

This was not easy work, cross-referencing source texts and com-
piling news for a letter to Warren. It probably served to extend and
reinforce her schoolroom education. Many young men of the mid-
nineteenth century rose to full literacy through their entry-level employment as clerks; Hellen matured as a reader and writer because the
war made some kinds of clerkship into women's work. Gradually, at
least: by the end of Doc Laverty's anecdote, Hellen seemed to grow
tired of copying, began abridging the original paragraph, and finally,
having reached the bottom of her second page, wrote, "but enough of
Old Zollicoffer." On the third page of her sheet, she began to relate
additional newsy particulars about folks in the neighborhood but drew
up short. She wrote "ther was A little boy came ther," then crossed
it out—perhaps concluding she had not enough time to finish that
story—and explained, "Now Warren Clem and Hannah is here tonight." Torn, it seems, between her visitors' immediate physical presence and the thinner epistolary bond with her brother, she wrote:
"Warren I would like to see you and have A long talk with you O

how I long to See you all but I guess I will just have to wait till you come home Warren." Hellen probably about had her fill of letter writing for this evening, but her little brother kept her going for a few more lines: "Green Says that he forgot one thing that he wanted wright he is in Federal Money in the Arithmatic he does not Cipher at School he just Cipher at home." Hellen signed her name at the bottom, encircled it with curlicues of ink, then folded the paper and wrote one last sentence on the back—seemingly a reference to something she was enclosing, though also a fitting image for the assemblage she had created at the desk: "I guess when you get all that is in these your noggen will be full good by Hellen Alford."[42]

THOUGH OFTEN LOST, forgotten, or apparently peripheral, women's letters—seen amid the tangles of wartime correspondence and stretched family bonds—sometimes turn out to stand right in the thick of the Civil War. When Harriet Creath wrote dejectedly to Owen on February 16, 1862, "I am afraid you will be deceived in your expectation that is about this war coming to a close so soon," all the children were in bed. She sat alone in her quiet Iowa house. "I hope the time will soon be that I can have my dear Husband^d here with me for everything is lonely and desolate without you." She did not know that hopes of a quick Union victory had been elevated that very Sunday. Several hours before, Ulysses S. Grant had written what would shortly become the most famous Civil War letter to date:

H^d Qrs. Army in the Field

Camp near Donelson Feby 16th 1862

Gen. S. B. Buckner

Confed. Army

Sir,

Yours of this date proposing Armistice and appointment of Commissioners, to settle terms of Capitulation, is just received.

No terms except an unconditional and immediate surrender can be accepted.

I propose to move immediately upon your works.

I am sir, very respectfully,

> your obt. srvt.,
>> U. S. Grant
>> Brig. Gen.

The fall of Fort Donelson, with which the Confederacy had held the Cumberland River, changed the course of the war and of the Creaths' lives. When Harriet went to bed that night, General Albert Sidney Johnston, the man then considered the first soldier of the Confederacy, was in Nashville deciding he must ready seventeen thousand rebel soldiers for a southward withdrawal from a city now open to Union invasion. The next Sunday, February 23, was Kate Creath's birthday. She, Mary, and Harriet all sat together writing, and when they folded their letters together into an envelope addressed to Owen in Missouri, the rebels were across the Cumberland, having abandoned Nashville and embarked on a march that would take them ultimately to Corinth, Mississippi. Armies were on the move, and armies on the move meant unreliable mail.[43]

That envelope reached Owen, as his family's Sunday letters usually did, on a Thursday, February 27. But on the following Thursday, March 6, no letter arrived. This disappointed Owen more than usual, for he knew it might be awhile before mail would reach him again. His regiment had received orders "to get our napsacks pact and to Dispose of our Clothing all only what we Could Carry." With the Tennessee and Cumberland Rivers now open to federal navigation, and Johnston's army on the retreat, thousands of Union soldiers in Missouri were being sent to join the Army of the Tennessee. On Saturday, Owen's regiment boarded trains in Jefferson City and arrived in St. Louis on Sunday morning. There, he shipped aboard the *Hiawatha*, one of more than 150 steam-powered transports that were carrying federal soldiers by river from around the western theater to a point of concentration somewhere near the Tennessee-Mississippi border, where the men under Albert Sidney Johnston were converging with other Confederate forces.[44]

As another man in Owen's regiment recalled, the *Hiawatha* had "110 mules on board and about 20 horses and something over one thousand men with all the waggons and regamental acquipage." The transport departed St. Louis on Monday, headed down the Mississippi to Cairo, Illinois, then turned and steamed up the Ohio River—following the route that, in Mark Twain's imagination some years later, Huck and Jim had hoped to travel to freedom. Owen, like a young boy on a raft, was a wide-eyed witness to incredible sights. At Cairo he saw ironclad Union gunboats, "mosters . . . huge construction[s] of mechanical skill" that Owen admired with a blacksmith's eye. The Ohio River was above flood stage, and he saw large steamboats running among tall trees on what normally was the shore. Some of the houses in Paducah, Kentucky, were underwater to their roofs. From Paducah, the *Hiawatha* turned up the Tennessee River. "Down here in this Dixes land," Owen wrote, "the wheat and grass looks as grean as the first of of June in Iowa and the buds are almost ready to burst on the trees along the bottoms."[45]

Owen wanted his wife to share in these experiences—"Harriet I wish you was here just one half Day just to see the fusse and bussle of the excitement"—but he had dwindling confidence that even his written descriptions of "fusse and bussle" could reach her. He had not received a letter in almost three weeks. The slow progress of the *Hiawatha* afforded ample time to write letters but not many opportunities to mail them. Then he heard a rumor that "they would not let our mail gow any further than Cairo for awhile." He supposed the army had good reasons for this measure but still thought "it is midling hard that you cant get my letters" and tied himself in knots thinking through the effects of being cut off: "I now you will be vary uneasy but maby it is all for the better but I no it will hard on you and the Children if it is so but I hope it is not so and that you will get this and if you should be so lucky as to get this letter and then you should not get any more for awhile Dont be uneasy for I think it is not long til I shall be at home."[46]

So little confident of the channel between him and Harriet, Owen changed as a letter writer. During the quiet winter in Jefferson City, he had written on roughly a weekly basis, most often on Sundays, just as Harriet and the children did. He had generally been upbeat and seen his army service as a kind of extension of his role as a provider for his family. Within a few weeks of Owen's arrival in camp at Jefferson City, the quartermaster had tapped his skill as a blacksmith. To be "at work at my trade" was gratifying, probably for its own sake and also because it earned him extra pay—only forty more cents per day, but that was something. He mentioned it to Harriet at least three different times. With "100 mules to shod" in his regiment, he expected the work to be steady, and he even thought he could get appointed regimental blacksmith and farrier. That would bring a significantly higher salary. He was able to send Harriet twenty dollars by express delivery at the end of January. In the letter he wrote the same day, he encouraged her to "buy a carpet for the front room" and also said, "Harriet you had better hire you a girl and try and take better care of yourself." All his predictions about the war coming to an end in the spring, round about April 1, were made during this period of steady employment. By early March, he thought he would have earned enough to send thirty dollars home, but it seems he didn't get paid before leaving Missouri.[47]

Now, aboard a riverboat in Dixie, he wrote more often than weekly, and he repeated himself a fair bit, as many writers did who doubted the ultimate delivery of any given letter. During the winter, the couple's regular exchanges had focused mainly on the children, the weather, Owen's plying his trade, Harriet's work at home, and the family finances. Now, Owen was clearly more than one remove from Iowa. By the time he ascended the Tennessee, he hadn't swung a hammer at hot iron in weeks. In new surroundings and without up-to-date information from home, he became, like Thornton Clark in Louisville, half diarist and half correspondent. Accordingly, he envisioned a different kind of reading experience for Harriet. "I expect you are vary uneasy by this time for I am told that our mail all stops at Cairo," Owen wrote on March 24, trying a second time—perhaps of no greater use than before—to explain why no letters were arriving from him. "If so you have not had any word from me for some time but this is five or six letters I have written to you sins we left St lewis and I suppose they are all lying at Cairo. . . . Harriet I shall write every few Days any how whether you get them or not and then when you Do get them you will hav a good time reading them all at one time."[48]

Resigned to the fact that his letters would no longer constitute a form of conversation with Harriet about family affairs and daily life, Owen imagined his letters becoming a kind of travelogue—something she might read like a book or a magazine. He related anecdotes about people he met during his steamboat adventure. Slaves fled plantations and came to the riverbanks, and the *Hiawatha* took three aboard. "I talked with one of the negros to Day," Owen wrote. "He had ran of from his old mas and he said the reason he Done it was that he had a young massa and he was in the Sesesh army and had taken his brother along to wait on him and he had ran of and gone to the union army and young massa had sent for him to gow and wait on him and he ran of he said he had swam one Creek that was about one hundred yards wide." Owen got to go ashore in Savannah, Tennessee. There, he saw a cotton gin ("looks some thing like a thrashing machine only in the place of teeth in the silender to thresh the grain it is more like the sausage mashine only in place of the knives it has fine saws all round the sylender"). He met more enslaved people ("I asked him if the negroes ware Secesh and he rather hesitated a while and stammered and then

said No Sah We brack folk union but misses secesh"). He particularly
wanted to tell his daughter, "Kate I hav been round over Savannah considerable sinse we stopt and oh the nice flowers there is here." Owen
tucked into the envelope one of those flowers and two samples of
cotton, one ginned and one with its seeds. He met a white Tennessean
trying to stay out of the Confederate army. "He had a wife and five
Children he had left at home and he says he is gowing to stay with us
til the thing is over he expects they will burn up every thing he has
and Harriet you think it is hard on you there whare there is no sutch
work as this but what would you think of such treatment as those poor
people have to encon^ter."[49]

While the *Hiawatha* lay ashore at Savannah, Owen received the
letter Harriet wrote on March 2. It had been two weeks coming and
must have been a little jarring. Fresh from strolling through town
picking flowers, Owen tore open an envelope to find Harriet describing
fresh snow on the ground and produce freezing in the cellar. Nevertheless, the fact that it arrived at all hinted at things returning to normal.
Owen had just slept his first night on solid ground since leaving
Missouri a week ago. Men on the transports had subsisted on hardtack
and river water that gave them "a bowel complaint," in Owen's
words, or, in the more colorful words of one of his shipmates, "a di-
reah [that] the boys here calls . . . the Tenessee quick stepp." (Some
resourceful men on the Tennessee River expedition figured out "the
trick of catching the surplus hot water ejected from the boilers" on
their transports and making coffee with that.) Now, Owen and the rest
of his regiment were cooking over campfires. After a brief camp on
shore at Savannah, they moved upriver to Pittsburg Landing, pitched
tents, and began laying floors in them with material scavenged from
abandoned cabins and fences in the nearby woods. These "old rail
fenses," Owen observed, "would blow away in Iowa." All around him
were the reassuring signs of spring. He'd seen wheat coming up "almost large enough to hide arabbit." Wandering a little away from

camp he came upon an abandoned house where "the folks had made
their garden before they left and their peas and little onions are up
nice the peas almost ready to stick the radishes was coming up too."[50]

Spring and the recent arrival of a long-awaited letter from home
provoked a certain ebullience: "Oh Shaw," Owen wrote after describing his adventures in Savannah, "wait til I Come home and then
I will tell you all about it and a great many other things that I Cant
write." But he and everyone around him also betrayed their anxious
anticipation of what would happen next. The Union concentration was
in evidence all around. Steamboats had been parked four and five deep
while troops made their landings, and by the end of March the area
around Pittsburg Landing was "alive with men," as one soldier recalled, the whole army covering "an emense tract of land." Owen
told Harriet, "the woods is full of tents as far as I have seen." "To give
you anidia," he wrote, "I would just refur you to the largest Camp
meeting that you ever was at and then just think of five or six miles of
tents only they are thicker here than the tents is at a camp meeting . . .
and they are still landing troops here every day more or less." Rumors
flew about the strength of the nearby rebel force. Owen knew it was
"a vary large body of the Secesh" and thought they were about twenty
miles away. William Warren, in a different company of the Thirteenth
Iowa, heard it was "over one hundred thousand men" within eighteen
miles. In any event, Owen wrote on March 15, "We are prepaired to
fight a big fight." A few weeks later, the writing was even clearer on
the wall: "We think there is gowing to to have to fight some in a few
Days but we Dont know any thing about it and we think if we Do it
will be the wind up of the rebellion."[51]

Owen had given the matter some thought. As far as he had come
from home, the thirty-three-year-old's bonds with his family remained
strong enough to estrange him from the younger men around him.
When it initially appeared that the Thirteenth Iowa would be held
behind the main army as a reserve, men in the regiment began "fussing

considerable about it." They were itching to fight. "I Dont want to see a battle if I can help it," Owen wrote to Harriet, "but if we Do get in to a fight I shall Do my best." Previously, he had thought his black-smithing would tend to keep him safe in the rear, among the mule teams—"I think I hav the best situation of any man in the regt as it regards Danger," he had written from St. Louis—but once he began to get the lay of the land in Tennessee, he wasn't so sure. "I think if the thing Does come to a test that I shall try and show at least as much bravery as some that make so much fusse about not getting to fight they seem to think it will be a Disgrace to gow home without haveing a fight but I want to be Disgraced that way and I Dont now it may be cow-ardice but if it is I Dont think so but harriet I should hate to gow home and now that I had shot any body or pierced some one with my bay-onet but if we Do get in an engagement I shall Do my best."[52]

Owen had traveled a great distance, physical and otherwise, since he received his daughter Mary's first-ever letter in Jefferson City, Missouri, near the beginning of March. Up and down the bends of three great rivers, into a different climate zone and a nominally dif-ferent nation, his channels of communication stretched, had at times seemed broken, and tentatively reopened. His bonds with his family ran circuitously across strange discordances of time and distance. It was February 10 when Owen predicted the war would end by the first of April, February 23 when Harriet asked if she might get up a Fourth of July dinner for him. (Harriet's idea was making the rounds either of the regiment or of eastern Iowa women: at least one other member of the Thirteenth wrote to his wife, "I shall bee home to take dinner with you on the fourth of July I gess.") Owen was aboard the *Hiawatha* looking at buds bursting from the trees on the Kentucky shore when he cautiously wrote, "I still think that you may fry a Chicken for me on the fourth of July but I expect to see a good Deal between now and then."[53] He had not spoken of it since. The first of April was one day past when Owen predicted the coming fight would be "the wind up of the rebellion."

Harriet had not traveled anywhere, but she likely felt the same twists and stretches in her bonds with Owen as he moved. On the day he arrived in St. Louis, she did not even know for sure he had left Jefferson City. She did know there was a measles outbreak in her neighborhood. It hadn't struck the Creath family yet, but she knew it would. She wrote to Owen about it that same Sunday he came to the banks of the Mississippi. The letter reached him on March 20 at the far end of his expedition, in Savannah, Tennessee. This was a more jarring reconnection with home than images of snow and frozen potatoes. His initial reply barely registered what Harriet had been trying to tell him, so full was he with observations of the miles of tents. If she received it, she may have wondered whether he even had read hers. Four days later, Owen wrote again, probably having reread Harriet's letter and calculated more carefully the passage of time, her worries having settled more fully upon him. "Now harriet it has been some time sins I heard from you but I am in hopes you are well thoug I am a fraid you are not all well for in the last letter I had from you you said you expected the children would have the meesles and I am afraid some of them have got them before now and I now you will have a hard time to take care of so many little children and them sick Harriet you had better hire a girl to help you or will make yourself sick with so mutch hard work and then to take care of your children too it will be too much for you to stand and I am vary sorry I cant be there to help you but it is out of my power."[54]

It had been almost three weeks. As if looking through a telescope at the light from an extinguished star, Owen realized, he was reading about the past. The measles had doubtless visited his children by now. By the time his suggestion of a hired girl came to Harriet—this letter went through quickly, arriving in Iowa on April 4—Kate and Helen and Tommy all were "having quite a serious time with the measles." Mary had already recovered, but her eyes had been so afflicted for a time that she couldn't see well enough to feed herself. Tommy was improving. Kate had them "com ing out very thick and that is a sign she is doing very well." Little Lizzie hadn't caught measles but worried Harriet nonetheless. "She has been vary bad with her bowels for the ^last week and I have been very uneasy about her she has been bothered this way all her life she is the most delicate babe we ever had." Harriet had been "up and down all times through the night" yesterday and felt "about wore out," besieged by childhood illness.[55]

It's hard to know whether Owen's suggestion of a hired girl—coming to Harriet's eyes three weeks after she first saw the measles looming, and this time without twenty dollars to back it up—struck her as a gesture of sympathy and support or as frustratingly irrelevant, or whether she even had time to give it much thought. By then, she had already weathered what may have been the worst: "I had four sick children to watch last night and I thought I had my hands about full." By now, Mary was well. Kate soon would be, too, and she was getting to be nearly as old as a hired girl anyway. When Harriet wrote back to Owen on Sunday, April 6, she explained, "Owen I did not hire a girl for this reason. It takes money to pay a girl and this is beginning to be very scarce with me." She was continuing a conversation with Owen that had been weeks unfolding. During those weeks, Generals Grant, Sherman, and Buell, Johnston, Beauregard, Bragg, and Polk had set the stage for a clash of warring armies unprecedented in the history of the continent. Harriet could not have known that at the very instant she was writing, more than five hundred miles away, Owen was near a small church called Shiloh, in the thick of what those men wrought. On this "very cold raw day" in Iowa, it was a warm spring morning in Tennessee, and Owen had gone into combat for the first time.

Late that evening, probably around the time Harriet was putting her sick children to bed, Hellen Alford's brothers, Wayne and Lafayette, were arriving at Savannah, Tennessee, with Don Carlos Buell's army. Somewhere along their way, as they rushed down the banks of the river, boarded a steamer, and descended on Pittsburg Landing, they

Owen Creath

passed near Kate Creath's father as he was ferried to the rear and ulti-mately to a hospital in Nashville. In the morning, the Alford boys would disembark, charge up through the woods toward the battle, and help turn the tide for the Union. The Sixth Indiana lined up just south of the Pittsburg-Corinth Road, on the same ground where Owen had fallen the day before.[56]

We cannot know Harriet's thoughts on Owen's many observations from his river expedition, for none of the letters she wrote between

March 2 and April 6 survive. The one she mailed on March 9 did reach Owen on March 20. Perhaps it remained in Owen's camp, which he would have left in a hurry on the morning the rebels attacked, and to which he never returned; or it was in his pocket, possibly ruined by blood and Sunday night's thunderstorms by the time he arrived at the hospital. Presumably Harriet had written on the other three Sundays between March 9 and April 6. As of April 2, Owen had not received those letters, and, if they arrived over the next few days, they too were with him on the morning he was called into battle. What Harriet wrote on April 6, the day Owen fell at Shiloh, still exists because by the time its delivery was attempted he had died of his wounds. These words had no reader: "This is a very dark gloomy looking morning it loks very much like rain I hope you are well and in good spirits O how we bad we all want to see you I did not think this war would be over by the first of april so I am not disappointed I must quit for this time good Dear Owen."

4

Strains

On errands of life, these letters speed to death. Ah Bartleby! Ah humanity!
—Herman Melville

THEY WENT up in flames. Arriving by the thousands, sifted by solemnly sworn clerks who plucked out the currency and photographs, a three months' accumulation of them was carried out, cartload after cartload, and lit. The bonfire burned for hours, and the quarterly spectacle of it attracted tourists. A schoolteacher down from Massachusetts, gazing through the smoke of one such fire in the late 1840s, saw "so much love and advice lost, so many hopes disappointed, such infinite treasures of love wasted, that might have strengthened and edified so many longing souls." Her lawyer husband, more jaded, figured that among the two million burning letters there must have been "thousands and thousands with bad grammar, bad spelling, and nonsense worse than the spelling or grammar, thousands more, impossible to read and not worth reading." Just think, he told his wife, of all the time saved in reading and answering them![1]

The Dead Letter Office had been an object of fascination for years before the Civil War. When postage got cheaper in 1845, people sent more letters—people who couldn't spell, who didn't know the proper way to address an envelope, who could afford now to take a chance on sending a letter into the blue. Undeliverable mail gathered in Washington, D.C., in great heaps. After the outbreak of war, it gathered faster, and in Richmond, too. The U.S. Post Office Department suspended mail service to the seceded states and sent southbound mail to the Dead Letter Office. The Confederacy created its own postal system, and its own Dead Letter Office, and did the same with Southerners' letters directed to the North. Both organizations tried to smooth the way for mail to and from the armies—soldiers generally could send letters without stamps, to be paid for on receipt—but still dead letters piled up. All Americans, whether they ever took a sight-seeing trip to the Dead Letter Office or read one of the countless magazine articles about it, knew well that many letters went astray, never to return.[2]

They also knew there were other reasons, terrible to contemplate, a hoped-for letter might not arrive. If the mail was uncertain, it was no more so than life itself. "Affection grows cold from fancied neglect," mused one writer in 1860, imagining all the people whose letters never came.[3] During the half decade to come, disappointment at mail call would still make men and women fancy they were neglected, but it would spark graver worries, too. "Dead letters!" Melville wrote, "does it not sound like dead men?"[4]

LUCRETIA THOMPSON'S HUSBAND, Henry, had little use at first for circuits, networks, or even the customs of letter writing everyone else observed. He employed none of the usual niceties—didn't even write "Dear Lucretia" at the beginning or sign his name at the end. What Lucretia thought about her husband's epistolary style is impossible to know for sure, but she clearly was taken aback when she learned that he burned her letters.

All the boys did it, Henry explained: "I burnt all the letters Sunday they are a burden to us for we have more than we can see to now the rest does the same. I would like to keap them." Lucretia probably did not appreciate hearing that her letters were a "burden," and she may have been unimpressed with all that Henry had to "see to." He was enlisted as a musician and posted on the Washington defenses—hardly the most grueling service in the Union army. In Henry's telling, it sounded a bit like a camping trip. He described gathering firewood and scaring up flocks of quail that put him in mind of hunting in the woods of Connecticut. His letters often ran on in the first-person plural about what he and "the boys" were doing, as if he had joined a kind of patriotic fraternity: "We have considerable fun among ourselves."[5]

It may not have been a camping trip, but it was kind of a jaunt, and Henry regularly regaled Lucretia with narratives of his adventures. He got a pass one autumn day and made a trip into the city: "I visited the Smith sonian Institute and saw every thing in this world all kinds animals Birds snakes minerals all the Preasant from diferent parts of the World I see enough here to pay me a thousand dollars as far as sight is concernd." He and some of the boys ventured into Alexandria, a town he said reminded him of New Haven. "We went into a saloon for our dinner And what do You think we met with 6 or 7 bad women, Curtice was rather struck for he a man of good principals and has a family he inquired the price for a dinner to get out of it, they said from 37 to 50 up to one dollar and from that for an extra one upstairs from 1,00 to 5 Curtice told them that he would look other whers as he had not so much money."[6]

Henry did not (by his own account) avail himself of the "upstairs" dinner, but it's still hard to imagine that the anecdote amused Lucretia. She had been filling letters with words of longing, and Henry's fullest expression of sympathy was to recommend, "You must get where there is plenty of company then You wont think so much about me." He had talked her out of traveling down to see him, even though she likely knew, and he acknowledged, that other Connecticut wives were making visits to the regiment. "Some of the boys has sent for their wives to come here But I dont think You had better come for it is is a bad place to be sick here Which You would be liable to be the change of climate is such as to bring on the diarea shure." She didn't let go of the idea, and Henry didn't relent either. Seizing on rumors that his regiment was about to be transferred elsewhere, he wrote again: "dont come down here for we may be a Thousand miles from here by that time there is no acomodations for You not bwat I would like to have Come Stay where You are & be Contented and think it is all for the best."[7]

It is little wonder that Lucretia's letters grew testy, Henry's defensive. She commented on his poor spelling. "You speak about bad speling," he replied; "if You was here You ^would^ not think I could write anything and hear the noise all from a loud Clap of thunder down is as near as near as I can compare it." She reported that other folks at home—his parents, his Aunt Anna—had complained of not hearing from him. "I have not wrote much to Father & mother for I thought Your letters would answer the same purpose," he answered; "perhaps you think we Musitians have plenty of time to write But its not so." She felt he had misunderstood parts of her letters or neglected answering her questions. On one occasion she let fly the sharp remark that he must burn her letters before he even reads them.

> As for burning up Your letters before I read them as You state in You letter is not so You may bet we read them but it is differcult to answer a letter corect for many times we are out practiceing or on drill and when we get a chance haul out our sheat of paper from our pocket and write a few words and then of agen and our letter that we ar answering will be in our tent in our kna psacks perhaps two miles from us we dont like to keep letters for we are apt to lose them out of our pockets or somebody will be reading them which is not pleasant for us so we burn them.

It may have been an honest explanation of why Henry did not always answer Lucretia's letters "corect." Nevertheless, within a month he would be admitting to her with no evident embarrassment, "I burnt up you letter the other night to kindle fire as soon as I read it, there was something You wanted to know but I dont recolect what it was now so You must do what you think best."[8]

Lucretia may have wondered what she had to do to get her letters taken seriously. In truth, there was probably little she could do on her own from that distance. But the war had its own way of changing Henry's relationship to her letters. When the Fifteenth Connecticut was called to join the Army of the Potomac on the Rappahannock River, Henry left the relatively comfortable environs of Washington and marched across the Virginia countryside through early December rain and snow. On half rations and with few supplies, he found Lucretia's letters, a few of which caught up with him on the march, now were too useful to burn. They were his only source of paper. Lucretia's missives began coming back to her with Henry's careless penciled lines running crosswise over her neat pen-and-ink script.

At first a desperate measure, this practice in time broadened the spectrum of the couple's communication. For Henry, re-posting his wife's letters offered a quick-and-dirty way of acknowledging them; some went back to her with nothing written on them except "I have Just received this but have not time 2 Answer it" or "dont forget & send stamps." Sometimes, it seems, Henry thought the more paper he could move back and forth along the imaginary zip line between Virginia and Connecticut, the more he could learn about how the mails worked. When one of Lucretia's letters took an unusually long time getting to him, he sent back not only the letter but also the envelope, presumably so she could see the postmarks showing a full week's lag between Fair Haven and Washington. On the envelope, he wrote, first, that he was enclosing a butterfly and, second, "this has been delayed at some place . . . . I am going 2 send it on a race after the one I sent yesterday & see which will get home first."[9]

Perhaps most important, writing on his wife's letters showed unmistakably that he had read them. Lucretia's questions did not go

unanswered if Henry jotted his responses into the blank spaces between the very lines in which she asked them. When, on one occasion, she was deliberating sending him a package and wanted to know
whether he would be staying put awhile, Henry drew a caret after
Lucretia's "if I was shure you would be there" and inserted "they say
we are going 2 texas next." Farther down the page, wherever Lucretia
again expressed hope that Henry might tell her his next movements,
he added "that is impossible" or "cant do it." One can imagine Lucretia
finding Henry's marginal notes frustratingly brusque and unsenti-
mental, but they also may have suited her better than anecdotes
about Alexandria prostitutes. At least she was getting answers to her
questions.[10]

For marginally literate Americans writing back and forth on scarce
paper via mail routes through war zones, just transmitting a message
and receiving a response could be a formidable challenge. If letters
were to do more than simply affirm a loved one was still alive, they
had to meet considerably higher standards than the ones Isaac Mann
set for Susan when he invited her to "make a b c s" or fill pages with
"black marks."[11] A letter bearing a message or question of any conse-
quence needed to be received with relative promptness; read (before
being burned) and comprehended (despite poor penmanship, misspell-
ings, or obscure phrasing); responded to in writing that, in turn, could
be deciphered and understood; and delivered before the original send-
er's now-altered circumstances had obviated everything.

In a word, communication by letter was asynchronous. This is
obvious to us, who can contrast it with phone calls and videoconfer-
encing, and it was no less obvious to people in the mid-nineteenth
century contrasting it with face-to-face interactions. Educated people
then were accustomed to the slow rhythm of epistolary conversation
and had devised ways of dealing with it, but the ordinary people
thrust into letter writing by the Civil War were less prepared for its
pitfalls. Henry and Lucretia came closer than most to approximating a

handshake in writing. Many soldiers and soldiers' wives, once the strains in their lives placed new burdens on their letters, once they tried moving beyond strings of conventions affirming continued affection, came up against the limits of their written words.

For highly literate people, writing a letter can hold special power, making it possible to express things too difficult or heartfelt to say in real time. (There is a reason love letters have never gone out of style.) But for inexperienced writers, conducting a relationship through writing—by necessity, not by choice—can be a recipe for misunderstandings and conflicts. Letters can be vehicles for the articulate expression of emotion, but they also can be frustrating filters through which feelings must be shoved, sometimes clumsily, in the form of words. Lafayette Alford responded angrily to something his mother apparently had said about his last letter: "You Said it grieved you to hear me wright So much foolishness Well Honestly if I rote foolishness I Dont remember it I am as much oposed to be writing folishness as you Can be Mother." John Lehman's father evidently wondered what became of John's army pay, provoking a long, acid letter in which he vigorously denied gambling or buying tobacco and whiskey (even though it does not appear his father accused him of such) and insisted that, if his father had to subsist on salt pork and hardtack and then got a chance to spend a dollar on "a loaf of soft bread," he would do the same. John signed his letter "My best respect to all I am your disobietient Son, John L."[12]

Countless soldiers felt misunderstood by folks at home who, they very reasonably believed, did not grasp the reality of army life. (Wives and parents back home generally wanted to understand their husbands' and sons' experiences in greater depth than a barely literate soldier's letters could reveal them.) Meanwhile, families bearing the burdens and privations brought on by men's absence could feel abandoned, disconsolate, and racked with worry. Sometimes they reached breaking points; sometimes they just wanted acknowledgment of sacrifices less celebrated than those on battlefields. Sarah Myers wrote to her husband, Joel, a Pennsylvania soldier, in response to a letter from him that does not survive: "you talk very quear to me. you say if i dont intend to rite i shall let you know . . . . what is the reasen that you rite so sasey to me? i think it is very little you care for me dont you think so? i think so. if you dont care as much fore me as i care for you you would not rite so to make me to mutch truble. i have not been well for too week but it dont make no difrence about that if i am diad or alive if you dont care for me no more." Sarah, evidently a dress-maker, wrote out an itemized list of the pieces she had made recently and how much she had sold them for (it added up to more than three dollars), then wrote, "Do you think that is nothing?" Though fearful that "the futher you go south the les you care a bout me" and that "if you come home you wont live with me no more," Sarah held out hope that she and Joel were suffering only from a misunderstanding and that letters were to blame: "i hope you will soon come home then we will talk to each other."[13]

In ways that virtually any human being can recognize, expressions of frustration and flares of temper, though they might have blown over quickly in the kitchen, could fester and grow when committed to paper. A recipient might stew awhile (many times, not surprisingly, soldiers who normally replied to home letters the day they were received waited a few days to answer letters that upset or angered them); then vent spleen in a letter back; then wait days or weeks for a reply that could bring clarification or contrition but could instead bring hurt feelings and escalating demands for attention. It's no surprise that, viewed the-oretically, real-time interaction trumps asynchronous communica-tion, or that most people today agree that some things just should not be done in e-mail.[14]

If letters could seem to bridge, almost magically, the vast distances opened by the Civil War, Americans found it a trickier matter to bridge time—to communicate with loved ones whose moods and circumstances were moving targets. Harriet Creath might press Owen's letter to her body and feel his distance lessened, but could she feel any closeness in his urging that she hire help when she already was staying up all night nursing a passel of measles patients? Even as the dream of instantaneous contact across distance was being realized—the overland telegraph connected the East and West Coasts of the United States the same year the Civil War started—countless Americans, stumbling into epistolary culture for the first time, had to figure out century-old protocols for taming the ills of asynchrony. Generals, politicians, and newsmen could have their messages tapped out in Morse code, but poor farming families had to remind each other to date their letters and to indicate by date the letters they had received. Many asked their loved ones simply to put numbers at the tops of their letters so they would know if the sequence was broken. Most significantly, they had to figure out how to interpret another person's words—carried intact, thanks to ink, paper, and the mails, over hundreds of miles, yet long detached from the moments of their writing. In time's gaps, letters could fall far short of talking face-to-face, yet it was precisely in those gaps that, sometimes, letters could exceed it.[15]

HISTORICALLY, THE ASYNCHRONOUS nature of written letters had been a business problem. The literate mercantile class of American colonists conducted most of their trade with England; they did business, necessarily, by letter, and their letters moved, necessarily, by ship. Ships moved at unpredictable rates. Sometimes they sank. Men of business often thought it prudent to send essentially the same letter by more than one London- or Liverpool-bound ship. The earliest transatlantic trading had been conducted on a roughly annual basis, but the pace of commercial letter writing soon quickened. In the 1740s, one up-and-coming South Carolinian sent a dozen letters, plus abundant duplicates by other ships, to a single London contact in a single summer. Each one began with careful recitations of the several letters he had

sent previously, and aboard what ships, captained by whom, and of the
letters he had received, and by what ships. These lengthy and laborious inventories of incoming and outgoing mail were an effort to
manage an acute version of the problem Civil War letter writers con-
tended with. As one historian of early epistolary culture explains:
"Because letters at this pace might cross paths somewhere in the middle
of the ocean, it was important to establish . . . a letter's place in the sequence of outgoing and incoming letters, so as to pinpoint exactly
what information it was responding to, and what information it was
following upon. Attending to this convention at the start of every letter
was meant to preclude any misunderstanding that might accrue from
the potential lag in transatlantic time—and from the fact that the most
recent letter for the writer might not be the most recent letter for the
recipient."[16]

The utility of this convention was obvious, both within and beyond
the realm of business, and it outlasted the age of tall ships (we see it
today when our e-mail software reproduces the message we just received below our reply to it). For the eighteenth-century man of business, it offered an effective if laborious solution to a formidable
problem. On occasion he had to spread out on his desk multiple letters he had received from his trading partner, as well as the copies he
kept of letters he recently sent, and minutely cross-reference these
overlapping exchanges to determine exactly what information the other
man possessed or lacked at the time he wrote something obscure or
ambiguous. It wasn't easy, but it was better than asking for a clarification that would be months in coming. It probably had ancillary benefits,
too. Studiously reconstructing another person's intellectual situation
is good practice for how to read a letter—even more, for how to understand another person's perspective—and it probably contributed to
the belief that people could know each other through correspondence
as well as through face-to-face interaction. As the author of an

eighteenth-century manual for young businessmen put it, "Thousands, in foreign trade, correspond for many years without ever seeing one another; but they can see the intelligent man of business as thoroughly by his letters as by his conversation; and sometimes better indeed."[17]

It was a hard practice to follow in spirit, if not in form. As letter writing expanded into personal life, marking a letter's place in a sequence became reflexive for experienced writers. By the mid-nineteenth century, the practice had ripened into one of the trappings of polite culture. Educated people habitually opened their letters by acknowledging receipt of, for instance, "your kind favor of the 24th *ult.*" or "yours of the 11th *inst.*" (from the Latin *ultimo* and *instante*—either last month or this month). Such notations were so widely observed and apparently obligatory that writers sometimes emulated them without quite understanding what they meant.[18] But the uneducated Americans whom the Civil War swept into epistolary culture, even if they found the convention unfamiliar, quickly discovered the reasons for it. A woman unaccustomed to correspondence who writes to her husband on a Sunday and receives a letter from him on a Friday may initially find it bewildering that the paper she holds has nothing to do with what she wrote five days ago—may feel confusion, disappointment, and exasperation, as her eyes pass over lines that seem a world apart from the questions she had asked and the worries she had confided, all because she didn't initially realize this letter was written before her last had reached its destination. Now imagine that the letter sent last Sunday informed her husband of the dire illness of their child and the one just received is light fare about soldiers' antics in camp.

If writing letters was hard work, receiving them was not effortless, either. Reading across distance could be fun. It brought impressions of strange sights in new places. Westward migrants of the early nineteenth century, who made the first significant wave of letter writing among poor and middle-class families, created sensations with their dispatches from the frontier. (The letters of Caroline Kirkland, a New York–born woman whose husband moved the family to Michigan in the 1830s, so enchanted her friends back east that she turned them into a novel, pseudonymously published.) Those migrants no doubt found time lags annoying, but they less often confronted their families' direst strains by letter. Husbands rarely were absent for years at a time; parents did not migrate away from their young children.[19]

During the Civil War, reading across distance could be enchanting from time to time, but reading across time was a grave challenge. Families needed their letters to do hard work. Spats between teenaged sons and their parents were one thing; privation and mourning were another. The disconnections of time easily exacerbated petty misunderstandings. In February 1864, Grant Taylor of Alabama learned that his wife's kitchen had burned. He did not learn it from Malinda, but from a man in his company who had gotten a letter from home with news of the neighborhood. Grant couldn't understand why Malinda hadn't told him this, and for weeks he kept asking her: "How is it you did not write to me about your kitchen being burnt up," and "Why have you never written me any word about your kitchen being burned." It took fully two months for Grant and Malinda to exchange enough letters to straighten the matter out. Tabulating their recent letters in mid-April, Grant determined, "I think I have got all your letters up to the 25th March except the one written the day after your kitchen was burned." The experience didn't prevent Grant from becoming short with Malinda, who had recently given birth, when she questioned him repeatedly: "You ask me again about naming the baby. I sent you names. What objection have you got to them. But if they don't suit you, name it just what you please. If you intended to name it yourself, why did you ask me about it at all."[20]

Worse news and greater pains, arriving out of time, could sunder letter writers' senses of connection across place. It was during his first months in the army that Larkin Kendrick could look westward from the coastal plain of North Carolina, imagine seeing his wife and children two hundred miles distant, and write to Mary Catherine, "I of ten maid the wonder when the son was a setting behin the western Horising if it was a shedding its brite Rays on my lovely home I often look at the moon and the countless stares and wonder if my belove ones is a behold the same seen." Four months later, the "strong ties of se-mented love," which Larkin assured Catherine "keeps my mind" with her and the children, had been strained by the irregularity of the mail. In a letter he got from her on March 16, written only three days be-fore, Catherine told him she had received no letters from him in six weeks, even though, he insisted, "I have sent you a letter every weak." Shortly after, Larkin went into the hospital, and Catherine's letters did not follow him. For more than three weeks he was too sick to write. Finally, in early May, he dictated a letter from the hospital in Everettsville:

My Dear wife I seat myself this Evning to drop you a few lines to let you Know that I Have been under the care of the doctors for the space of twenty two days in the hospital with the Chills & fever & then pneumonia & now I have the Reumatism in my hips & Legs but I am some better . . . . I can Say that I have not Receved A Single letter from you since I have been in the hos-pital & I hope when these Lines come to hand they may reach you in perfect health. I can say My Dear Wife that I would Like to come home & see you but I do not Know now whether they will Let me come home or not but if I get the chance I shall ac-cept of it one thing Sure But for fear I do not come I want you to write as soon as this comes to hand & Let me know how your health is & how you are getting along My Dear Wife I can say to you that our Rigment had gone to virginia they are at guineas station & I cannot tell you kow when I shal go to the Regment but if I get well I shal go soon & if I do not get well I donot know

where I may be sent to. . . . how long I Shal Stay here I do not
know.

Writing through, or rather speaking to, an unknown amanuensis,
Larkin's thoughts generally turn on what he wants to "say" to Mary
Catherine—what he *can* say, since the letter abides in the absent and
unknown. Larkin knows little of his own future—whether he will
live or die, be well or ill, sent here or there—and, cut off from Catherine's letters, knows nothing of her recent past and certainly nothing
of her present. He would learn nothing more until he completed the
journey to rejoin his regiment, all the way up in northern Virginia,
at the railroad town where Stonewall Jackson would die one year
later.[21]

Sometimes letters long delayed came through in a sudden burst.
Epistolary traffic that had slowed almost to zero raced back up to speed.
When Thornton Clark rejoined his regiment after his illness and
recuperation in Louisville, the first thing he did down on the Kentucky-
Tennessee border was "run all over the Camps to see if there was any
letters" from his wife, Nancy. Sure enough: "you dont know how glad
I was when I found four letters all from you and then they was all in
your own hand write I want you to write me as often as you can for I
can read your hand write very well then it dose me more good to read
a letter in your own hand write than any body elses." Reading Nancy's letters, he rejoiced to feel once again connected, though he also
saw the bitter fruits of their long period out of sync. All those several
weeks, Nancy had kept writing—and kept receiving letters from
Thornton in Louisville that never acknowledged her own, displayed
no awareness of what she had written, and showed no concern for the
troubles she had confided to him. At least once, Nancy voiced the fear
that he was forgetting her, and Thornton, his heart wrenched, replied
effusively: "I dnt want you to think that I have forgot you for that is
all I want to live for in this world is to make a liveing for you and the

Children and to prepare for eternity if I had not enlisted when I did I should not havev enlisted atall not as I am sorry that I am in the army only for your sake I would like to be at home for there is no body els in this wourld that I think as much of as I do of you and Children that God has given to us I will come home as soon as I can."[22]

Thornton now also had weeks' worth of accumulated family business to attend to. Nancy had been writing to him about their financial plight. The neighbor named Brooner to whom Thornton had entrusted his first army paycheck used it to pay off one of Thornton's debts. Nancy thought Thornton might have arranged it this way. He spent many sentences explaining just what he intended, promised Nancy all the support he could provide, and held back none of his anger at Brooner: "if he keeps back that money to pay that judgement he is not the man that I thought he we for I wrote to him and told to pay Jim Brown five dollars and to let you have the balance as you stood in nead of it the next money that I send home I will send to you for you to spend to please your self."[23]

Only a day later, Thornton received another letter from Nancy. Sent before she had received his euphoric first letter home from Tennessee, it of course made no reply to anything he had just written. Far from rejoicing at their epistolary reconnection, as Thornton might have hoped, it carried more fears of forgetting and worries about money. Thornton therefore repeated himself: "I am very sorry that you are so dissatisfied but you hav had enough to discourage you to some extend I think that Brooner acted very wrong in keeping back that money that I sent to you I did not give him any orders to pay off that judgement all the orders that I have him was to pay Brown five dollars and to let you have the balance." Straining harder now to allay what his previous letter, perhaps still on its way north, had not stopped from coming, Thornton detailed all the small sums of money he thought she might be able to collect or borrow from folks in town. He assured Nancy he would send money when he could and would come home

when he could, but her expressions of need plainly outstripped anything he stood able to provide:

> Nancy you want me to come home and I want to come home as
> bad as you want me to come but that is out of the question for
> when one once gets in to the army it is a hard job to ever get out
> again while they are fit for duty. . . . I will try to get a furlow and
> come home and see you and the Children for I do want to see
> you very bad you are never out of my mind when I am awake
> and when I am a sleep. I am a dreaming about you you talk about
> me a forgetting you when I am so far from you my prayre it is
> daily that God will bless you and give you grace and strenghth
> that you may be able to bear with patience your lot in this world
> I want you to cheer up and put your trust in God and all will work
> out for the best yet. . . . now Nancy for my sake do try and cheer
> up and do not take things to heart so do not grieve so much about
> my dieing before hand write as often as you can and do not think
> that I will make fun of your spelling for I think that you do very
> well besides I think that I would have little to do to make fun of
> your writing.

Little changed through the winter. Thornton's letters, barren of the
reveries of his easy days in Louisville, became repetitive and pon-
derous, constantly urging Nancy not to be discontented and to put
her trust in God, constantly assuring her he would send home his pay
just as soon as he got it. She got a particular rise out of him by saying
she would start forgoing coffee. He replied, "I dont want you to scimp
yourself too much for any thing dont quit useing coffee on the account
of the high price for it will not take much to do you." Like a colonial
merchant sending the same message by multiple ships, Thornton repeated this admonition two days later—"I dont want you to suffer for
anything dont quit useing your Coffee as long as you can get it for it

dont take much to do you"—but this time he backed it up more practically. He enclosed five dollars borrowed against his next paycheck from the captain of his company, Cyrus Medcalf.[24]

Then Thornton was detached from his regiment and again cut off from the mail. Some officer having identified his skill as a carpenter, he was assigned to General William Rosecrans's new engineering detail, the Pioneer Brigade. He told Nancy this would gain him thirty-five extra cents per day (whenever he got paid) but also make him less able to write letters, as he would be busily moving across the Tennessee countryside building bridges. On December 22, he wrote out exactly how Nancy should direct her letters:

> Thornton Clark
>   first battalion
>   of pioneer Corps
>   army of the Cumberland
>   in care of Lieutenant Culow

But by the time she would receive this model and a reply so addressed could make its way back to Thornton, he would have rejoined the main army. Having worked through the night on a bridge over Stewart's Creek, outside Murfreesboro, Thornton's crew received orders at four o'clock in the morning on December 30 to move up to Stones River.[25]

They rang in the new year fighting Braxton Bragg's Army of Tennessee in the bloodiest battle of the war. The two days of fighting at Stones River involved some of the fiercest artillery fire anyone had yet witnessed, and bodies were destroyed in astounding ways—"torn to pieces," one of Thornton's fellow Hoosiers wrote, "and throwed in every direction one leg here and another there." The commanding Union general, William Rosecrans, was seen riding along the line of battle splattered with the blood of a staff officer whose head had been torn off by a cannonball. Positioned to support artillery regiments, the

Pioneer Brigade was somewhat shielded, but it was a chaotic scene even behind the line of guns, whose deafening roar so terrified horses that dismounted riders seemed almost as thick in the air as bullets.[26]

Thornton came through "safe and sound with out a scratch on me," and soon afterwards the mail caught up. After four weeks without hearing from home, he got two letters from Nancy the same day. Perhaps Nancy said something that taxed his patience, or perhaps, witness to a bloodbath, he had hardened. He wrote back in smudged pencil: "you must quit your grieving for it only makes you more miserable put your trust in god and ask him to give you grace to bear with your troubles and all will go well with you."[27]

Up in northern Virginia, when Larkin Kendrick arrived back with his regiment after his hospital stay, letters from Mary Catherine were awaiting him. One of them contained a different kind of grieving, to which he responded:

Dier wife I this mornin take my pen to try to drop you a few lines but wated down with the heav affliction I hardeley Know whethe I will be able to give you sadisfaction or not. I never heard that mychild was ded till yesterday and tongue cant express my feeling about it my mind ran back home and I see in amagination all my famley but now I see them siperated nevr to mee in this world. I look back but a short time ago when I left you all in health but Monster death has com and lade its hand on my infant and taken it away. but let this be hard as it may be we must be submisive to God for the Lord giveth and the Lord will take away. and blessed be his name. I Know the large rivr of simppath cant fetch my little Elisabeth back to me but the strong ties of pure love is so close I cant help it. I am sadisfid that she is in Haven walking the Golden streets of that upper and better world thare to be happy forever and ever but still it strikes my soule with *terrar*.

After giving over most of one page to grief, a grief that seems worse for having been delayed ("I never heard that mychild was ded till yesterday"), Larkin finally comes around to his letter's customary beginning: "I am as well as common only tired from the fatigue of my long trip. I seresley hope these lines may find you injoying the blessing of god." This convention was born of epistolary communication's slow pace: no one can do more than hope the lines he writes will find his loved one—at some unknown time, subject to all the uncertainty of the future—doing well and enjoying blessings. Larkin, now more mindful than ever of how much can change during a letter's transit, means it seriously.[28]

AS IN VIRTUALLY every aspect of the nineteenth-century United States, gender mattered a great deal in epistolary culture. The "particulars" that went into a proper letter might be sorted between men and women. Charles Beecher, brother of Harriet Beecher Stowe, used to say in his family letters that he supplied the "philosophicals" while his wife, Sarah, took over the pen to cover the "domesticals." When the war broke out, women were not only called upon to take over men's roles as managers of farms and finances; they shouldered new epistolary responsibilities, too. Their letters now were expected to sustain the morale of soldiers. In the South, where men's valor and fighting spirit were counted on to match the North's bigger and better supplied armies, concerns about morale were acute. "DON'T WRITE GLOOMY LETTERS," the *Huntsville Democrat* warned Alabama wives, and a Georgia newspaper fretted that women were giving up under strain, writing "very desponding letters" that would cause soldiers to "lose confidence in themselves."[29]

Some historians of Civil War soldiers have likewise reproved women whose letters detailing hardships at home added to the woes of men suffering through a horrific war. Bell Irvin Wiley, writing in the 1940s,

scarcely contained his scorn for the "regrettably prevalent" genre of
the complaining letter from the Southern home front:

> They complained of bad crops, of fear of Yankee raids or of
> havoc already wrought by Federal visitation, of trouble with
> overseers, of slothfulness and insubordination of slaves, of scar-
> city of food and clothing, or of apprehension of such scarcity, of
> the undue prolongation of war, of the hopelessness of victory,
> of deprivation of the company of their absent sons or spouses,
> of sickness or the anticipation of it, and of innumerable other
> woes. One wife, after apparently exhausting the supply of ordi-
> nary complaints, upbraided her soldier husband for fathering the
> several children already born to her, and while complaining of
> his absence, expressed dread of his return lest she again be sub-
> jected to motherhood.

Illness, hunger, and the approach of an enemy army would seem to
be more than "ordinary complaints," and the prospect of a fourth or
sixth or eighth pregnancy might well strike fear into any woman in
the nineteenth century. Even more recent historians have subtly be-
moaned the ways women's letters sapped the high-minded patriotism
of men at war. James McPherson, after reading thousands of soldiers'
letters, concluded that "the wrong kind of letter" from home—
meaning, those "complaining of loneliness and hardship and expressing
fears that the war would leave them widows and their children
fatherless"—lowered morale in both armies. The notion that women
"complained frequently" may be a "false impression," McPherson
acknowledges, created by the archival evidence. When women "wrote
encouraging letters to their husbands or sweethearts," the men did
not send back reassuring or defensive explanations for themselves.
"Most evidence of women who encouraged their husbands' or lovers'

commitment to duty, honor, and country is lost to history, for most collections of soldiers' letters home do not include letters coming the other way."[30]

In fact, an examination of more than three dozen manuscript and published collections of soldiers' letters that also include letters received from a woman at home, as well as hundreds of isolated letters written by Civil War women to soldiers, suggests that it is no false impression: pep talks are rare, descriptions of hardship are plentiful. This is unquestionably so in the South, where women's letters played a major role in inciting their husbands to desert the army.[31] It is even true in the North, where the typical white soldier's family suffered relatively less than in the Confederacy. But there is more than one way to interpret the "complaining" aspects of women's Civil War letters. In the case of Nancy Clark, it is easy to assume—because her letters do not survive and we do not know exactly what she was "grieving" about—that her hardships do not compare to Thornton's having just witnessed men's bodies being ripped apart by screaming artillery shells in the Battle of Stones River. Still, it is only an assumption. The letter in which Mary Catherine Kendrick informed Larkin of little Elisabeth's death also does not survive, but surely no one—least of all Larkin—thinks she should have curbed her grief in favor of cheering her husband's honorable devotion to the Confederate cause. As two scholars of the New England home front have observed, civilian correspondents had to "walk a tightrope between therapeutic remembrance to prop morale and sincere disclosure to maintain intimate relations."[32]

It was when they walked that tightrope, when they were under the greatest personal strain, that people stretched themselves as writers. Then, their letters did not merely record the meaning of the Civil War—which was, after all, none other than a protracted personal strain for millions of ordinary Americans. They created its meaning out of

the interpretations, inventions, and expressive turns they used to hold
families together with pen and paper.

BETSY BLAISDELL'S INFANT child was already buried when her husband, Hiram, joined the Union army in the fall of 1864. Looking ahead
to a cold winter in upstate New York, she closed up their farmhouse
and moved in with her parents a little farther south in Cayuga County.
A few years older than her husband and already past thirty, Betsy now
found herself childless and a little childlike—in some ways older than
her years, in some ways younger. An effectively single woman, she had
some pressing responsibilities on the farm—chickens, a pig, a cow, a
horse, and a corn harvest that needed shucking—and few resources
to meet them. Alternately striving toward independence and resenting
her belittling dependency on other men, such as her father, Betsy suffered the inward strains of a shaken home, an unmoored identity, and
crippling anxiety. Letters crossing in the mail seemed a hopeless means
of sustaining the connection with Hiram that alone in her mind offered
a recognizable future.

The war must have seemed at first a far-off affair to the Blaisdells.
As a healthy man in his mid-twenties when the war broke out,
dwelling in a heavily Republican area—home of one of the party's
leading men, William Seward—Hiram would have seemed a prime
candidate to enlist early. In fact, whether from political misgivings or
a sense of obligation at home, he waited until the fall of 1864, when
his conscription was imminent. During the presidential campaign
that summer, a family like the Blaisdells might have thought, if
they only kept their distance from the war a little while longer, it
would pass them over—either because Union victory was around the
corner, or because a new administration would pull the plug. But by
September they apparently concluded the draft would not wait long
enough, and they were right; Hiram's name came up less than a
month after he volunteered.[33]

Betsy likely nurtured hope he would be deemed unsuitable, for it was not the moment he left home to sign up at Auburn, the county seat, that most affected her. It was when she got word he was mustered into the Third New York Light Artillery and leaving for the front:

> O Hiram if you could have seen your Bet when you left Auburn I dont know what you would have said for I could not controll my feelings I cried for days untill I was sick I could not eat when I went to the table you was not there and I was full I could not eat it seemed as thoug my heart was broke for I would have to leave the table for crying. . . . O Hiram you know it is an awful trial for me our famely is broke up and I am left alone our littl one is laid in the grave and you are to war.

The looming threat that her family would be permanently "broke up"—that Hiram would not return and she would be left a childless widow—unleashed regret, desperation, and panic. "Keepe out of danger all that you can," she pleaded, "for I want you to come back to me O Hiram it seems to me I never shall see you again and you dont know how bad I feel it seems I cant give it up I cant be reconciled if I had knowed I would ever felt one quarter as bad you never should gone I would went to canda with you." They probably contemplated a draft-dodging flight to Canada before Hiram signed up—at least Betsy had contemplated it, even if Hiram did not seriously—for she returned to the idea regularly and ruefully: "I am so sorry you went I dont know what to do I never shall for give myself for not saying you should not go and went to canada."[34] Drawn though Betsey was to such solacing visions of a restored family, they may have only intensified the sense that her life now lay scattered—at her parents' house, on her farm, with Hiram's regiment, within a small grave, at some notional spot in Canada. Far from accepting this time of trial, she continued to imagine alternative realities, only then to scold herself for doing so. When her foot began swelling up shortly after Hiram left—"it pains me all o the time from my toes to my ankel and it has for a fort night or more"—she believed she was destined to be crippled, she told Hiram, as moral retribution "for wishing you had a leg or arm broke." Hoping her husband would suffer just enough injury to get sent home was not Betsy's only "wicked" thought. She confessed to Hiram that, after reading his first letter from the field, she was "glat to know that you felt bad when you left auburn," for his homesickness reassured her their bond would survive distance: "you will not forget me if you feel lonely and bad."[35]

It's not surprising that Betsy would find the asynchronous quality of letters singularly aggravating. Her sentences sometimes became tangled in knots as she tried to situate matters in sequences of letters in transit: "you said you had got all the money I sent you," she replied once to Hiram. "You have not unless you have got it since you wrote that letter for there is three dollars more on the road beside what you have got unless you have received it since you wrote." It disappointed her when Hiram's letters didn't talk about what she expected them to. Around the time she sent Hiram a care package, something began delaying mail from the front. When she finally got a twelve-day-old letter, all she noticed at first was what the letter was not: "I thought I should got one to night that would told about your box and told how you enjoyed eating my victuals."[36]

Hiram could be more sanguine about the pace of the mail. He spoke frequently of letters that were "on the road" and seemed to care rather less about their sequencing and responsiveness than simply about there being plenty of them in the pipeline. "I have received your letter last night and . . . I had just written ᵒⁿᵉ the day before th I got yours so thare will be f three on the road to you and you keep as many a you can on the road to and we can hear from ~~one a~~ each other often." But a long wait for letters could leave him anguished, too. After he left Auburn, he traveled first to Elmira, New York, then Baltimore and Fortress

Monroe in Virginia, and finally arrived in New Bern, North Carolina. Only after he had been encamped three weeks at New Bern, well more than a month after he left Auburn, did Betsy's letters finally catch up to him. In Virginia, he was demanding: "Dear Bet I have got tired of waiting for an answer. so I am going to write again when you get this stop work and sit down write me an answer and then hitch up and put it in the office for I want to hear from you so bad." In North Carolina, when he wrote his seventh apparently unanswered letter, his tone had become despairing: "O Bet I have got almost tired of waiting for a letter yet I have been waiting and putting of writing expe cting a letter from you I cannot think that you have not written but that thare is some mistake about it some way."[37]

Even once the bottleneck opened, it took awhile for the epistolary channel—and the air between Hiram and Betsy—to clear. Overdue letters made it hard for each to grasp the other's present situation. Betsy wrote near the end of November, "Dear beloved Husband I Have just received your letter wrote the 18 [of November] that you had got my letter 17 of october it has been a long time going to you you wrote you was disappointed in not geting my letters they must be delayed for I write often last week I wrote 3 and this is the 3d one I have wrote to you this week so you see Hiram I write whether you get them or not Hiram I to get disappointed for I sent tuesday and I went thursday night myself and did not get any." With letters halting and then flowing, the husband and wife oscillating between curt disappointment and sac-charine pining, their correspondence lurched accordion-wise like an ungainly army column on the march. Unaccustomed to communi-cating with each other in such ways—as they were, probably, to being apart at all—Betsy and Hiram may have felt they were so ill equipped for separation that, after all, emigration to Canada would have been wiser. Ironically, it was from precisely that direction that Betsy would see the Civil War coming even closer to home—and kick-starting her faltering efforts to connect with Hiram via letter.[38]

Even as she was writing her first plaintive letter to Hiram on October 13, following his departure from Auburn, a cadre of Confederates was quietly slipping across the border from Quebec into Vermont. By the time Hiram made it down to North Carolina, Betsy had been able to read in the papers of what happened on the other side of the Adirondack Mountains on October 19.

The young Kentuckian Bennett Young had seen far more of the North than the average rebel soldier. He rode in John Hunt Morgan's cavalry raid across the Ohio River in the summer of 1863. At the end of a thousand-mile incursion that terrified civilians in Indiana and Ohio, Bennett was captured with the rest of the group and sent as a prisoner of war to Camp Douglas in Chicago. From there, he escaped to Canada, traveled the long way around to Richmond, and secured—along with a new commission as a lieutenant—the Confederate War Department's approval to organize assaults against the Union's Northern frontier. Back in Canada, he mustered twenty-odd men, all young Confederate soldiers who had escaped north from federal prisons, and plotted a surprise raid on St. Albans, Vermont, one of the northernmost towns of any significance, only about fifteen miles from the border.

The men arrived sporadically during the week leading up to October 19, unassumingly checking into St. Albans hotels. Some volunteered that they belonged to a Montreal hunting and fishing club and were taking their fall outing. Did the townspeople have any extra guns they could borrow? Once the whole party had arrived, they waited for the quiet of a Wednesday afternoon. Bennett put on a grey Confederate uniform, walked out of his hotel, fired a revolver into the air, and announced he was claiming the town for the Confederate States of America. Some of the raiders herded everyone they saw onto the town green, while the rest proceeded to rob the downtown banks. Among the hostages was a former Union army captain who sneaked away, got a horse, and quickly raised a posse of armed townsmen.

The raiders fled back across the border, having mortally wounded one man and stolen more than $200,000. They tried to set the town afire, but most of their incendiary bombs fizzled. One woodshed burned down. The whole thing lasted about forty-five minutes.[39]

However minor an event in the military history of the war, the St. Albans raid was more than sufficient to shock the people of the town, and that shock quickly rippled outward, rattling nerves across the North. The night of the raid, a woman of St. Albans wrote to her son, Marshall, detailing the day's events. "We will not go to bed to night," she told him; "I now hear the train whistle I hope it is the soldiers or the Arms or something." She included a message from another member of the family: "tell Marsh to send me a revolver." Cadets from Norwich University, a military academy in central Vermont, were sped north by train to defend other towns along the border. Anxious Vermonters looked over their shoulders for rebel infiltration. A bank clerk outside Montpelier, in a letter to a friend in the army, said darkly, "The State is full of strangers prowling around with no apparent business"; but, he reassured him, "the towns are taking measure to protect themselves. . . . Revolvers have been in good demand." Within days, the popular *Frank Leslie's Illustrated Newspaper* had sent an artist to St. Albans, and he created eleven woodcuts for a double-page spread illustrating the progress of the raid. By early November, readers across the North were gazing on images of neatly dressed Vermonters standing with their hands in the air as ruffians pointing guns forced them to swear allegiance to the Confederate States of America.[40]

Rumors swirled that the St. Albans raiders were the advance guard of a rebel army massing in Canada and preparing to descend on the placid and undefended northern tier of the nation—possibly to coincide with the upcoming presidential election. Beneath alarming headlines about "THE FRONTIER WAR," northern papers propagated stories about imminent raids "which will cause the whole country to shudder with horror and cry out with indignation against the diabolical hearts which conceived and were ready to carry it out, to the extent of pillage, arson and murder." In the first days after the Vermont raid, one paper reported an attack on Plattsburgh, New York. No such thing was occurring, but Plattsburgh residents nevertheless tore up their own railroad tracks to frustrate invasion. The *New York Herald* declared that "murder, burning, and robbery" were in store for the city of Buffalo. Rebels reportedly were massing across Lake Ontario for an attack on Oswego, New York (Hiram heard a rumor around camp—no doubt wishful thinking—that his regiment would be sent back near home to defend Oswego). Confederates were said to be launching boats from Halifax and planning raids into Cleveland, Detroit, and Chicago. Secretary of State William Seward sent a letter of warning to the mayors of several major cities near the Canadian border. Newspapers reprinted that letter, as well as an October 28 order issued by Major General John Dix, which predicted that rebel incursions had both military and political objectives: "large numbers of [southern] refugees, deserters, and enemies of the Government," the order warned, would be coming across the border "with a view to vote at the approaching Presidential election."[41]

On the southern shore of Lake Ontario, Betsy Blaisdell did not know what to believe. Two days after the St. Albans raid, she wrote to Hiram, "they think they will have out the drafted men to guard the falls" (probably Niagara) and that "they are holding secret meetings in every city they say and they thinks they will burn houses." In the coming weeks, as rumors of Confederate infiltration from Canada multiplied, Betsy's vaguely conspiratorial "they" became more specific. She wrote to Hiram about "awful threats" from Canada. "I do not know but we shall all be massacred. . . . they think they will come through here as the gurilas do south cayuca has ordered every house to be armed."[42]

As if besieged by anxiety, Betsy would view nearly every aspect of her life during these weeks with fear. Critters were eating the cabbage up at her and Hiram's farm, and the last time she went up to tend to things there, the door of the house was stuck—which she interpreted as possible evidence of Confederate incursion. "I belive some one had been in the house or tried to get in," she explained to Hiram, "for I like to never got the door unlocked and I never had any trouble before there is lots of stealing around and canada is making awful threats." She was suffering a mysterious pain in her side, which she believed was worse because Hiram was away at war:

> yesterday Morning I went out to the barn and done My chores and came back and had to go to bed I tried three times to sit up and every time I would have just such a spell and the pain was so severe it would set one right in a chill I never had any thing like it before Hiram I am afraid something new has set in it worries me dreadfully if I aint no better to morow I shall have the Dr O how I wish you was here to help take care of me and go and get something done O Hiram you dont know how I miss you and now it is worse than ever I should had the Dr yesterday if you had been here how I wish you was here I tell you there will no one do like an own Husband O Hiram.

Betsy's sister, Adeline, left her children with her and went to pay a visit to friends. "I am perfectly willing to take care of them," Betsy wrote to her husband, "but I like to see folks think some one els does something once in awhile as well as them I dont like to be shit on I knew it would be just so when you went away for you know there was no one only you and Mother that any pitty for me." Betsy heard that a man in the neighborhood, Bruce, was headed south to exhume and bring home the body of a relative who had died in an army hospital. Bruce apparently said he planned to ask some of the Cayuga County boys in Hiram's regiment to help him. At this, Betsy panicked. "I dont want you should go no how," she told Hiram, "for you are weak and will take disease a great deal quicker I shall worry about it all the time till I heare I am afraid ~~you~~ he will get there before the letter does I dont think it is right to dig any body up when you dont know what they died with and it aint a going to make it any better for him and it will be a great deal worse for me to be left than it is for them and if any one of you should catch any diseas and it should go through the camp it might take you all off so dont go none of you." Put simply: not a single person who might breathe the same air as Hiram should dig up this corpse because, according to Betsy's risk analysis, Bruce's family suffers less having a loved one buried in Southern earth than Betsy will suffer if widowed.[43]

Paranoid, bitter, hypochondriacal, Betsy Blaisdell may call to mind Harriet Beecher Stowe's characterization of Marie St. Claire. (Then again, the strains of the war drove other people clear into psychosis.)[44] If Betsy seems the epitome of the complaining wife, sending discouraging letters that sap her soldier-husband's morale, she is also a study in the emotional contortions women had to perform as they held the straining tethers between war and home. When the question of whether she and her husband should get out to Canada turned into a question about marauding enemies getting in, the geography of her emotional life flipped over. Letters between her and Hiram, delayed, crossed, and missing, were less strings of connection than tangles of mismatched feeling.

In one of her lengthiest epistolary excursions, Betsy narrated the episode in which it seemed the Civil War had come verily to her doorstep.

they was a spy along the other day and I dont see what folks let her go for without stoping her and shut her up is what thay ought to done but they all seemed to be afraid of her or him it was it was no woman I know as well as I want to if they are afraid of one I do not know what they will do when a whole band comes she was dressed in bloomers and dressed very nice and had a splendid cane likley it was her weapon she called to a good many houses and she would take out a book and set some thing down wherever she stoped. . . . she pretended to be a prophet she warned all the farmers to take care of all they could raise for they was agoing to be four years more war and four years famine when she said she was a prophet she said they would be more along in a few days she was nothing but a man dressed in womens clothes just a spying what she can to tell the rest as she would not note every thing down and folks think they will be a band along to rob and I do not know what else it is awful times were are in a bout as much danger as you are I think sometimes[45]

It's hard to know exactly what to make of this report. Betsy evidently believed the great rebel incursion from Canada had begun, was coming straight through her town, and had taken the curious form of a cross-dressing spy with the odd habit (for a spy) of announcing exactly the coming invasion ("she said they would be more along in a few days") for which she supposedly was casing the town. Betsy's vacillations—insisting the figure is a man and just as insistently using "she"—reflect an apparent indecision about whether to take what she has seen seriously. In the guise of a woman prophesying in biblical tones, "she" may be nothing more than an eccentric millenarian wandering across what had, after all, been called the "Burned-over District," so hot had been its evangelical fervors during the Second Great Awakening. Yet Betsy seems earnest in seeing the more sinister image, however implausible, of an armed Confederate disguised beneath those bloomers.

If she was seeing things two ways, it was not just the dizzying effects of anxiety. After a month adrift in an unsatisfying correspondence she used largely to vent longing and frustration, Betsy was beginning to discover how letter writing could open a person's eyes to multiple perspectives. We are in about as much danger as you are I

think sometimes. This apparently passing thought, inspired by the
general atmosphere after the St. Albans raid, took firmer hold in the
days after the "prophet" episode. A notion of emotional reciprocity—
a conviction that she and Hiram held feelings in common despite their
physical separation—seemed to spring from Betsy's sense (however
distorted) that they both were at war, each "in a bout as much danger"
as the other. Such mirroring became the leitmotif of Betsy's letters
as fall changed to winter.

A few more days after writing to Hiram about the prophet, Betsy,
still apparently rattled, dispatched one more deeply self-pitying
letter. Her horse is sick, her hens will starve, "it snows and blows like
fun," and she has lost so much weight that when she put on her Sunday
dress "it did not touch me no where hardly." (By way of summing up
her report on daily life, she quipped, "this living without a man in
the winter and such wether and away from home aint what is cracked
up to be.") In a crescendo of pining, she wrote, "I hope you will be
spared to come home for I cant think that you will forget your Bet or
but [illegible] you will love me just as well as you ever did Hiram you
think one yar is a short time but it seems very long to me. . . . I wake
up nights and lay awake hours and hours thinking of you." Nearing
the bottom of a page, she squeezed several of the most crucial words—
"will forget your Bet or [illegible] you"—beneath the last faint blue
line of her ruled paper. The ink running unevenly, Betsy possibly
writing through tears, she inscribed several cramped words difficult
to make out. One or two are almost impossible to decipher. They may
or may not say, "or but expect you will love me."[46]

Hiram may have been unable to read these lines exactly, or he may
have been unsure about Betsy's convoluted syntax. (She can't think he
will forget her, meaning she doesn't think so? or meaning it is too
painful for her to contemplate what she fears is the truth?) Perhaps he
was hurt to find her thinking along these lines at all even if, nominally,
she was lodging no accusation. In any event, he replied in force: "Bet

do you think that I could ^{ever} cease to love t̶o̶ to love O Bet I could not harbor such a thought in my ^{heart} for a moment no neve can I cease to love my Bet O Bet you can not think that I do not love you just dear when I am ^{here} as at home do you do you think for a moment that I do not O Bet I know that you do not."[47]

This letter reached Betsy more than two weeks after she wrote the words that provoked it. Hearing her words come back to her in Hiram's phrasing, and in tones as aching as her own, plainly affected Betsy. What the spy-prophet had prompted her to think—that she and her husband were mutually endangered by the war—was proving true in their emotional lives as well. Husband and wife were threatened equally by the strains of misunderstood letters, of fear and anxiety about the other's constancy. Now, far from taking selfish pleasure in knowing Hiram "felt bad" when he left Auburn, Betsy seemed at last to recognize that Hiram's suffering might match her own and that, in their shared longing, they were bound together. Her letter of December 8, 1864, replying to Hiram's plaintive asseveration, is suffused with the sympathy previous letters lacked.

She determined not to cause Hiram the anxieties she has suffered: "Hiram you wanted to know if I thought you would cease to love me no never nor I you are nearer and dearer to me than ever and I trust I am the same to you I do not want you to think any such thing if I have wrote any such thing I did not mean to and am sorry for it." She studiously avoided complaint about her hardships: "Hiram I dont want you should worry any thing about me or our things i will take just as good care of them as I can and as for me I am well real well Hiram for me or I could not do as much hard work I milk and lug water to the barn to the horse now dont worry about me at all for I can get along any way I want you should keep up good courage and good spirits." During the preceding weeks Hiram had several times tried to calm Betsy's exploding fears, imploring her not to "borrow trouble," and Betsy now, for the first time, adopted her husband's pet phrase for her own use: "Hiram do try dont borrow any trouble about about any thing." On the heels of this rhetorical role reversal, she imagined herself likewise taking on some of Hiram's responsibilities as a protector and provider: "if you want any thing Hiram send for it and you shall have it as long as your Money last I dont want you should go hungry if you want any paper envelos or stamp just let me know it or Money or anything else you shal have it."[48]

Showing an emotional generosity of which she had scarcely seemed capable in her earlier correspondence, Betsy now sent letters replete with warmth and reassurance. Nearly every page she wrote for the next month included the words "dont worry." If there is anything you want from home, she told Hiram again and again, with almost ritual echoes of the Sermon on the Mount, you shall have it. She remained a deeply nervous person: though determined to send money, she worried about it getting lost in the mail, asked Hiram how much he needed, fretted that he was without money while she awaited his answer, panicked at the thought of sending a ten-dollar greenback and having it go astray, resorted finally to getting a stack of fifty-cent notes and enclosing one at a time in weeks' worth of letters.[49] But she was feeling her way toward a correspondence with Hiram that might calm rather than inflame her anxiety.

It was with her December letters that Betsy began confining herself to the first two pages of each letter folio, so that Hiram could tear off half the large sheet and use it himself. His letters now would come to her on the very paper she had tucked into an envelope a week or two before, and Betsy seemed hopeful of achieving, within this closed circle of their material exchanges, more of inward directness and connection. After writing, as she had many times before, "It makes me feel agreat deal better to hear from you and hear that you feel better," she was careful to add—plainly concerned for the authenticity of their letters—"but dont tell me you feel better when you dont." Rotating the page, Betsy continued up the left margin, making sure to preserve the other half sheet for Hiram: "write just as it is wont you dear Husband." With this commitment to "write just as it is," the Blaisdells abandoned the pretense of hoping their letters would find each other "enjoying the same blessing." It would be enough, and truer, for their letters to find each other suffering the same hardship. After the December turn in Betsy's letters, Hiram rarely told her "don't borrow trouble." Now he encouraged her to "write all your troubles to me."[50]

Though invited now to lament—and she still did from time to time—Betsy seems actually to have found it relieving to do less of this. A more easygoing and conversational voice crept into her letters. "Wicked" and self-serving wishes that Hiram might break his leg and come home gave way to lighter thoughts about what they would enjoy together on his return, whenever that came. "John killed my pig yesterday," Betsy told him; "he is pertty nice I wish you had part of him to eat he think you are Mad at him because you dont write to him so write some to him in my next letter." If Hiram was amused by the notion of writing a letter to a dead pig, he didn't say. He did respond in kind, with his own imagining of what they might do if he were home, besides eating fresh pork. "I have just washed up all clean and nice," he wrote in his reply. "I guess if I was there I would have a kiss and it would not mess up your face much."[51]

The arrival of the new year found Betsy hopeful—"they think the war will not last any Longer than spring"—and feeling confident of victory, too, in her struggles with letter writing. Asynchronous though they were, the letters between her and Hiram were working—holding them together in time, across however much space. "I think of you all of the time," she wrote, "constantly Hiram and I lay awake night hours thinking of you so when you are thinking of me you can think I am thinking of you." Like a New Year's resolution, she took up a new habit, simple but hard-won: "Hiram I have numbered my letters and I will the rest so after this you can tell me is one lost and I want you to yours so I will know if I get all of yours." At the top of the page she had written "No 1."[52]

SAREPTA REVIS EMERGED from winter's despondency into a lively summer of 1863. Like Betsy Blaisdell in the wake of the St. Albans raid, she felt the war had come to her doorstep. A band of Confederate deserters returned to their Henderson County, North Carolina, homes, including the men of several families the Revises knew well: among the band were "three Statons three Longs bob Beding field and sevral others." When the state militia came after them, a gunfight ensued. A letter over Sarepta's name included a lengthy narrative, probably composed mostly by her brother, Clint, that detailed the killings and injuries on both sides. The deserters killed the lieutenant commanding the unit trying to apprehend them, but the militiamen "shot at rube and Ambers and wounded them but tha never got them but Ambers wound kill him he only live about one day and night and rube was wouned in the shoulders and I dont no whear he is I hear that the men is runing a way fast hear of late and the malishey is out a trying to gether them up." (None of it was news to Daniel, who had written a few days earlier, in a letter Sarepta had yet to receive, "I hier bad acounts from your contrey I hier that lieutenant garen went to take Ruben staton and he kild him and I hierd that 1 of the staton boys was kild and another wonded.")[53]

Perhaps for a sense of safety, Sarepta's extended family gathered closer together. Around the time of the clash, she moved in with her parents, and so did Clint and his wife, Ellen. From this consolidated household, Sarepta sent Daniel letters more gregarious than the ones, probably ghostwritten by Clint, that had gone out during the winter. Although Clint still acted as her scribe, the voice began to sound a little less like an older brother speaking on his sister's behalf, a little more the way Sarepta herself may have sounded. Salutations like "Mr daniel W revis" gave way to "My Dear loving hus ban." News reported rather stiffly in earlier letters—"I have move to fathers and clint and Ellen has move there too"—gets repeated in more conversational tones: "I recend you have heard that I have move to paps." Sarepta began using letters to attend to household duties: "I want you to rite to me and let me no how you are geting along about your cloths I be leive you are a bout naked I want you to rite about your clot^hing I have got you some pance made."[54]

Illiterate though she was, Sarepta attended with some care (and perhaps some of Clint's help) to the coming and going of the mail: "i have jest receive aletter from you that was ^rote July the 9 and I receive one ^the 19 that was rote the first of July." Still, their crisscrossing letters and the vagaries of the Confederate postal system could spark small misunderstandings. Daniel had written in May, prompted by no specific event he mentioned, "I want you to rite to me as often as you can but it is not worth while to start aleter wthout pying for it for it is a axident if we get them for if we aint at the post ofise they wil not folow us." To Sarepta, this had the sound of a slight. She bristled but maintained her sense of attachment to and through the correspondence: "you began to think I dident think enough of you to Pay for the letters that I sent to you but I pay for all the leters I send to my little sweet Daniel."[55]

Whatever glimmers appear in Sarepta's summer letters of a growing comfort with the medium, she developed no further as a wartime correspondent. If she ever wrote a page in her own hand, it does not survive; if she felt a yearning to inscribe her own letters, it faded when Daniel came home. He had made intimations he would do it. In mid-July, he sent home a letter in triptych form—the two inside pages of the small folio addressed to Sarepta, the front page addressed to his sister, Ellen, and the back page to Sarepta and Clint's younger brother, Joseph Ward. The letter to his wife had pride of place as well as a certain propriety (to Sarepta he said, "I hav got the bowel complaint"; to Ellen it was "I hav got the shits very bad"), but all three recipients got a hint: "I want to see you very bad and I dont think I can stay from you much longer"; "I want to see you verybad and I think I will before long if I hav good luck"; and "you must bee a good little boy til I come home."[56]

At the time of that letter, Daniel was swept up in a Confederate withdrawal across Tennessee. Having just moved forward to support General Braxton Bragg, his regiment as quickly turned around: "the yanks has whiped our men at tulehomiey . . . . generl brag was in full retreet and we got out of thair in quick time." The rebels fell back as Union general William Rosecrans's Army of the Cumberland advanced southwestward from Tullahoma, Tennessee, toward a late-summer showdown just across the border into Georgia. In one of several blue columns, snaking between the ridges of the Cumberland Plateau, marched Thornton Clark.[57]

But these men would not meet. By the time the contending armies clashed near a creek called Chickamauga, Daniel Revis was gone. He had deserted and gone east over the mountains, making it as far as Jackson County, North Carolina, only about sixty miles from home, by the middle of August. There, he was apprehended by the state militia. He got off a letter to Sarepta: "me and John Revis and Jonas pace and fransus farmer started to come home and got hier to aplace called webster and met with some of the malitia started out to ketch up conscrips and they stopt us hier and wont let us go any further. . . . we wold hav got home in 2 days more I stil hope I will get to come home before long and seemy little sweet one time more."[58] In the seven months since Daniel had last been up in these mountains, about twenty miles northeast at Shelton Laurel, the tables had turned. Now he was the one ensnared by faithful Confederates out to "ketch" the disloyal.

❧ 5 ❧

Breaks

Open the envelope quickly,
O this is not our son's writing
—Walt Whitman

I N   T H E   W O O D S along Chickamauga Creek, communication broke down. Confederate general Braxton Bragg's orders to his division commanders during the night somehow never arrived, and when the morning sky lightened on September 20, Bragg heard none of the sounds he expected to hear—no artillery, no musketry.[1]

As the morning hours progressed and the rebels organized for their delayed attack on this battle's second day, the commanding Union general, William Rosecrans, received reports that John Brannan's division was not in its appointed place; that there was a gap in the center of the Union line between the divisions of Generals Thomas Wood and Joe Reynolds. This was a dire situation and required immediate attention. Rosecrans saw that his preferred scribe, the punctilious future president James Garfield, was busily engaged, so he asked another aide to send a message to Wood. It read, "The general commanding directs that you close up on Reynolds as fast as possible, and support him."[2]

It had haste's brevity. Receiving no explanation of the rationale for what seemed to him a highly unusual order, Wood could not reply by pointing out that Brannan's division was, in fact, right where it was supposed to be. The reports Rosecrans had received were false. Wood could not "close up" across a gap that did not exist. The only way he could "support" Reynolds was by pulling his men out of position and moving them around behind Brannan's division to join Reynolds. This he dutifully did, thereby creating what had not been there before—a break in the battle line. No sooner had this been accomplished than Confederate soldiers under James Longstreet, just arrived from Virginia, came barreling through the new opening in the federal front. Union regiments were sent into disarray, and hundreds of soldiers were captured. One of them was Thornton Clark.

It had been exactly one year since Thornton sent his first letter home to Nancy from Camp Morton (then Camp Joe Reynolds) in Indianapolis. After a rough beginning—the delays of its first autumn months, the strains following the wintertime Battle of Stones River—the couple's correspondence had finally caught its stride during the spring and summer of 1863. Mail had been slow during the winter, taking almost a month to move from Indiana to Tennessee, and Nancy's letters remained despairing ("I recieved your this morning of the 24," Thornton wrote home, "and was glad to hear that you was all well but was sorry to hear that you had given up all hope of seeing me any more"). The Pioneer Brigade, to which Thornton had been detailed before Stones River, undertook a major engineering project during these months—building Fortress Rosecrans in Murfreesboro, the largest fort built during the war—but Thornton was not a part of it. He fell ill with "a very severe cold" that, he said, "settled on my lungs" and was kept with his regiment doing light guard duty until May. Then he finally got an up-close look at the great fort under construction—by virtue of a transfer to the "convalescent camp" inside its walls.[3]

As it had been in Louisville, separation from his regiment was a boon to Thornton's letter writing. Inside the Army of the Cumberland's nerve center, he enjoyed more regular mail delivery, and his and Nancy's epistolary relationship grew warmer and more relaxed than it had ever been. Thornton had received several months' back pay and sent home his largest remittance of the war, forty-two dollars, in March. Such support, along with the coming of spring, brightened Nancy's outlook at home. She wrote to Thornton about how finely her garden was growing. When the gooseberries ripened, she told him she was canning some and expected him to help eat them up. She sent him pressed roses. He sent her a lock of his hair, a ring he carved out of a briar root, and "a small heart that I mad out of a mussle shell that come out of stone River you can keep it untill I come home and then I will put a pin in it for you so you can wear it for a breast pin." He asked her to send him a braided lock of her hair "long enough to go around my wrist."[4]

With these exchanges of sentimental tokens came also a renewal of the intimacy of domestic life. Their letters were moving back and forth quickly enough that Thornton could participate in kitchen-table conversation and minor neighborhood drama: "I think that the least that you can have to say to Nanc parker the better it will be for you I think that she must have a little feeling and a very low principle to talk to you as she dose when she knows that you are there a lone and in trouble about me any how you must not mind such talk if I could have things my own way I would be at home in a very short time." The stubbornness of Thornton's illness raised hopes he would be discharged and return home very soon indeed. While he awaited examination at the convalescent camp, he was encouraged by the sight of other men around him receiving discharges. His mind bent more and more toward home. A carpenter who had not planed a board in months, he wrote to Nancy: "I want you to examine my tools and see if they are a getting rusty and if they are I want you to take them out of the Chest and given air and get some sweet oill and oil them and then put back in the Chest a gain."[5]

As summer advanced and no discharge came, such eager anticipation waned, but a certain serenity remained. Living the family's life through letters was working, more or less. It could tide them over until they were reunited. "Tell alice to write to me," Thornton wrote, "and let me know how she improves in writing." She soon did and received a reply of her own, addressed to Miss Alice Clark.

> Murfeesboro, April 5th, 1863
>
> Dear Daughter, I received your letter of the 22 and was very glad to hear that you was all well. I am glad that you are a learning to write. I don't wish to find fault with your writing, for I think that you done very well for a Girl of your age, but I must give you some instruction about writing. You crowd your words too close together and then you bear too hard on your pen which makes your letters hard too understand. Make your letters as light as you can and commence all names with a capital, and when you speak of yourself, use a capital "I". Thus: I am a going to school, I have been, I am a going to, I am well, and so on. I am glad you are a going to school. . . . As you grow in years, to grow in grace and the knowledge of the Lord so that all good people will love and respect you. I am not well but I am a getting some better than I have been. Tell your Mother not to get discouraged but to keep in good heart. I would to come home and see all of you, and will as soon as I can. Don't get mad at me for talking to you about your writing and not write anymore, but write often as you can. I remain your loving and affectionate Father,
>
> Thornton Clark[6]

The Clark family resembled a little correspondence school for writers. That summer, Nancy grew curious to know how much her own skill had developed since the fall, and she asked Thornton to return some of her earliest letters for comparison: "you wanted me to send you one of your first letters to see if you had improved any in writing here is the two first that I got from you I have got all of your letters that I have recieved."[7]

Thornton was judged fit for duty and returned to his regiment in time to join the southward push toward Georgia before which Braxton Bragg's army, and Daniel Revis until he ran off, was receding. Finally feeling healthy—"better than I have for six months"—Thornton took courage from the awe-inspiring landscape: the Cumberland Mountains were "towering up towards heaven though as if they were sencble of him who gave them being here," and water flowed from a sparkling mountain spring "as the weary Christian does from the foundtain of Gods mecies and love." He tried to convey some of his new resilience to Nancy: "I dont want you to get downhearted and discouraged because I did not get to come home but rather rejoice to think that my health is improveing so that I am still able to help defend our countries rights." In his last letter before the Battle of Chickamauga, he included a separate note to the children: "your Pa wants you all to be good Children and love and mind your Mother and attend sabath School for when Pa comes home he wants to find his dear little ones that he left good Children be loveing and kind to each other and keep out of bad company and there all good Children will love to be in your Compa ny your loveing father."[8]

Nancy did not hear from him again for more than nine months. When she did, the letter came from Andersonville, Georgia. Taken to the rear of the Chickamauga battlefield by Longstreet's forces, Thornton ultimately became one of the first inhabitants of the war's most notorious prison camp. Though possessed of three-quarters of a year's bottled-up news, sights, and thoughts to share with Nancy, he could fill only a single page if he wanted his letter to get past the camp censors, up to Richmond, and across the Virginia battle lines by a flag of truce. The summer of 1864 was probably half gone by the time Nancy received it.

June 16 1864 Camp Sumpter Dear Nancy I just recieved 2 letters
from you the first that I have heared from you sience last August
you dont know how glad I was to hear from you oh how I would
love to see you and the Children but when I will be at home God
only knows but I hope it wont be long when I do I have a great
many things to tell you I am dreaming of home evry knight I still
keep well with the exception of a lameness in my legs and that is
not very bad I still look to god for help my love to you and all
the Children Direct your letters to Camp Sumpter andersonville
Georgia 29 detatchment 2 mess your loveing and affetionate Husband untill death Thornton Clark[9]

CIVIL WAR FAMILIES agonized over the long wait for letters, but
there also were letters whose arrival was worse than the wait. They
came stamped with unexpected postmarks, from hospitals or prisons.
Worse still (in a society that felt the touch of people's hands in their
distinctive penmanship), they bore unfamiliar handwriting. That could
mean only a few things—illness, injury, death—no matter what the
words said. Asynchronous communication was never more painful
than when the excitement of a newly arrived letter concealed the darker
truth that, at that very moment, hope had been extinguished. In one
of Walt Whitman's best-known war poems, a letter arrives for an Ohio
farm family, and the mother panics instantly, seeing that "a strange
hand writes for our dear son." The text on the page "swims before her
eyes . . . *gunshot wound in the breast, cavalry skirmish, taken to hospital.*"
The soldier's sister struggles to calm her parents—"*Grieve not so, dear
mother . . . the letter says Pete will soon be better*"—but the poem's
all-knowing speaker interjects, "Alas poor boy, he will never be
better . . . while they stand at home at the door he is dead already."[10]

Letters of mourning, memorial, and condolence already were traditional forms, but the scale of Civil War mortality put new pressure

Thornton Clark

on them. Grieving families suffered even more acutely when their loved ones died—as they almost always did—away from home, among strangers, in uncertain spiritual condition. Deathbed gatherings, last words, mourning rituals: everything that dignified and palliated loss now had to be replaced by letters, which challenged writers to improvise. Men and women at the front wrote what they knew would be a dying or deceased soldier's family's last glimpse of him. Mourners had

to carry on what they considered the proprieties of grief amid the hardships of war.[11]

In the northeast corner of Texas, Arminda Kite had no well-stocked
shops to visit, even if she could have afforded their wares. When she
learned her husband, George, had died she took ordinary letter paper
and envelopes and drew heavy black borders on all their edges. On
this homespun mourning stationery, Arminda replied to the man who
had informed her, a Confederate corporal in George's regiment, the
Eighteenth Texas Infantry, named Bluford Alexander Cameron: "I re-
seved your sad leter stating that my dear beloved husban was ded &
gon to rest I hard [it] on the 3 of this month o hant it hard my frend you
now how he suferd & I dont." Just as she had taken care to adapt her
paper to the solemnity of the occasion, she tried to coach Bluford in the
writing of a proper report of George's death—one that could correct
the distressing irony that this man should know how he suffered while
George's own wife does not.

> I whant you to wite to me what he sed abou[t] dy ing & what he
> sad about me & his der bab all you can recolect I whant to now
> it all for he is gon & I now it & I cold not see him & I what [to know]
> [want] he talked about [before he did] did he think he was prepared to met
> god I supos ther had bin agrat chang in him in the last 10 monts
> I hop ther was did he look matcherd after he did was he berred
> in his own clos did you shav him I dont recon he ever shaved after
> he started I whant you if you can send me his clos what time in
> the day did ~~day~~ [he dye] was he bered ~~after he~~ the sam day he dyed
> did he say any thing about wher he whant[ed] me to liv was he in his
> write mind when he did did he talk to the last der frend did he
> dye hard did he strugel for bret

In Arminda's barrage of questions are the ingredients—for her and
her husband, all missing—of a "good death." Although she could not

be at George's side to draw out his dying wishes or ask after his readiness to meet his maker, she might recreate in her mind's eye the scene she missed: the time of day, his last words, his struggles for breath. Although she could not prepare his body for burial, she might at least picture him at rest: his clothes, his beard (or not), his "matured" look.[12]

Pleading to have all this knowledge transferred from Bluford's mind to her own, Arminda created what could have been a manual for how to write a letter of condolence.[13] At the same time, her written words resemble vicarious ministrations. Driving her pen across the page, line after questioning line, she occasionally slips into what sounds like familiar conversation with and about her husband. Her asides have the faintly, teasingly henpecking tones that might have inflected her deathbed murmurs. I don't reckon he ever shaved. Had there been a great change in George in the last ten months? I hope there was. She tends to the narrative of her husband's death as carefully as she would have to his body, and her writing reflects her vigilance. Having begun to write what apparently was the question "was he buried after he died?" she crosses out "after he"—presumably realizing the ambiguity of it, or imagining a reader poking fun (well we didn't bury him before!)—and inserts the impeccably precise "the same day."

If much of Arminda's letter is composed with the deliberateness and delicacy of fingers adjusting the bedclothes on a dying man, it also betrays her practical anxieties (did he say where he wanted me to go live?) and her grief-stricken horror. The imagined scene behind her final question—did he struggle for breath?—may have taken her to the brink of composure. In any event, it took her to the bottom of the page, and for Arminda, as for millions of letter writers, turning over her leaf of paper meant what the idiom had meant for centuries. On the verso, she is self-possessed and proper: "my frend write soon & giv me all the satis faction you can der frend you mut excus my bad writing & spelling writ soon."

"All the satisfaction you can" still might not be much. Arminda could spell out for Bluford just what kind of letter she wanted, but even the fullest and most consoling letter imaginable would not banish grief. Sometimes the only tangible remnant of a soldier's life, a letter reporting his death bore tremendous burdens. Like rock under the great heat and pressure of earth, such letters metamorphosed. Personal missives might bristle with excitement as they zipped through the postal network or droop with forgettable clichés, but dispatches of death took on the character of memorials. In their recipients' hands, delicate paper had some of the quality of marble.

When John and Letty Long got a brief letter from a soldier in the former regiment of their son Ben describing the location of his grave on the battlefield at Fredericksburg—"you will finde him by going up th Fridericsburg railroad as far as hamiltons crossing theare take the lefte hand ond the military road from hamiltons crossing go up the road to the firste house about three miles about one hundred and fifty yards to a double cherry tree from the house"—they took care to recopy it for preservation. It arrived on a torn scrap of what apparently had been another letter, addressed on the back to "Emelyline Jones." Either John or Letty—or more likely, since neither of them was highly literate, someone else whose services they requested—transferred the soldier's note to a clean sheet of higher-quality paper (it bears an embossed stationer's mark, unlike most other documents in the Long Family Papers). The scribe wrote neatly, regularized the spelling, corrected the date (the soldier had written December 31, 1863, instead of 1862), and set the last line apart in the center of the page:

You will find on his head board
   B. N. Long Co I 57 Regt N. C. T

It gave John and Letty a paper version of the wooden inscription they might or might never be able to visit.[14]

Rebecca Pitchford Davis, the mother of four sons in the Confederate army, spent the first years of the war busily moving letters to and fro—forwarding those from brothers serving in one place to the other ones elsewhere—and occasionally chiding her sons for the quality of their writing. When the family's first bad news came—twenty-five-year-old Weldon, the fourth son, was captured in the Battle of Rappahannock Station in November 1863—Rebecca's many epistolary circuits buzzed with even greater intensity. George, the third son, who served with Weldon in the Thirtieth North Carolina, wrote on November 9 to tell his mother Weldon was a prisoner, and probably wounded. Rebecca sent George's letter to Mat, the oldest son, on November 14, and shared a secondhand report from a neighbor that Weldon was not wounded at all. She asked Mat to forward George's letter to Burwell, the second oldest, who had served in the Thirtieth regiment with George and Weldon but had been wounded in the spring and, now recovered, was working in a hospital in Raleigh. Mat did as Rebecca asked on November 17, relaying to Burwell his own hope that the report of Weldon's health was true. On November 21 Rebecca wrote to Burwell directly and said Pa was so worried about Weldon that he had "no appetite and is almost sick." On December 7, a brief note came to the Davis household from a cousin who said he had heard from Weldon and that he was wounded in both legs. Rebecca forwarded that note to Burwell, but quite likely by now she just wanted this month-long epistolary panic attack to end.[15]

On December 10, Mat wrote to Burwell, enclosing the last worried letter he'd received from their mother, to say there was a notice printed in a Richmond newspaper that Weldon Davis had died on November 22 at Douglas Hospital, in Washington, DC. He believed Ma must not have seen it and apparently did not intend to tell her. She did finally, in mid-December, learn definitively what the whole family had come to expect. She received the rare letter whose journey to Warren County, North Carolina, was initiated by the U.S. Post Office. It was written in the unfamiliar hand of a Mrs. Elizabeth Blount from Washington, DC, and it was a model of the kind of letter a family would hope to receive, if they had to receive the kind of letter they most dreaded. It delivered with perfect propriety what Arminda Kite craved.

Washington City, Dec 8, '63

Mrs. Edward Davis
Warrenton, N.C.
Dear Madam,

In the discharge of a most painful duty, I address you, sympathizing most truly in the sore affliction which it has pleased God to appoint you. Your son, Capt. Weldon Edwards Davis, was wounded and brought to this city & placed in the Douglas Hospital, receiving the most careful attention and provision. Capt. Davis' wound, a severe fracture of the right leg, rendered amputation necessary. At first surgeons were hopeful, but on the 19th symptoms of tetanus appeared, rendering unavailing all skill and attention of the surgeons in his behalf. He expired 40 m. after 4 o'clock on Sunday, the 22nd. I was permitted to visit him every day, was with him the whole of the last day of his life, witnessed his baptism, his holy & happy death, & received his last message to you, his dear mother, assuring you that he died a Christian in the hope of a glorious immortality. I attended his funeral to cemetery of the soldiers Home. At his request, the effects found on his person when captured are in my hand to be delivered to you.

With sincerest respect, your fellow sufferer,
Mrs. Elizabeth Blount

With the arrival of this letter, Rebecca's relationship to the papers on her desk became quieter, slower, and more deliberate. Before, it seemed letters were getting refolded and dispatched to new places almost as soon as they had been read; now they lay open before her quite a bit longer.[16]

After reading this dignified letter, Rebecca took a blank sheet of paper and wrote a letter to no one, a sudden and uncharacteristic outburst of diary keeping: "I have just now received a letter from Washington City, from a lady who signs her name Mrs. Elizabeth Blount." Rebecca proceeded to repeat everything the letter had told her—"she was permitted to visit him every day during his confinement, and was with him the whole last day of his life, witnessed his baptism, his holy and happy death"—and then wrote, "The above is pretty, yes, exactly the words of the lady." Then or soon after, Rebecca wrote out "exactly the words of the lady" at least three more times, for she sent copies of the letter to each of her sons. In fact, she created for each of them a kind of paper memorial to Weldon, a commemorative edition of the correspondence between their mother and Elizabeth Blount. An undated sheet among her papers (apparently an unsent draft of a letter to one of the boys) reads: "I have sent you a copy of the entire letter of Mrs. Blount. . . . On the other side is pretty much what I wrote in reply. I wrote it on a whole sheet of nice letter paper which your Uncle Tom gave me, as I had none."

Soon after, a letter came from the youngest of Rebecca's absent sons. The boy named after his uncle was only fifteen when the war started. Tom itched to join his older brothers, but his father would not allow him to enlist until he turned eighteen. Several months before Weldon died, when Tom was seventeen, he left a note pinned to his pillow, slipped out of the house in the middle of the night, and ran off to join George and Weldon's regiment. Tom's letter home was apparently the first of the surviving boys' reactions to the confirmation of Weldon's death, and Rebecca wrote about it to Burwell. "It is one of the best letters I ever read," she told him, "and really has a good deal of consolation in it. . . . He says if he had lived the life Weldon lived, he would not fear to die." Rebecca's eyes drifted again and again, away from her own letter to Burwell, to the letter from Tom that lay next to it on the table. She filled most of a page with paraphrases and quotations from Tom: "He says . . . And then he says . . . And then he says . . . He says." Rereading Tom's letter, Rebecca found another and another sentence she wanted Burwell to hear, but she could not simply fold Tom's letter and enclose it in the envelope to his brother, as she had done with many others before. This particular sheet of paper she intended to keep.[17]

In the face of grief, even fear of grief, letters came to be valued less for their mobility than for their permanence. During the autumn following Weldon's death, Rebecca wrote to one of her sons: "I *did* think I would send you Tom's letters, but have concluded Otherwise. He got lost after the battle at Fisher's Hill the 21st, got over into the Yankee lines, and straggled off into the mountains." Tom got safely back to his regiment, but the fright of the episode made Rebecca want to preserve his letters in what was by then a growing collection of treasured, if mournful, Civil War keepsakes. As the family archive grew, Rebecca's own epistolary output slowed. Her intimations of Tom's mortality quickly proved true. He was killed at Cedar Creek in October 1864. Rebecca wrote Burwell to tell him but said, "I feel like I had almost as live die as to write to George and tell him that Tom is killed." When a third-hand rumor came to her that George too had been killed, she wrote a brief letter to Mat about it and concluded, "Send this to Burwell. I do not feel like writing. As ever, Your Ma."[18]

SO WIDELY SHARED was the anxious waiting for a letter from someone gone silent; so real the threat, especially as the war progressed, that an empty mail call signified the ultimate silence; and so deep the yearning, when a family lost a loved one, for some tangible memorial, that people like Elizabeth Blount could not mistake their responsibility. Nurses and hospital volunteers wrote letters as frequently as they changed bandages. One Northern nurse's journal chronicled eighteen-hour days in which she "dispensed medicines, served breakfast, wrote letters, dispensed medicines, served dinner, wrote letters, dispensed medicines, served supper, wrote letters." When twenty-three-year-old Cornelia Hancock rushed from Philadelphia to the Gettysburg battlefield, she was deemed too inexperienced to meet the carnage as a nurse, so she did the next most urgent thing: "I went from one pallet to another with pencil, paper, and stamps in hand, and spent the rest of that night in writing letters from the soldiers to their families and friends." Louisa May Alcott's nursing experience formed the basis for a book called *Hospital Sketches* in which Alcott's alter ego, Nurse Periwinkle, observed that "the letters dictated to me, and revised by me" in a single afternoon "would have made an excellent chapter for some future history of the war."[19]

Hospital workers wrote for men who were too sick, too weak, or too badly injured to write for themselves, for recovering men whose writing arms had been amputated, for barely literate men grateful to have an amanuensis. Some of these letters were ordinary installments in a standing correspondence, barely distinguishable from the soldier's own letters except by their handwriting. When Thomas Warrick of Alabama was in a Tennessee hospital with jaundice, he dictated several letters for his wife, Martha, and he availed himself of standard epistolary rhetoric—"I take my pen in hand to inform you," "I remain yours by signing myself"—despite the fact that he held no pens and signed none of the letters. Whoever wrote for him dutifully recorded the voice of a man who, though "now lying flat of my back," preferred to maintain the fiction that he was inscribing words on paper just the same as always: "I don't know wife that I've got much news to write you but I shall Keep Scratching a long untill I get Some more of this filled up."[20]

Other times, volunteers wrote on their own initiative to the families of men too ill to do more than utter a name and address or mutely yield up a home letter from a pocket or knapsack. An envelope not in a soldier's handwriting would worry his family, but finding his familiar voice inside, speaking in the first person, could reassure them. A letter composed entirely by a stranger painted a dire picture, no matter what words it used. Probably many such letters do not survive. Rather than being folded carefully and bundled in a safe place, they were—like the telegram that beckoned Mrs. March to her sick husband's side in *Little Women*—cast aside in the bustle of departure, or clutched while speeding by train or horse toward a distant hospital. Some have become well known because of who the concerned volunteer happened to be:

> Mr and Mrs Haskell
>
> Your son Erastus Haskell, of Co K 141st New York, is now lying sick with typhoid fever here in hospital. I have been with him quite a good deal, from day to day, was with him yesterday & indeed almost every day, & feel much interested in the young man. He has been very sick, & seems to be so now, as I should judge, but the doctor says he will recover. I had a talk with the doctor yesterday, & he says so still. But Erastus seems to me very sick, & I thought I would write to you. He had some one write to you about two weeks ago, but has received no answer. Erastus does not talk much, so I do not understand much about his affairs. I am merely a friend. The address of Erastus is Ward E, Armory Square Hospital Washington D C should you wish to write to him direct.
>
> Walt Whitman

The poet wrote for many soldiers who, he found, had "not written home to parents, brothers, sisters, and even wives, for one reason or another, for a long, long time. Some are poor writers, some cannot get paper and envelopes; many have an aversion to writing because they dread to worry the folks at home—the facts about them are so sad to tell."[21]

Letters like Elizabeth Blount's, reporting the saddest fact of all, could not have been easy even for talented writers to produce. Still, countless nurses and volunteers carried out their solemn obligation to inform and console a dead soldier's family, even across enemy lines. Kate Kern, a Tennessee woman who cared for a dying federal soldier in her home, wrote to the man's mother "by flag of truce" (as many people had to on the contested borderlands of Union-occupied Tennessee) and signed herself "your sympathizing friend." The soldier uttered no last words for Kate to share with his mother, but she insisted, reassuringly, "I feel confident he knew he was dying, and did not fear death." Not everyone, though, put such reassurances above their allegiances. When Thomas Barker of Maine was killed at the First Battle of Bull Run, he was carrying a letter he had written the night before to his brother. At the bottom of it, he gave these instructions: "If I am slain, whoever finds this will please state the fact in this & forward it & confer a favor on the ashes of Thomas B. Barker." Perhaps he imagined his body falling under the care of some maternal figure, some Elizabeth Blount or Kate Kern. Instead, it was a staunch Confederate surgeon who found the letter. He conferred the favor but not before writing a note of his own to Thomas's brother: "This letter was found on the body of a man sacrificed by the Lincoln government in the unpatriotic, unholy and hellish crusade against a people struggling for their rights under the Constitution, and in accordance with the Declaration of Independence that 'all men are entitled to life, liberty, and the pursuit of happiness.' A sad fate to fall in an inglorious cause!"[22]

When men died in a well-supplied Washington hospital or a private home, there usually was ample material for a consoling letter of memorial—a days-long pattern of attentive care, the provision of every comfort, the deceased's last words, his burial in a known place. Hospital workers became experts at the genre. Most common soldiers got less practice and weren't as literate to begin with (they had trouble enough spelling "hospital" and "pneumonia," which sometimes came out "hors spittle" and "new money"). Yet to them fell the peculiarly difficult task of informing the families of men who died with their regiment or were slain in battle—disappeared from earth, sometimes, with scarcely a trace. To meet this challenge (and there is no telling how many men contemplated writing such a letter but shrank from the task, or tried and gave up), soldiers availed themselves of different strategies of condolence.[23]

There was no approximating a peaceful deathbed scene in the case of African American corporal William Guy. He was killed in the horrific Battle of the Crater, in which predominantly black soldiers—trapped inside the great pit that opened after Union forces detonated eight thousand pounds of explosives in a mine deep below Confederate lines—were mercilessly gunned down by Southern soldiers standing above them. James Freeman, a comrade in the Thirtieth Maryland Colored Infantry, wrote to William's mother, Rebecca, and he avoided nearly all mention of the circumstances of William's death: "I am sarry to have to inform You that thear is no dobt of his Death he Died A Brave Death in Trying to Save the Colors of Rige in that Dreadful Battil." William's valor in saving the regimental colors may have filled some of the void where a "good death" would be, but there probably was little else James would want to tell William's mother. If he was like many black soldiers at the Battle of the Crater, William was killed under circumstances which, had he been white, would have resulted in his capture, not his death. James said nothing of this. To fill out a letter, he had to turn away from the scene of dying and, like a eulogist, celebrate William's life: "Billys Death was unevesally by all but by non greatter then by my self ever sins we have bin in the Army we have bin amoung the moust intimoat Friend wen every our Rige wen into Camp he sertan to be at my Tent and meney happy moment we seen to gether Talking about Home and the Probability of our Living to get Home to See each other Family and Friend."[24]

Just what such a letter meant to Rebecca Guy is, of course, impossible to know. She had to hand it over to the army as proof of William's death when she applied for a pension. (Thus does it survive.) Did she first carefully recopy it or have it recopied for her? Was there a twinge of grief's return when she pulled this artifact of loss from its box or drawer? The way letters of memorial acted upon their recipients is mostly unrecoverable; so is the way they affected their writers. To create such letters was to assume a literary position unlike any most soldiers had held in their lives, even if the war had made them prolific letter writers. They became the scribes of a life that had passed. It is difficult to assess the influence such work may have had on a man's development as a writer, since most letters of memorial were sent to someone outside his own family—maybe to someone in the same county or neighborhood back home, though maybe to a stranger—and so remain separated from everything else that individual wrote. The richest way of understanding letters of memorial today is by considering them where they lie—where their recipients put them, most often at the end of a bundle of letters from the deceased soldier. In many archival collections, the last letter in the file is the one in different handwriting, and it can show the common soldier's war experience from a new angle.

GEORGE WORDEN WAS twenty-three years old when he married nineteen-year-old Amanda Haney ("Fannie") on December 13, 1860—one week before South Carolina declared it was seceding from the Union. Whatever his politics may have been, the newlywed Indiana farmer was in no rush to help put down the rebellion. By the time George was recruited at the end of 1863—it appears he volunteered, although by then he faced the draft if he did not—he and Fannie had been married three years, and they had a daughter, Adelaide (or "Adda"), who must have been old enough to talk. "Tell Adda she must not call you Fannie, but call you Ma," George would soon write home from camp.[25]

George left home in January, and by the first of February he had joined his regiment, which was encamped for the winter in northern Alabama. "I have at last found time to write a little while, I will improve it by writing to you," he wrote to Fannie. "I have been on guard Duty this fore noon for the first time & expect to be called out again before I get this wrote." He told her about his good health, the fine weather, how his tentmates made a table, that he had been detailed to cook, and what he had to work with: "we are Short of cooking tools, in our mess of 6. we have 2 knive & forks 4 cups 2 spoons, 1 plate, 1 Spider, we have to borrow a coffee Boiler." To George's pleasant surprise, he completed this first letter home before he was called away: "by writing fast I have finished before Duty time. I have wrote all I can think of this time." If a little proud of filling three pages for Fannie's eyes, he was nevertheless concerned that it could have been better, or at least neater. Turning to the back of the paper, he told Fannie where to address letters—"Co B, 12th Regt Ind Vol, 15th Army Corpse, Scottsborogh Allabama"—and finally wrote, "P.S. excuse bad writing as I am writing on a board on my knees, George."[26]

Within a few weeks, the novelty of camp life, and of reaching out to Fannie by writing letters, had lost some luster. On February 14, 1864, he wrote:

My Dear Fannie,

It is with a very sad heart, that I commence this letter, to one that is more to me than all the world. Although I did not know what it was to leave you, until, now, I feel so very lonely, this morning, thinking of the Dear ones at home that it is very hard work to keep the tears back, in fact they have fell on this paper while I write, but you know it is said, there is relief in tears, I feel it is so with me, I went for a letter this morning, feeling very sure I would get one, but O! Judge my feelings when I found there was none, I waited all the week verry patiently, for one but it has not come yet I have received but one cince I have been here, but I blame the mail for it, for I know you would not fail or neglect writng to me, Stoney Starts for home this evening and that makes me more lonesome, now Dear Fannie dont let this letter grieve you. I know I am doing wrong in writng such a letter, but I cant help it, I write Just as I feel, this is the first attack of such a feeling since I left, home, now dont let anyone see this for the world, for fear they will say I am homesick, it will pass off in a day or, two. . . .

Now dont laugh at me. for being homesick, it is a complaint that is not dangerous, neither is it pleasant, but I have writen enough of this, I think

Fannie, I shall stay in the ranks, and when we march I think I can give out without much trouble, now be sure & let no one see this, & write to me, but dont discourage me, take good care of Adda & Mother, I will write to Ma this week. Give my respect to all & keep a good share, with my love for yourself

Like many soldiers—like every soldier, probably—George found he hadn't really known what he was signing up for. Even without fighting any battles or seeing their carnage, he was experiencing something without precedent in his own life. He "did not know what it was" to leave his home, to be away from Fannie. Everything, now, was new to him: the feeling, the challenge of putting it into words, the turn in his marriage that involved such powerful feelings without any way but a letter to communicate them.[27]

Almost immediately after sending his Valentine's Day letter, George began to regret it. Even in the moment, he had believed he was "doing wrong in writng such a letter" and insisted Fannie keep it private. The very next day he wrote again to say, "yesterday I wrote a very mournful letter, but I feel better today . . . . I have writen so many that I am getting ashamed to mail them." Although Fannie's letters to George do not survive, we can reasonably surmise they showed George's letter had affected her profoundly—as, in a sense, any writer hopes his letter will—but also that it made her very worried. If George's homesickness attested to his devotion to his wife, it was not that which most occupied Fannie's mind; it was her anxiety about George's state of mind. What, in turn, most occupied George's subsequent letters were efforts to calm her fears.[28]

After mid-February, each time George got a letter from Fannie, he began his reply by apologizing for "that homesick letter." On February 28:

> what to write, I dont Know, I have writen so many lately. it is the same thing over all the time, but in the first place I will say that I am ashamed of that home sick letter I sent home, it was the impulse of the time being it was of short duration I had not been here long enough to get used to Camp life, and the boys, and then Stoney going right back home, I felt just as so I ought to go to, And because I could not it made me home sick, but I have got all over that now, I have enjoyed myself first-rate ever since I came here except that day.

On March 1: "Fannie I hope you will excuse this holy paper, as I have to be saving of paper. Fannie I am sorry I ever sent that homesick letter home." The letter on "holy paper" has an abrasion across the middle of the page. Before he started, George circled the torn part of the paper, wrote "I am ashamed of this," and proceeded to write his letter around it.

Not yet two months in the service, but separated from his wife for the longest he ever had been, George's emotional life had come to be dominated by shame. He is ashamed of the "homesick letter"; ashamed of the number of letters he has written and mailed (an indication of just how homesick he is); ashamed even of the quality of the paper he

Scattsborough Alle

March 1st 1864

My Dear Wife

I received your letter of the 28 to day, it came through very quick, I am glad you are so punctual in writing, I hope you will keep it up, I also received one from you last Sunday, I answered I am ashamed .... this the same day, Fannie I hope you will excuse this holy paper, as I have to be saving of paper. Fannie I am sorry I ever sent that homesick letter home, it was all on account of Stoney's going home that made me feel so miserable, it was all over as soon as he was gone

George Worden to Fannie Worden, 1 Mar. 1864 (page 1)

is writing on, which he probably sees as another measure of his failing fortitude, since he has written so many letters home that this is the best sheet of paper he has left. Rampant homesickness among soldiers generated much sympathy in the sentimental culture of the time, and some in the medical establishment regarded it as a genuine malady—occasionally even assigning it as a cause of death. But it also provoked scorn as a sign of weak character; one army doctor considered homesickness as damning a reflection on the sufferer as gonorrhea or syphilis.[29]

George may also have been ashamed of the other side of his absence from home—not what he felt but what Fannie was enduring. As Fannie's letters kept coming, George less often apologized for having worried or upset her and instead expressed increasing concern about the practical hardships that befell her because he was not there. His perspective shifted from his own sadness, his embarrassment about the "unmanly" tears that fell on his paper, to the real burdens Fannie bore doing "man's work" in his absence. "Fannie I dont want you should work so hard as to make yourself sick," he wrote in his March 1 letter; "and as for getting up in the morning, I dont get up very early. generaly a little after sunrise. I dont blame you for laying abed these cold mornings if you can. . . . Fannie I want you should ejoy your self the best you can." George did not entirely discourage her from overworking—the work of the farm and the household *did* need to be done—but also commended her management of the family's business. A letter Fannie wrote on February 29 evidently described her recent sale of livestock, and George replied: "I think you done first rate with Prince. I was glad to hear that you sold old Prince so well. I expect that you done better with him than I could, if I had been there."[30]

As George learned to move with some agility between his own and Fannie's perspective, between the army camp where he sat and the home he could only imagine, he discovered in writing an almost wondrous possibility for letters to become their own place. The couple's correspondence could substitute for the kitchen table, a place of consultation about household and neighborhood affairs. In a postscript to one letter, George offered "a word of Privacy for Frank Bidwell, if he goes in partner ship with Cassel, tell him he will have to watch him. I think he is a little tricky, but this is Privately tell him." Their letters could evoke the bedroom, too: "Fannie you dont miss *the kisses* any more than I do, and I sncerely hope and trust your prayers will be heard."[31]

But upon finding what warmth and intimacy letters were capable of bearing, George despaired anew about his deficiencies as a writer. On March 8, he received a letter from Fannie and replied: "It was very welcome you can bet, and I was very much obliged to you for such a long one. If I could, I would write you one Just as long, but you know what hard work it is for me to write. . . . Fannie I am very sorry you was so disapointed, in that short letter but I write ~~so many~~ so many that I cant write long ones. . . . Fannie you must excuse this very bad writing as I feel a little under the wether. Day before yesterday I had the head ache, and I took some of them pill & it makes me very week, you may think this is not my writing but it is." After four pages alternating between warm conversation with Fannie and apologies for himself, George drew near the end of his last page and, in a small cramped hand, squeezed three more lines into the last half inch of paper: "Now Fannie excuse for not writing more this time, & remember Fannie that everyday strenghens my love for you your ever loving husband George."[32]

This is a marriage understandably under strain, tethered but also tested by letters—at once powerful and frustrating in their distinctive, asynchronous way. On one day, Fannie, in Indiana, tells George how much she misses his kisses. On another, her letter comes before his eyes in Alabama, and—with a pleasing sense that, across five hundred of the eighty-fifth meridian's miles, they are connected, simultaneously—he feels the same. But by the time his expression of their shared sentiment comes to her, she may be preoccupied with selling a cow or buying furniture, and George, once called upon to sympathize, may now be only wondering why his headache won't go away.

It would not go away. The next letter Fannie received, dated six days later, was in someone else's steady and practiced handwriting. It was George's voice, though, and it bore his signature. It came from the modest hospital serving the Fifteenth Army Corps in its winter quarters at Scottsboro.

> I have some fever and am weak but do not think I shall be very sick and hope for the best. I hope you will not be over-anxious about me, as I have good attention from physicians and nurses. If I get worse or better I will let you know. . . . Most of the boys in the hospital are getting better. Some of them have been worse than I am, and are rapidly recovering. So long as I can see others improving I am cheerful and hopeful. I do not allow myself to become discouraged which is a great advantage in sickness. Do not worry over it and make yourself sick over my illness. I will write to you often, and keep you informed of my prospects and will tell you frankly if I am better or worse.

There are different ways of imagining this scene of writing. George, genuinely upbeat, dictates these lines to an encouraging nurse who buoys his spirits and emboldens his reassurances to Fannie. George writes a letter himself, laboriously scratching out those reassurances in a hospital bed, but is so ashamed of the penmanship that he asks a nurse to recopy it. George, prostrate and fearful but desperate to convince Fannie that everything's all right—mindful, after all, of how much anxiety he has caused his wife already—repeats his injunctions against worrying as the doubtful nurse gently humors him.[33]

Whatever his intentions, his promise to inform her of any change in his condition went unkept: Fannie did not hear from him again. He

may have grown too sick to write or been unable to find an amanuensis, or perhaps he just could not bring himself to send Fannie what
would have been his most worrisome letter yet, telling her he was worse
and would not be getting better. George had typhoid fever and was
dead within a week. The final letter Fannie received, dated March 21,
1864, came from Frank Saltzgiver, a private in the same company as
George. He enclosed six letters addressed to George that had arrived
in the mail too late, and he said: "Mrs Worden with Sorrow I Take my
Peninhand to inform you of the Death of your Husbend. one that I
Loved and hav Ben with Ever Sins we Started from our Beloved Homes
in the Defence of our Coundry however it Proved fatel with him By
Doing So."[34]

Frank would have known little if anything of George and Fannie's
prior correspondence. He could not have anticipated the way his letter
of condolence, obviously written with the best of intentions, may have
undermined George's month-long efforts to disavow his homesickness. But it is hard to imagine that Frank's memorial letter did not fix
in Fannie's mind a narrative of what happened to her husband after
he enlisted:

> inregart to his Sickness he was Takin with a Chill in the first Blase
> and I think home Sick with it. and then he Took the Typoid feaver
> and it apeared that medeson Dident help him atall he ran Down
> untill his Death I onterstood that his mind was on home all the
> Time untill he Died. . . . George was Som Disapoinded wen he
> got hear for he Didend find thinks as tha wair Promis to him So
> he Set Bad I will Tell you moore about it after Wile. . . . affter
> Stoney Starded home he Took Sick and got Wirs all the Time.

It was the same story cast in a different light: George had explained
away his "homesick letter" by saying Stoney's departure provoked one
hard bout of misery, after which he rallied. As far as Frank perceived,

the same event initiated an affliction that "got wirs all the Time" until finally George died—about half from typhoid, in this letter's account, and half from homesickness.

Were George's letters of reassurance to Fannie all inauthentic? If they weren't deliberately so, were they essentially panicked responses to whatever profound worry Fannie was expressing in her letters? Was he ready to say anything to calm her? Or did he in fact rally, if only in ways not visible to the men around him? Did he, by sitting down and writing to Fannie, exorcise demons, achieve inward reconciliation, feel an intimacy with Fannie that, even if it made him long to be at home, invigorated more than it depressed him? Was letter writing a form of therapy that was working, until bacteria interfered? Perhaps George Worden's illness and death were what Frank saw—the culminating effects of George's (to him, shameful) homesickness. Perhaps they were what George's own letters would have us think—a tragic irony, coming just as he was successfully adapting to the army.

Fannie lived until 1917 and never remarried. She and Adda lived together many years, probably until Adda married at age thirty. George's nine letters and Frank Saltzgiver's single memorial—the family's complete archive of the Civil War—were somewhere under their roof. How they may have interpreted that archive to make sense of George's life and death and their whole family's sacrifice is impossible to know. The breaks in correspondences rarely speak above a whisper.

In many letters of memorial, customs of the prewar years staged a resurgence. The sentimental mood of antebellum America and the rhetoric of evangelical Christianity melded in the formulaic stylings that long had defined epistolary culture. Letters about death constantly verged on cliché. Familiar and timeworn sentiments may have been all someone like Frank Saltzgiver could muster; they may also have been exactly what Fannie Worden wanted, or thought she wanted, to hear. Frank echoed countless similar letters when he encouraged Fannie to tell herself, "thye will Be don not mine," and to remember that she and George may hope to meet again "wair Trobbel Can not Com nor Parting will Be Know moore." Grieving Americans had clung to just such comforts—the inscrutability of the will of God, the eternal rewards of heaven—for two centuries. The Puritan poet Anne Bradstreet, in an elegy to one of her grandchildren, who lived only a month, struggled to accept that God had called this "pretty babe" to the "endless joys" of the hereafter: "With dreadful awe before Him let's be mute, / Such was His will, but why, let's not dispute." Barely six weeks after George Worden's death, Jefferson Davis made the same effort at acceptance as he paced back and forth in an upstairs room in Richmond. Shocked by the sudden death of his five-year-old son, the Confederate president repeated aloud for hours, like a mantra, "Not mine, O Lord, but thine. Not mine, O Lord, but thine." It was the sentiment Abraham Lincoln would invoke on a staggering scale when he told the nation in his Second Inaugural Address, "if God wills that [the Civil War] continue until all the wealth piled by the bondsman's two hundred and fifty years of unrequited toil shall be sunk, and until every drop of blood drawn with the lash shall be paid by another drawn with the sword, as was said three thousand years ago, so still it must be said 'the judgments of the Lord are true and righteous altogether.'"[35]

Most ordinary soldiers could easily avail themselves of such sentiments and such language when they had to write letters to the families of fallen comrades, for they had practiced them in letters of reassurance to their own wives and parents. "I dont want you my dear to think long of my absence," an Alabama soldier named William B. Gilliland wrote to his wife, "for if its gods holy will I will soon return home & may his will be done with us all and may we be resined to his will." Thomas Warrick wrote to Martha, "You dont know how glad I would be to see you and them but God only knows when the time will come when we will all meet again on earth If we never do meet again on this earth may we all meet again in heaven." An Indiana man wrote home, "may God spare us as a Family that we may meet again on earth, if not let us be prepared to meet in the next world where there is no war."[36] Countless Civil War letter writers—from Fred Hooker to Thornton Clark to Hellen Alford and Betsy Blaisdell—experimented with new modes of expression, but when mortality loomed a great many sought the comfort of sameness.

Still, if memorial letters seemed very much the same in the aggregate, they were always irreducible to the person who received one. For that person, the last letter's meaning might lie less in its unoriginal words than in the distinctive epistolary relationship to which it announced a dreaded end. For Veronika Lehman, a twelve-year-old immigrant girl in Michigan, that relationship—a fast-evolving correspondence with her brother—was also an education in the social dynamics of language and literacy.

Veronika was two years old when her family left their home in Württemberg, and her older brothers were not quite teenagers. A decade on, those young men enlisted in the Seventh and Twentieth Michigan Infantry regiments; to them, the sister they called Verona was probably still the baby of the family. In the Lehmans' adopted home west of Ann Arbor, Verona would have enjoyed more time in school than her brothers, whose labor was needed on the farm. It was she, therefore, who became a kind of wartime family secretary. Johannes, who went by John and signed his last name "Leeman," could barely write German. His parents could read no English. Verona became their link.[37]

"Dear Father Mother sister and Brothers," John wrote from his first stop at Detroit Barracks. "I am sorry that I cant write our native language but some of you can read it." If John at the outset blithely assumed his family could work the matter out, his efforts to communicate home by letter soon would sow frustration and worry. When he joined his regiment at the front in early December, he had drawn

near his brother, Jacob Friedrick ("Fred"), who had enlisted a few
months earlier in a new regiment, the Twentieth, born out of summer
1862's fevered enlistment drive. Fred had been at the front since just
after the Battle of Antietam in September. Though in different corps
of the Army of the Potomac, the two brothers could visit each other
from time to time. John, still a green recruit, could see the epistolary
habits that had sprung up during the several months of Fred's service.
Hearing from home at secondhand through his brother could seem to
promise a bond of double strength. There was convenience in it,
too: "Fred spoke something about having a box sent to him by a man
from Anarbor," John wrote to his parents, and he went ahead and ordered up mittens, dried fruit, "writing paper and infelops and sta^mps."
But John quickly realized that his brother was getting more letters
than he was. "I see by the letter which Father wrote to Fred that you
was all well and received that mony ^that I sent which I was very glad of
but it would seem better if I could get a letter myself." A week later: "I
have had no letter from you nor any body else since I ve left Detroit
but heard from you when I see Fred."[38]

Though only two years apart, the brothers were very different
writers. John, the elder, evidently had received more English-language
schooling—with the result that he lost more of his native tongue. Fred
could and did write intelligible German. In fact, despite his ten years'
residence in the United States, he had greater facility with that language
than with English. He wrote to his parents in relatively fluent German,
but the few letters he wrote in his adopted tongue (to his grown and
married sister, Mary) consisted mostly of a phonetic representation of
German-accented spoken English: "we have a handsom plase to Camb
on it is nise leveb sandy drie ground close to Jamesriver where we can
git blindy of Oisters. . . . yeu most exews me for not writing bertter
becase yeu no Im a poor Scholer and besides where I have to set down
on a Nebsec and take my paber on my Nees." Whether Fred received
more letters from his parents because he wrote to them in the language

they preferred is impossible to say; it could have been simply a problem with John's mail delivery. Nevertheless, John came to suspect he was out of favor at home because he couldn't write German.[39]

For the time, John could tolerate having his connection with home routed through his brother. Fred was nearby, and they could meet frequently enough to collaborate, in a way, as correspondents. John's regiment was one of the first to cross the Rappahannock River in the Battle of Fredericksburg, and he took advantage of the brief Union occupation of the Virginia town to secure more writing paper—in the form of some townsperson's checkbook. He used a page of blank bank drafts to send home another unreciprocated letter of his own. He also promptly tore some sheets out to give Fred, whose regiment had been held in reserve during the battle. For John, putting some of his purloined paper into Fred's hands meant Fred could write more letters that might get replies; it gave John a functioning if indirect conduit to his family. In his own hands, blank checks were more suggestive. As he ran his pen beneath dollar signs, reminding his parents that he had "had no letter from you nor any body else," it seems to have crossed John's mind that he was an epistolary creditor, sending out the emotional currency of "respects" and receiving little in return. Out of blank space, he closed his letter on the empty lines of a check—"*Pay to* Give my respects to all my *or bearer* inquiring friends from your son and brother *Dollars*"—and signed on the signature line.[40]

Soon after Fredericksburg, Fred's regiment was sent to Kentucky, but John remained in the Army of the Potomac. Now, even his second-best option—contact with his family through Fred's translations of German-language letters—was not available. For a few months, John apparently did not even try to fill the void. He wrote at least one letter to Mary, his grown sister, and he exchanged letters with Fred, but there is no evidence that he wrote to his parents, or heard from them, between December of 1862 and April of 1863. He did receive, early that April, a letter from his one sister living at home, Verona. Whether at

Papa is rather ... hear with me that is writing sheets but
I found this book this forenoon and thought I could put it to no
better use than writing to you I wish I could send you some
things which I have seen distroyed books there is no end to them
in every house and some of the most valuable libraries I ever saw
I have had no letter from you nor any body else since I ve left
Detroit but heard from you when I see Ned I hope you are well
as I am Dont worry about me because I am engaged in a good cause
and if I should loose my life it would be no worse for me than
many other men

Bank of Virginia — Fredericksburg
Bank of Virginia — Fredericksburg
Bank of Virginia — Fredericksburg

John Lehman to "Dear Parents Brothers and sisters," 15 Dec. 1862 (verso) her urging, or simply because he had grown desperate and finally was willing to give his parents what he believed they wanted, John then tried writing a letter to his parents in German. He got out several lines then switched to English, saying, "If I was to write this sheet with german writing it would take me all day and part of tomorow so I concludet to fill it up with english."[41]

Writing in his parents' language wouldn't work, but Verona, he finally realized—perhaps because she had told him so in her recent letter—could help. When John wrote home the following month, he apologized—"I hope you will excuse me for not writing in german for I make such wretched work of it"—but, he offered reassuringly, "If Vrona is at home she can work it over into your own language." He closed his letter by signing himself "your homly Son, John Leeman," then added below that—in *Kurrentschrift*, or German cursive—"Johannes Lehmann." With this symbolic gesture, he gave Verona, now formally enlisted as his translator, something she could show her parents—a testament to their son's good faith and unbroken ties to the country of his birth.[42]

This glimmer of tenderness toward his parents—where, a few months before, John had seemed peevish about receiving fewer letters than Fred—may have sprung from his own frights and longings. Barely six months in the service, he had participated in two of the Union's bloodiest defeats of the entire war: it was one week after the Battle of Chancellorsville that he decided to style himself "Johannes Lehmann." Thoughts of his mortality well might have made John forgiving—of his parents' favoritism toward Fred, their deficient English, or whatever he thought hampered their epistolary relationship. John's reviving bond with his parents may also have owed to Verona's intercession. In fact, it was largely a bond with her that John's letters home were forging. The month after Chancellorsville, John wrapped up a letter to his parents and, on the last page, below his signature, began a second missive: "Dear Sister Vrona seeming as here is room I'll scratch off a few lines to you I supose you go to school this sumer hope you do anyway you must read and interpred^t this letter to father & Mother."[43]

Appending notes to Verona at the ends of his letters to his parents became customary. It sparked a new kind of relationship between these two siblings. From being merely a translator, Verona became a confidant. She and John enjoyed privacy in their correspondence, after all, since their parents could not read what either wrote. In July, for the first time since her pivotal intervention in early April, she began writing to John in her own voice, as well as serving as her parents' scribe: "was very glad," John replied, "to find that part of Fathers letter was filled up by you." In return, John began devoting more of his literary efforts to her. Having looked more carefully at the way she signed her own name, he no longer wrote "Vrona." Hitherto only a few lines on the last page, John's notes to "Dear Sister Verona" expanded until his letters home became evenly divided—two pages to his parents, two to his sister. When he neglected these attentions, she noticed. In November he wrote, with an apparent mixture of umbrage and guilt, "To Miss Verona Well sister I see that you do not write to me unless I direct a few lines to you."[44]

At the end of the year, John got a thirty-day furlough and returned home. He and Verona, newfound epistolary allies, saw each other face to face again. There is no way for us to hear what they said to each other, these twelve-years-distant siblings who perhaps never had spoken as peers before the war. We do know that when John returned to his regiment in early 1864 he gave up the pretense of writing to his parents through Verona. Now, he addressed her alone. She was his foremost correspondent and his principal tie to the world outside the army.

Although only John's letters survive, his and Verona's exchanges plainly had the steady rhythm, the reciprocity of virtual embrace, that characterized intimate correspondence—and that John had not been able to achieve with his parents. John's replies would begin with acknowledgements of Verona's just-received letters: one that "came to hand last night," another that "arrived about an hour ago," another "about half an hour ago." John's closeness to Verona showed in more than his promptness. Some letters to his sister had a philosophic strain that none to his parents had: "I wonder where I'll be next year this time. Who can tell? Perhaps I'll be at home, perhaps in the army somewhere and I may be under the sod, time alone will determine. . . . I am glad to hear that you learn so fast and like your school so well hope you will improve your time how I wish that I could live part of my life over again I think I could spend some of those school hours to better advantage than I did but there is no use in wishing."[45]

Verona internalized her role as a liaison between her brother and her parents. Presumably she now told them how John was getting along and relayed to him what they wanted to say, but she did so on her own authority. She neither took their dictation nor, it seems, read them John's letters aloud. The latter now displayed the kinds of mischief and sarcasm a grown and Americanized son probably suppressed around his more traditional parents. At the end of a particularly poor specimen of his penmanship, he added, "Dont you think that I improve writing. I talk some of coming home to teach writing school." Elsewhere he wrote, "Give my love to all the goodlooking gals."[46]

Freed up for a new role, Verona tried matchmaking. John evidently had met several of her friends—the "goodlooking gals"—while he was home on furlough. In one of his first letters after returning to the front, he had offered "my love to all the girls and Catherine in particular." But it was a young woman named Charlotte, not Catherine, whom Verona ushered into their correspondence. One day he opened an envelope from his sister and was surprised to notice another person's handwriting on the paper inside. "I little expected to receive a few lines in my Sister's letter written by an intire stranger," John wrote, but he gallantly replied "To Miss Charlotte, Lady Friend." "Since I have been in the service," he told her, "there is nothing more interesting to pass away the many lonly hours than to read and write letters. . . . I would be glad to get letters from you any time and shall allways answer them to the best of my abilities."[47]

No epistolary courtship flourished. John wrote Verona in mid-April to say that his mail service would be interrupted. He did not know why; probably it was because the Army of the Potomac was short on wagons. Ulysses S. Grant had been put in command the month before, and preparations were underway for his Overland Campaign. On May 1, 1864, John wrote Verona a hasty letter saying he was about to strike his winter quarters: "We have orders to tare down our loghuts tomorrow and pitch our sheltertents in their place, dont know what its for unless it is to get us used in laying on the ground. . . . Well Sis this is a short letter but you will excuse me this time, when we get on a march I shall have more to write about, if I only find time to write. You must write soon and often, improve your school hours well. My love to Father, Mother and Martin my best respects to all inquiring friends from your soldier brother John."[48]

The Army of the Potomac had set forth on what would prove a long and deadly march to Richmond, and John had sent Verona his last letter. Five days later, on the second day of the Battle of the Wilderness, his regiment charged up the plank road in a dawn assault on Confederate forces under A. P. Hill. John was shot in the chest and carried to a hospital in the rear. A regimental chaplain named Franklin Schoonmaker took the small pocket diary John kept and turned to the page where it left off. For May 6, 1864, John had written, "The weather pleasant fireing commenced at daylight and kept up steady." Schoonmaker filled the rest of that page and two more with a narrative of John's dying hours and beyond: "He did not suffer much pain but seemed inclined to sleep. Everything was done for him that his condition demanded. . . . He seemed aware of the possibility of his death and asked me, in writing to you, not to inform you that he was so badly wounded." Schoonmaker's lines ran down and across the diary's pages, through the printed headings for May 8, May 9, May 10—days John Lehman would never see—though the narrative barely got past the afternoon of May 7: "He died very easy near sundown we wrapped him in his blanket and buried him near the Hospital on the side hill where there was a house and a garden. I put a headboard at his grave with his name company and regiment. I send you all the effects found on his person."[49]

The chaplain mailed the diary home to the Lehmans. Only Verona would have been able to read it.

THERE IS SOMETHING fitting about Verona opening John's diary and leafing through the pages covered in his writing until she comes to the one in a different hand. John's translator and the intermediary between him and their parents, she now found herself addressed by another intermediary, the chaplain who translated thirty-six hours of dying into three pages of narrative. Verona could read to her parents the kind of letter Arminda Kite wanted—a detailed account of the scene, a written approximation of keeping vigil at the deathbed. At the same time, she held in her hand a token of John's physical presence, something she and her parents could stand near and touch as she perhaps intoned, in English or in German, what must stand as his last words: "The weather pleasant fireing commenced at daylight and kept up steady."

Perhaps the chaplain had struck upon this practice once, amid the cruel assembly line of fallen soldiers and the unyielding necessity of sending letters to their families, and kept it up with intention, whenever he attended the death of a diary-keeping soldier. If loved ones must receive the fateful letter in different handwriting, he may have thought, let them at least find it alongside words in their son's or husband's or brother's familiar hand. But perhaps it was simple practicality. Like hospital workers, chaplains had to write such letters in wearyingly large numbers. As the work piled up, it could tell two tales of destruction: that many men were dying, most obviously, but also that the sheer number of deaths was leaching away identity. As writers rehearsed the same litanies of assurance—provision of care, acceptance of death, hope of eternal reward, last words (if any), and proper burial—the dead came to seem bereft of individuality. A Confederate officer replied to a widow's request for "the particulars" of her husband's death by explaining: "So many die in the Hospital that those employed there cannot remember how each one passes from this world. For your comfort however, I will say that a Chaplain visited the Hospital regularly; I have no doubt that your husband during his sickness availed himself of his pious conversation." Chaplain Schoonmaker, by using the diary, may have been trying to keep the living John Lehman in view; or maybe he had to do this so often that, for efficiency's sake alone, he had stopped using clean paper and looked for dead men's effects to recycle.[50]

Wartime mortality could wear letter writers down or drive them to fall back on cliché, and men and women at the battlefront evolved ways of coping with the fatiguing demand for letters to dead men's families. But grief did not afflict only those at home. When Emily Moxley of Alabama died in childbirth in the spring of 1862, her husband, William, was in Corinth, Mississippi, serving in Braxton Bragg's corps of the western Confederate army. Their oldest child, George, was ten. William had never written an entire letter directly to George, and he did not know quite what to say. He evidently knew that counseling deference to God's will, assuring him he would meet his mother in heaven, would not go far with a ten-year-old. He also knew—as countless men intimated, especially during active seasons of fighting—that the letter he sent home might be his last. He was twenty miles south of the spot where Owen Creath, on the same day, wrote to Harriet,

worried about the hard time she must be having with the kids' measles.
Between the two men lay what would become the Shiloh battlefield.

> My dear Son,
>
> I write you afew lines to let you know you have a Father who
> loves you dearly with your little Sisters & Brothers. George, I
> have often told you to be a good boy, mind your Mother, and take
> care of your Sisters & Brothers. George, I cant say so any more.
> Your dear Mother is gone now, George. Mind your Grand Pa &
> Ma and evry person that teaches you to do right. George, you
> are the eldest. As you have no Ma, always take care of your
> little Sisters & Brothers. Be good to them & be a good boy. If
> your Pa should die or get killed in Battle, then you would have
> niether Father nor Mother to advise you.
>
> George, keep this paper; get it by heart. Your Grand Pa will
> read it for you. Besure to keep it untill I go to see you, & if
> I should die, keep it untill you are a man. Read it to your sisters
> & Brothers.
>
> George, be a good boy. Betty, you & Laura be good children.
> Mind when told. Take care of little Willie & Thomson. You are
> all dear children to me. Your Pa loves you dearly & will do all
> he can for you. I do hope to see you before a great while.
>
> Good by, my dear children.
>
> Your loving Father,
>
> W. M. Moxley[51]

Moxley lived. On the other side of the Tennessee River, the following
week, an Illinois private named George W. Collard read the letters
he pulled from the pocket of Owen Creath in the field hospital
at Savanna, Tennessee. He sat down and addressed a page to Mrs.
H. E. Creath:

Dear Lady As chainges that will Perhaps Mar your Happiness has taken Place I thought I would aprise you. I see in your letters to your Husband the Mark of a good Christian Wife. And nowing how to simppathise with Dear Wives at home I address these lines to you my dear lady it Pains me to tell you the sad intelegance of the Death of your Dear Husband of Whom you So Kindly Speak. your Stile reminds me of my own dear Wife.

He reminded Harriet that Christ is a husband to the widow, expressed his hope that her small children would live to be a blessing to her, and—finally remembering, near the end, the duties of such letters—added at the bottom of the page the brief report that Owen Creath "died of Gun shot through lef Lung and shoulder at the battle of Pittsburgh Died April 10th."[52]

6

Unions

Such as we are in word by letters when we are absent, such will we be also in deed when we are present.

—2 Corinthians 10:11

SEVERAL MONTHS away from home, regularly writing to his wife on the same pages she sent him, Henry Thompson signed off with kisses. At first he sent a simple "Kiss for You," encircled in curlicues of ink beneath his signature, then "7 kisses as 7 days is a week." Soon inflation set in. By springtime in 1863, it was "99 thousand Kisses," then "24 million Kisses." Lucretia responded in kind, sometimes with a pert addition. "A thousand kisses," she would write at the bottoms of her letters, and, on one early-summer evening, "Good night, 3000 kisses PS If you was at home the would some thing done besides sending kisses."[1]

The erotic undertones in their correspondence seemed to be on Henry's mind even in battle that summer, as he charged toward Richmond under General John A. Dix: "shells was going and comeing through the air saying {I want You, I want You, I want You { Il have You Il have you Ill have you { Ive got You Ive got You &c they speak it as plain as You can by mouth." No shells ever got Henry, and in 1864 he received a furlough and came home to Connecticut and Lucretia. The couple's letters ceased for about three weeks between late March and

April 19, when Henry boarded a southbound train in New Haven and rejoined his regiment in North Carolina. That summer he wrote to Lucretia "hopeing this will find You on good footing {*& not with child*}."[2]

Though many epistolary relationships were broken off before soldiers and their families had mastered letters, those fortunate enough to survive years of war and separation found that letter writing was no mere stopgap. It had become the fabric of their marriage or family, as real as a fleeting or dreamed-of reunion. Their challenge was to discover whether letters could do more than bide time until a homecoming. Could words on paper conjure the same depth of connection people enjoyed in each other's presence? Ordinary Americans who achieved the heights of creativity in their correspondence, who graduated the wartime school of letters, often did so by writing about precisely the allures of physical togetherness. Contemplating coming home, accepting that they must remain apart, soldiers and their loved ones reached new frontiers of expression.

FRANCIS POTEET, WHO was conscripted by the Confederate army in the fall of 1863, exchanged letters with his wife, Martha, for about a month before leaving his regiment and coming back home. He had talked about doing it almost from the outset. "Sumtimes I think that I Will Runaway," he wrote just a few weeks after leaving his small farm in McDowell County. He had come 250 miles from the North Carolina mountains, down across the Piedmont to within 50 miles of the ocean. "This is the levlest contry that I ever saw," he told Martha; "it tis as leval as your Garden tha ant a hill that can be seen about hear."[3]

Initially, Francis desired to flee back into the mountains for his own sake. He was homesick, and he chafed against the restrictions of army life: "My Dear Wife I cant tell how mutch I would giv to be at home this morn ing to go With you to Preachin and stay With you as long as I live I youst to Read my Bible till I got tired and then I could talk With you and go where I Pleased but now I hant got the chance of

anegro." Week after week he felt torn between desertion and discipline—"I cant stay hear no longer but I have to stay but it tis hard for
me to stay"—and sometimes he seemed overwhelmed by despair: "if I
nown that I had to stay in the army till the war ended I would as soon be
Ded and I would any how if it wasant for you and my littel Children."[4]

The hardships facing Martha and their children did more than keep
Francis from committing suicide; they turned his talk of running away
into action. On November 23 he received a letter from Martha telling
him the family's landlord had forced them off their place. "If I had of
bin at home when Bill Rented you out of house and home," Francis
wrote back, "I think that I would of heart him and I Dont now but what
I will yet but I ought to pray for our inmas but it is hard to pray for any
Speclator when tha doo so." Most unjust, and most worrisome, Bill
pushed Martha off the land after she had sown winter wheat, and the
loss of that crop set off a scramble for sources of income and food.
Francis, who did a lot of milling and carpentering, had customers who
still owed him for jobs done before he was drafted. He urged Martha to
"tell Joseph Landis to pay you for them coffins if he asks you what you
charge you can tell him if he will let you have wheat at one Dollar per
bushel that he can give you 6 bushel." Maybe Francis initially was timid
of collecting payment from a man who had occasion to order multiple
coffins, but his own family now had a monopoly on his sympathies.[5]

This outraged and worried letter was the last Francis would send
for some time. The next news he got from Martha set a match to the
powder of his home feelings. Their thirteen-year-old son, Alvis, was
gravely ill. Francis left his regiment without permission, set out westward, and made it home in time to see Alvis before he died on December 21, 1863. Francis had written Martha weeks earlier that he
hoped to be home for Christmas, and he was.

IN 1861, AMID the excited formation of companies and regiments in
individual counties, men volunteered and were publicly cheered by

their families and neighbors as they left to fight a glorious war of short duration. Men like Owen Creath could confidently declare their expectation that the war would end, and they would return home, by Christmas or April or the Fourth of July, in 1862. By 1864, men entered the two armies under less auspicious circumstances. Recruiting rarely was the fervent grassroots effort it had been in the beginning; it was the work of national bureaucracies trying to fill the tens of thousands of spaces in the ranks left empty by shot, shell, and disease. Men were drafted, or feared they soon would be; they were hired as substitutes for drafted men; they were running away from something and trying to claim a bounty. Their families, if they had any, may or may not have known they were going, or known why, or felt the least enthusiasm for their enlistment.

As predictions of a fast-approaching peace proved false, and year followed year of seemingly interminable war, letters between soldiers and their families increasingly dealt with alternative forms of homecoming. Countless soldiers and their wives, sisters, and mothers wrote about seeing each other in dreams. To a generation fascinated with the spirit realm, dream visions seemed to provide the purest evidence of true attachment. They transcended the quotidian world of delayed mail and prognostication about the end of the war, banished fears that a loved one had been forgotten, and raised hopes that a return was imminent. A Georgia woman wrote to her brother, "Joe you must try to get a furlow if you can i dreampt the other nite you come home i saw you so plain i hope you are coming home." Daniel Revis had written to Sarepta, "Sereptia I do want to see you I dream about being with you and I want to be thair but times wil not emit of it now." Margaret Baggarly wrote to her husband, Tilmon, "I dreamed a few nights ago that I saw you I thougth I was somewhere and you came to me before I knowed you here if that was only so it would be a joy that I never experienced before." For his wife, Lucy, Eli Fogleman inscribed one of his dreams on a piece of "old paper that I found in the court house"

of Jones County, North Carolina, which "the Yankees has torn up."
On one side, the paper documents the birth of a now-fading nation-
alist dream—the record of the votes cast in Jones County in the first
and only Confederate States presidential election, November 1861—
and on the other, Eli's narrative of a different birth: "I dreamed the
other knight that you had a baby and I came home and it came to me
and I kissed it."[6]

For families in profound distress, like the Poteets, dreams were not
enough, and letters brimmed with hopes, pleas, and declarations that
men would not wait for the war's end to return home. Where folders
in archives today fall silent—a researcher leafing through regular
weekly letters comes abruptly to the end, or to a long gap—
correspondents may in fact have burst into voluble conversation, only
in person, not on the page. Some returns home were authorized. Discharges, like the one Thornton Clark hoped for, were permanent and
usually granted to debilitated men. Temporary furloughs became
rare in the Southern army, which was chronically short on men, but
common in the North, especially during 1864, when Henry Thompson
returned home. The three-year terms of men who had volunteered in
1861 came due that year, and the Union army, at risk of losing thousands of its most seasoned troops, offered them furloughs as incentives
to reenlist. 1864 was an election year, too, and the Lincoln administration encouraged furloughs so that men from states that did not allow
absentee voting could go home and cast ballots.

Though the strapped Confederate army could not offer many furloughs, the proximity of the fighting to Southerners' homes afforded
many men opportunities to return. Some Confederate soldiers were
encamped within a hundred miles of their homes; some were marched
along routes that passed even closer. As Confederate general John C.
Pemberton led his troops east out of Vicksburg, Mississippi, after sur-
rendering it to Ulysses S. Grant, he found that nearly all the men who
lived west of the Mississippi River or in the state of Mississippi had al-

ready deserted. He fully anticipated that those who lived in Alabama, Tennessee, and Georgia would leave, too, as soon as they got nearer those places. The men had been besieged in Vicksburg for weeks, reduced to eating mule meat and deprived of most mail service. "It is not to avoid a camp for paroled prisoners," Pemberton wrote, "but a determination to see their families." Considering their desertion inevitable, he offered a thirty-day furlough to his whole army so that at least some of them would come back.[7]

The captain of a company might wink at a soldier's brief slipping away to his nearby home (though in time the Confederate army stripped subordinate officers of the power to grant leaves), or the soldier might venture off on his own authority in what men termed a "French leave." Stories circulated in the South of stray soldiers moving about the countryside who, when asked to produce official furlough papers, patted their guns and replied, "This is my furlough." Nor was desertion uncommon in the North. More than 100,000 Confederate soldiers deserted, but more than 250,000 men deserted the larger Union army. Both figures are likely underestimations, given the secrecy that often was involved.[8]

Questions about men's volition cast shadows over home letters. Could he come home? Would he? Why wasn't he coming home? Wives and parents constantly encouraged soldiers to pursue legitimate means of getting out of the army, especially when a soldier was sick, and they often had a hard time understanding why their husband or son wasn't receiving the furlough or discharge they had heard of some other man receiving under similar circumstances. Betsy Blaisdell, in her plaintive way, urged Hiram to seek a furlough on account of his wintertime illness. "O Hiram try hard to get a furlough," she wrote repeatedly during the winter of 1864–1865; "dont wait for them to offer you one ask for it there is nothing like trying." A friend or relative named Mort was home on furlough, evidently on account of illness, but Betsy didn't think he looked as sick as Hiram sounded, and it seemed to her only logical and fair that Hiram should receive the same consideration as Mort. Once he got home, she told Hiram, he could even get his "furlough lengthened the rest do Mort does and he looks as well as any body and is I guess he is around all the time in one place and in another and works some."[9]

Men responded to such urgings in a variety of ways. Some explained, a little defensively, why this was impossible or impractical. They reported in detail the forbidding military restrictions on furloughing, especially in the Confederate army: "there is one furlow to evry hundred now"; "I canot get but 24 hours furlow and it wood take that long for me to go home and back"; "a man can get a furlow now for 40 days if he will get a recruit in his company first but I dont aim to tri that at all for if that is my chance to get a furlow I will never get it in this life."[10] Just as women on the home front compared notes on men who returned from the army, deducing from them tactics their husbands could use to come home, men in camp took notice of the reasons fellow soldiers received furloughs and discharges. A Confederate soldier from Texas named Patrick Divine wrote home, "I dont expect that I woul be able to get a furlow to go home from here at all, the only chance would be by you sending some good excuse, such as you been sick and some of the Children and you and your family in a bad Condition." Northern soldiers believed the same thing would work in their army. Joseph Diltz of Ohio wrote to his wife, Mary, "I dont see as their is eny chance for me to get home very soon maby if you Would rite some big yarn about bing sick and send to me I mite get a furlow to go home I dont Know how it Would bee if you do dont let eny body Know it."[11]

What people thought would work was not always accurate, of course, and what really would get a man a furlough varied at different times in different commands. It depended on how individual surgeons assessed cases of illness, what directives generals had given their subordinates, what military actions were anticipated. Such factors were generally opaque to the rank and file, but men could tell which way the wind blew. They also had opinions about when such a valuable thing as a furlough—if you got one, you might never get another—was and was not worth taking. Hiram Blaisdell's reason for not seeking a furlough showed careful calculation on his part: "I do not want to get a furlough without I could for sixty days for it would take some twenty five days to go and come and I would not have a very long time at that stay it would pass off very quick and then I should have to part with my Bet again and that would be awful hard." Mindful of his wife's sensitivity and the epistolary strains of their recent past, Hiram doubtless knew Betsy could interpret this to mean he did not really want to see her. She had previously written, "I would give a hundred dollars if you could come and stay with me one Night if no longer," and if Hiram, marking out the days of a notional furlough, thought this was a silly, sentimental sort of talk, he never said so. He did not press his measured argument about the lengths of furloughs; he never expressed the least unwillingness to endure twenty-five days in transit.[12]

Instead, he mounted a noticeable effort to show just how much he did want to see Betsy—to reciprocate her most romantic sentiments and convey through his letters the depth of his desire to be with her. Almost every letter he wrote during the month following his demurral on the furlough featured some form of imagined physical intimacy. Sometimes he voiced simple wishes: "O Bet how I would like to press you to my bossom O how happy I should be I guess I would squeeze you some"; "I have just washed all up clean and nice I took off shirt and had a general wash I guess if I was thare I guess I would have a kiss." In three different letters within two weeks, he described kissing his photograph of Betsy: "I have just been looking at your likeness O Bet if I could kiss you in stead of that but that is some consolation to me."[13]

These were clichés, of course, and plenty of Americans might have viewed them cynically. Melissa Dalton Baker of Iowa teased her husband, Obadiah, that his photograph of her soon would "get all rubbed out" because he kissed it so often. "But dont please wear your lips out," she wrote, "for I want the pleasure of kissing them again when you come home." A South Carolina woman was blunter: "when you get this letter dont go on with any of your nonsense crying over it kissing it putting it to your heart and pretending that you love it." Still, for Betsy Blaisdell and many other Americans, tender asseverations of romantic attachment were precisely what could salve the hurts of absence. Photographs carried images of the body, and letters narrated the workings of the spirit. Only furlough, desertion, or peace could bring both together.[14]

Even Betsy Blaisdell could be a realist about such matters. "I want to see you so bad I do want you to come if they will let you," she wrote to Hiram in the first days of 1865, before checking herself: "I do not want you to dessert for it is awful to read how many is shot for deserting O I hope they will let you come." When the extreme step of desertion came up, the tone of a correspondence often changed. Many letters resembled the sharing of news on front porches, family conversations over kitchen tables, tense exchanges of worry and hurt feelings, or solemn eulogies. In letters that broached desertion, writers assumed the whispering tones that bring heads leaning close to each other. Tilmon Baggarly wrote to Margaret on a small square of paper, "My Dier Wife ceep this a seecret an dont you think that i am distrest in my mind for trien to get of." Grant Taylor wrote to Malinda, "And now I will write you a secret which I want you to keep. It is this. If I live God being my helper I intend to come home next April if I do not get a furlough before then and they do not pay me off or I will be caught and brought back in the attempt." Lucy Fogleman discreetly advised Eli, "if you ever get into a battle if I was you I would not try to fite I would run to the yankeys if there was any chance without geting hurt then you could get to come home and stay awhile."[15]

Such confidences plucked taut strings between marital and family unions, on one side, and on the other a sense of duty, patriotism, honor, or simple resignation to military discipline. The increasing commonness of desertion dispelled some of its stigma. By the third year of the war, Confederate officials were acknowledging it was "no longer a reproach to be known as a deserter," and that deserters were "shielded by their families and by the sympathies of many communities." But the shame associated with dereliction of duty never disappeared entirely (nor would it: almost a century afterward, Bell Irvin Wiley published *The Life of Billy Yank* with an index entry on "Desertion" that notes "*See also* Cowardice"). Sons writing to their parents—young men whose chief concern was to prove themselves—often took pains to insist they never would desert and expressed indignation if anyone suggested otherwise.[16]

Frederick Hooker had struggled in mingled print and cursive through twenty letters to his mother by the time the Second Connecticut Heavy Artillery was called off the Washington defenses and into the field. The paymaster came just before the regiment left Fort Ellsworth, and when Fred disembarked on the opposite side of the Potomac, some thirty miles downriver at Belle Plains, Virginia, he posted an express package home containing sixty dollars. On May 18, 1864, in Fredericksburg—where, two Decembers earlier, John Lehman had appropriated blank bank drafts and Henry Thompson had begun writing crosswise over Lucretia's letters—Fred took a torn half sheet of paper and hastily penciled this note: "dear mother i am well i am going to the Front you must not write to me u n till you hear From me agi n you may Look at the oFice For money i enclosed 60 doLors night Before Last." He marched off to replenish the ranks of the Army of the Potomac, badly depleted by the fighting in the Wilderness—where John Lehman had been killed twelve days earlier—and at Spotsylvania Courthouse, where Fred arrived just as nearly two weeks of carnage was drawing to a close.[17]

The springtime drive toward Richmond was not yet a month old, and the Union army had already suffered nearly forty thousand casualties. Grant stripped the forts ringing Washington for reinforcements (thrashing Lee on the way to Richmond, he reasoned, was as good a defense of the capital as heavily manned garrisons). Men like Fred Hooker, after months at routine duty in the safe confines of places like Fort Ellsworth, found themselves suddenly engaged in exhausting high-speed marches and some of the bloodiest and most grueling trench warfare yet fought anywhere in the world.

The Army of the Potomac's veteran infantry viewed these green bands of artillery boys with mixtures of amusement and scorn. Full complements of men filing by in tellingly pristine uniforms drew jeers and bemusement from men who had been in the field for years. Stephen Crane imagined the archetypal scene in *The Red Badge of Courage* years later: "some perambulating veterans, noting the length of their column, had accosted them thus: 'Hey, fellers, what brigade is that?' And when the men had replied that they formed a regiment and not a brigade, the older soldiers had laughed, and said, 'O Gawd!'" Fred Hooker's Second Connecticut Heavy Artillery was one of these, more than 1,500 strong when it arrived at the front. They received a particularly jolting welcome. Some veterans only hollered at them, "Why, dearest, did you leave your earthworks behind you?" Others, fresh from the Spotsylvania battlefield's "Bloody Angle," said, "This is what you'll catch up yonder," and showed their mutilated limbs.[18]

Fred was quickly swept up in a fast march—Grant's southbound race with Lee along and across the Pamunkey River. The men of his regiment were driven to exhaustion. One took advantage of a halt in the march to eat something and woke up later with a mouthful of half-chewed hardtack. The swift-spreading news that a fight was brewing led some to declare, "I'd rather be shot than marched to death." A regiment from North Carolina would oblige when, later that afternoon, the first of June, the Second Connecticut Heavy Artillery charged across an open field at an entrenched rebel line—what one remembered as "a sheet of flame, sudden as lightning, red as blood, and so near that it seemed to singe the men's faces." More than 300 of the regiment's 1,500 men, 20 percent of the total, fell on that field. In what one observer called "a mute and pathetic evidence of sterling valor," the bright blue uniforms that two weeks earlier betrayed this regiment's inexperience now, on the bodies of its dead, marked their path of attack, "in a dotted line[,] an obtuse angle, covering a wide front, with its apex toward the enemy." The survivors had not yet learned that the little crossroads where their long march had stopped was called Cold Harbor.[19]

Men who survived Spotsylvania and Cold Harbor constantly said, for years afterward, that the ferocity of the fighting there defied expression. "I never expect to be fully believed when I tell what I saw of the horrors of Spotsylvania, because I should be loath to believe it myself, were the case reversed." Of the Union charge at the Confederates' Cold Harbor breastworks, a veteran later said, "Language cannot describe the fearful picture" of the scene of "a thousand men falling in every minute." A private in the Second Connecticut wrote home just after Cold Harbor—for him as for Fred and every man in that regiment, the first time "seeing the elephant"—"the real battlefield with it's woe & carnage & bloodshed, pain & misery, groans & cries, curses & prayers of the wounded & dying is indeed a scene which my pen cannot describe."[20]

Any thought of putting into words what he had just seen and endured was likely far from the mind of the barely literate Fred Hooker. But something soon compelled him to take out what must have been his last scrap of paper, now stained and dirty, and scratch out a letter with his pencil. A mailbag caught up with Fred's regiment on the front lines at Cold Harbor, two and a half days after their severest fighting.[21] It brought a letter from his mother, and that letter carried two pieces of news that alarmed or upset him: the sixty dollars he sent home to Jeannette Hooker had arrived in Farmington as a package addressed

Frederick Hooker to Jeannette Hooker, undated (between 4 and 10 June 1864)

to Mary Hooker containing ten dollars; and someone had told Jeannette that Fred deserted.

> deᵃr mother i got your Lettr i am sory to hear tha i am a diserter But it ant true so dont mind what he say the reson why i did not write sooner was Becaus we have Been on a Force March For three week & hant had time to there is amistake about the money in the name & amount oF money For i sent (60) home the 16 oF the month From Bell Plain VA By the Bay master so take the

Rackage out oF the oFice & look ever it is or rihere [?] we have
Been in Battle & Lost KiLLEd & wounded 350 men some one is
triYing to cheat you so Look out oPen the package it will come
out wright

diReCT to hooker COL 2 CV arT

First Brigade

2 diViSion

6 army Core

Washington dC[22]

During the ensuing days, as the groans of wounded men between the
lines diminished and the smell of the dead worsened, Fred remained
entrenched, pestered by mosquitoes. It would have been understand-
able if he was stewing in outrage. To have been called a deserter! It
was false to begin with but must have seemed a particular injustice now,
just when he had finished doing work as hard as Union soldiers ever
were called upon to do. I wish I had deserted, he may have been
thinking; or, better for hundreds of his comrades to have deserted than
to have sacrificed their lives for a few yards of ground. Either another
letter came from home, frustratingly repeating what the last had said,
or Fred's indignation reached a boiling point on its own. He somehow
acquired a complete, clean sheet of paper and took a step he had
not taken in more than two months: he asked a more literate person to
write for him. The first letter since early springtime that Jeannette
had received in someone else's handwriting said:

Dear mother and Nancy, I receaved a letter the other day that
you directed to Fort Ellswo[rth] you sead that the express man had
brought a package directed to Mary Hooker and thare was $10
in it now I think thare must have been a mistake made bothe in
name and amount for I sent $60 $60 by the pay master and as I

had no utensils for writing I got a Sargt to direct it. I saw in your
letter that it was rumored about home that I had deserted.

He momentarily retreated from the charge of desertion and returned
to the problem of the missing fifty dollars—"now then look into that
and not let them cheat you"—but he could not let the rumor go. "Now
I think that it is rather hard to be caled a deserter when the idear never
entered my head of deserting I suppose that you have seen by the papers that we have had a large battle near Cold Harbor our Regt lost a
grate menny kiled and wounded."[23]

For Fred Hooker, nineteen years old and seeking to prove himself
a man, it may have been hard to say which was worse: seeing fifty dollars of his earnings disappear (equivalent to nearly $800 today) or
hearing himself deprived at home of the reputation he probably
believed he had just earned. Some young men, more fluent in their
writing, less beset by misunderstanding, could make confident,
preemptive declarations. William Allen Clark wrote to his parents in
Indiana, "You need not be afraid of my Deserting or taking a french
Furlough. I think to much of my Character and my Country." But
thinking of character and country was a privilege that other men—
ones on whom children depended for sustenance—might not have
been able to afford.[24]

Husbands writing to wives tended to discuss the prospect of return
with greater candor, sometimes more urgency, and often a palpable
ambivalence—like Francis Poteet's back-and-forth, "I cant stay hear
no longer but I have to stay but it tis hard for me to stay." Grant Taylor
wrote to Malinda, home nursing a two-month-old infant Grant had
yet to meet, that he could not bring himself to run away but, having
seen many of his comrades paroled by the Yankees, would not try very
hard to avoid capture, either: "I do not intend to desert, but I shall not
make strenuous exertions to get out of the enemy's way." Such exchanges rarely flared with young Fred Hooker's indignation. Many

men gingerly prodded the idea of desertion, while many of their wives stabbed directly at it.[25]

LETTER WRITING UNQUESTIONABLY made military enlistment and separation more tolerable for most families than they otherwise would have been. The keenness to write among even barely literate men and women obviously testifies to that. But some Civil War letters made separation intolerable. Probably the best-known genre of wartime letters by civilians are those from poor Southern women urging their husbands to come home. The thousands upon thousands of letters in which soldiers' wives described their families' sufferings encouraged desertion from the already outnumbered Confederate army and probably helped tip the military conflict toward the Union. They even figure in cultural memory of the Civil War in our own time. In the film adaptation of Charles Frazier's novel *Cold Mountain*, it is a letter from Ada Monroe calling to Inman, "Come back to me," that starts him on his odyssey to the mountain. Newton Knight, the legendary deserter who inspired the 2016 film *The Free State of Jones*, left his regiment after receiving a letter from his wife, Serena, saying the Confederate cavalry had seized the only horse the family could use to go to the mill.[26]

Letters from Southern women were in the public eye at the time, too. Thousands of women, their families often near starvation, wrote individual and collective petitions to public officials pleading for relief, state aid, or the discharge of their husbands.[27] Even private letters to husbands, making direct pleas to desert, came into the open. One was introduced in a Confederate court-martial as part of a deserter's defense of himself:

My dear Edward:—I have always been proud of you, and since your connection with the Confederate army, I have been prouder of you than ever before. I would not have you do anything wrong for the world, but before God, Edward, unless you come home,

we must die. Last night, I was aroused by little Eddie's crying. I
called and said "What is the matter, Eddie?" and he said, "O
mamma! I am so hungry." And Lucy, Edward, your darling Lucy;
she never complains, but she is growing thinner and thinner every
day. And before God, Edward, unless you come home, we must
die. Your Mary.[28]

Numbered in the thousands, letters like Mary's really could turn the
tide of a great war. Other women, either less desperate or inclined
toward a different calculus of risk, were circumspect. Elizabeth James
of Mississippi surely wanted her husband to come home as much as
anyone. "I dreamp night before last that you come home and when
I awoke I was sadly disappointed," she wrote to him; "when I ask
Jimmy where his pa is he points his fingers up the road and says now
now." Nevertheless, she insisted, "I donot want you to ever come
home with out leaf if you hear that wee are all dying they have shot
several up hear for coming home."[29]

Accounts of men being shot for desertion are strikingly abundant
in soldiers' letters home—quite out of proportion with the frequency
of such occurrences. Military executions numbered in the hundreds in
a war in which more than seven hundred thousand men died, yet scores
of surviving letters recount soldiers' experiences of being ordered to
stand and witness executions.[30] Men wrote home about these harrowing
scenes because they made a powerful impression on them, as Thomas
Warrick made clear:

Deare Louving Wife I hant got a grate deal to say at this time I
can inform you that I saw a site to Day that maide me feel mity
bad I saw a man shot for Deserting there was twenty fore guns
shot at him thay shot him all to pease so they sed I did not go to
see him he was shot for Deserting he went home and thay Brote
him Back and then he went home a gain and so thay shot him for

that Martha it was one site that I did hate to see it But I Could not help my self I had to Doo jest as thay sed for me to doo.[31]

Thomas did not go up and take a close look at the body, as others did, but he was compelled to witness the shooting.

Army commanders intended such displays to deter men from deserting. When men recounted these harrowing spectacles in letters, they reminded their loved ones—maybe intentionally, maybe not—of the risk a man would be taking if he came home without leave. Henry Thompson's letters to Lucretia began dancing around the question of desertion in the wake of the Battle of Fredericksburg. "Our leders are good for nothing," he wrote, and a great many of the men, if only they could get back north of the Potomac "would take their walking ticket." He intimated he might take one "long step" all the way to Connecticut. Lucretia was mainly amused by the wit of Henry's phrasings: "when I read that perhaps you should take a long step it was all I could do to keep from laughing out loud." But after Henry had taken his furlough—and, upon returning to his regiment, witnessed an execution—no such jocularity attended talk of desertion. He devoted almost the entirety of an August 1864 letter to every detail of the incident, even drawing a small diagram of its arrangement: a rectangle of watching soldiers on three sides and, represented by a dotted line on the fourth side, the six deserters seated on their coffins; the firing squad in the center; and, marked by a heavy black dot, like a widened pupil, the place where Henry was standing, "within 20 feet of the first" of the condemned men.[32]

The letter Martha Poteet wrote to Francis telling him of Alvis's illness does not survive. Whether or how strenuously she urged him to come home is unknown. Even if she had not then fully appreciated what it meant for Francis to desert, she would soon enough. Barely a week after Alvis died, Francis had to leave home again. He was just about to slaughter the family's hogs when the Raleigh Guard came to town. This militia band, like "home guard" units across the Confederacy—heirs to the legacy of Daniel Revis's company at Shelton Laurel—was known for ruthlessness toward deserters and their families. Francis took no chances. Whether he made it back to the Forty-Ninth North Carolina's winter quarters on his own or was apprehended along the way, by January 12, 1864, he was 250 miles from home in Weldon, a prisoner in a Confederate guardhouse.[33]

At his first opportunity, Francis composed a letter home. He had left under duress, making hurried good-byes to Martha and their eight surviving children, but his first words to them since were staid and proper: "My Dear Wife and Children I take the pleasure to drop you afew lines to let you now that I am will at this time hoping these lines may Reach your kinds hands and find you injoying the same blissing." Such rhetorical customs were instinctive and habitual for Francis, but he now had an extra fillip to epistolary decorum. He was being watched. "Tha have to Read the letters that I git from you and Read my letters," he told Martha next. And then he picked up where the family had left off: "I want you to Rite to me whether you have got your hogs kiled are not I am in the gard house and I dont now when I will git out I hope that god will Bless you and my littel Children and gave you plenty to eat as long as you live."[34]

Francis did not know it, for no mail was reaching him here, but Martha had already written to him in care of his regiment. Her long, flowing letter had the relaxed, garrulous quality many writers found hard to achieve amid the time lags and miscommunications of aching absences. It was just over a week since Francis left, and they had conversations to continue. Martha wistfully began, "The Raleigh gard never come back no moor I wish you could hav staid with me," then moved on to business. The butchering did get done: "Mr Walker and Johnathan kiled my hogs the day after you left." The threat of eviction still loomed: "I cant get the William house he is a going to move to it and I dont know what to do Bill Cowen come hear a teusday and told me to get out as soon as I could." The weather was not good: "you thought it was cold when you was hear but it was nothing the 1 & 2 days of this Month was the coldest I ever felt." Martha had turned her paper over before she realized she did not exactly know where this letter was headed—"I want to know what they don with you for runing away"—and as she drew near the bottom of the page, winter's darkness closed around her: "O my dear husband you dont know how lonsom I am sins you left I dread to see Night come.... O Francis it dos seem like it will kill me to be parted from you with no one to protect me and your little helpless children I pray the Lord to save your sole and body fom harm if I never see you no moor I want you to write soon I am so cold I must quit."[35]

Martha did not yet know a prison guard would be opening the envelope. Throughout the winter and into the spring, she and Francis corresponded with someone looking over their shoulders. "Gard please send this to my Wife if you pleas," Francis would inscribe below his signature; "please gard give this to my husband," Martha would reply.[36] Once Martha knew her letters would not be private, she clammed up in certain ways: "I would write you some about My self but I cant let evry Man read what I would be willing for you to read." At the same time, she seemed inclined to give her new audience a piece of her mind. Francis already had a fair idea of the hardships Martha faced in his absence; the Confederate prison guards did not. She described some challenges that were news to Francis: "I went to the cross Roads last Saturday and got two dollars worth salt and Sunday Night some body stoled about half of it." She also, apparently more for the benefit of official eyes, summarized the situation: "I thought wen a man went back with with in themselves they did not put them in the gard house but George Tay lor told he tuck you up and is to get thirty Dollars of your wages and I expect that is the of you being punished it is Just one Month to day sins our little son died and I dont think they ought to blame you for coming home to see him Die."[37]

Martha believed George Taylor—someone they knew, plainly, a relatively near neighbor—conspired to get Francis arrested and claim a reward. She would return to this injustice amid increasingly desperate laments of her family's suffering and increasingly fiery denunciations of everyone she held responsible: George Taylor, her landlord, the entire secessionist South. "You wrote for me to stay hear," she wrote to Francis in February. "Bill Cowen says if I stay in the house I shant work the ground that I shant as much as hav the garden I hav walked my self down this week trying to get aplace and hav got non me and my children are bound to perish. . . . I am in a great deal of trouble Doctor Young charged me three dollars in gold or silver or thirty dollars in confederate for coming to see Alvis one time and george Taylor to hav thirty dollars for his kindness leting you rid to the head of the road he ought to be double quicked to the armey if I was a man I would kill him." The symmetry of the thirty dollars seemed to compound George Taylor's betrayal: he had taken exactly the money that would have paid the bill that was incurred for Alvis, whose death had brought Francis home, which was the reason—together with George's action—that Francis was in prison now with no hope of returning home again anytime soon.[38]

That Francis was away and George Taylor was at home represented, to Martha, an indictment of the whole war. "All the honest men is gone," she wrote, "and a set of speckalating dogs is left to press the lives out of the poor Woman and children while the soldiers is standing as a wall between them and the enemy they are standing between them and there wives to snatch evry thing the can get I think there ought to be astop put to it if it aint we all will be bound to perrish." In its politics, Martha's complaint resembled those of many poor Southerners who resented the richer men who stayed home. The Confederacy's draft rules—including a notorious exemption for men who owned at least twenty slaves—fueled charges of "a rich man's war but a poor man's fight." Small-time men of means could evade the draft, too. Bill Cowen went off to Richmond, according to Martha, saying "he would give 12 hundred penny weights of gold to get off "—gold she no doubt saw as the fruits of his "speckalating" ways, including forcing her and her children off his land so that he could rerent it at a higher price.[39]

Martha's sentiments were not unique, but she expressed them with a striking visualization of Southern society during wartime: Confederate soldiers were "standing as a wall between" the Yankees and Southern stay-at-homes, while the latter were "standing between" the soldiers and their families. Written to Francis out in Weldon, Martha's letter charts a west-to-east, mountains-to-tidewater geography overlaid by twin fights: the Confederacy's against the North and her own to survive. With this four-part formulation—women and children, then speculators and stay-at-homes, then soldiers like Francis, then Yankees—Martha critiqued a core tenet of secession. At the outset of the war, Southern men were called to fight amid loud cries to protect Southern women from the defilements of Yankee invaders. But as Martha saw it, Southern men fell into two classes, and the departure of one left women and children vulnerable to exploitation by the other. She described the Confederate army's role with the same words—"standing between"—that she used for men taking food from her children's mouths. The Yankees, at the furthest remove, barely seemed to matter, and Martha expressed little fear of them. If anything, she might rather see the "enemey" let loose on the "speckalating dogs." All this "standing between" made for a merciless war. "I hope they wont punish you allways," she wrote to Francis. "I dont think they ought you did not stay at but 8 days and then went back." But she seemed increasingly resigned to the fact that Francis's imprisonment was all the mercy the army would show him. As for herself: "I told you when you left I was left to the Mercy of the people there is about as much mercy shown me as a dog would show a peace of meat."[40]

If Francis's imprisonment got Martha riled up, it certainly expanded her as a writer. The intrusions on the privacy of their letters accustomed her to the idea of addressing, or maneuvering around, an audience beyond her husband. Visualizing the war as a succession of hostilities stretching eastward down the mountains, Martha did more than express a political view; she defined for herself the challenge her letters faced. They had not only to conquer distance; they needed to rise above and reach over the malign forces that separated her and Francis. As winter gave way, mercifully, to spring, Martha became adept at writing letters that could.

Back in February, she had made a request that, to a prison guard opening Francis's mail, might have seemed curiously precise: "I want you to get a furlow by the 12th of May and Come Home to take care of me." Francis knew exactly what this meant. When he had returned home in December, perhaps even before reaching Alvis's deathbed, he discovered that Martha was in the second trimester of another pregnancy, conceived shortly before his conscription in October.[41]

Now, as month followed month and Francis remained in the guard house, Martha must have realized the furlough was wishful thinking. Even if Francis got out of prison by May, it was highly unlikely that he—a man just punished for desertion—would be granted a leave for any length of time. Running away a second time could very well land him in front of a firing squad. So, Martha carried on, eight months pregnant, nursing children with croup, getting a few crops in at planting time. "I have got 2 bushels of sweet potatoes and planted them," she wrote in early April. "I haint planted Corn yet I want to plant next Week if it dont rain." Springtime brought a pale, distorted image of life as usual. "Last week some body stold two of Allens horses," she wrote, giving Francis the neighborhood news, "and left two old poor no count ones in there place." Everything around her underwent a gradual version of those horses' overnight transformation. "They say that the yankeys can come here at any time they please," she told Francis, "but they dont want to come for there aint any thing to come for but a parcel of half perished woman and children."[42]

As Martha's time drew near, Francis's regiment was on the move. He was transported to Richmond, Virginia, still under guard. "I do not know how long I will be kept hear or what will be don with me," he wrote home on May 4. Five days later, he was released and returned to duty. Probably a commander decided that punishing deserters was less important now than protecting the vital rail junction at Petersburg. Francis was sent to the front at Bermuda Hundred to help General P. G. T. Beauregard block the advance of Benjamin Butler's Army of the James. That's where Francis remained while Frederick Hooker and the rest of the Army of the Potomac marched down across the Pamunkey River, came east around Richmond, and besieged Petersburg. It's where Francis was when Martha gave birth. As the last of Ulysses S. Grant's troops were crossing the James River on June 16, 1864—focusing the entire eastern theater of the war on a siege that Robert E. Lee knew his army could not survive—Martha Poteet sat down and wrote to Francis for the first time since her delivery. He was in a trench outside Petersburg when he opened the long-awaited envelope. Inside he found three items. Two were letters. The other was a small piece of scratch paper, edged with ink outlining four fingers and a thumb. On it Martha had written, "the sise of the babys hand."[43]

By now Martha knew Francis was out of the guardhouse. If she was relieved that their letters could be private once again, she probably also felt resigned to the likelihood that Francis, away off in eastern Virginia, would not be returning, if he ever did, as long as the war lasted. Newly determined to make the best of their separation, as optimistic under the conditions as the start of summer could make her, and by now a relatively seasoned writer of letters, Martha set to work with an inventive pen.

In the two separate letters Francis pulled from that envelope, Martha had divided her goals as a writer. On one sheet of paper, she composed her words for precisely the kind of outside audience she had disdained during Francis's imprisonment. With no epistolary niceties and little pretense of addressing Francis at all, she wrote:

> Dear husband I cant get no person to cut my wheat the men says that they dont know what will be don with the wheat for there aint men to cut it and if I dont get Mine cut me and the children will be bound to suffer I would like for you to show this to your Capt and tell him if he pleases to let you come home a few days the first of July to take Care of it for me I hav about 8 bushels sowed and no person to cut a straw of it.

For the benefit of Francis's captain, Martha inscribed a litany of hardships: the mare has distemper, the cow gives no milk, "I haint got no money," and she saw no relief in sight "if this cruil war dont stop." She wrote it on the mostly unused half of a relatively good-quality letter folio Francis had sent her in March; on one side, Martha's narrative of wants wraps around her own home address, in Francis's handwriting, and a C.S.A. postmark. Perhaps she had no other paper at her disposal; perhaps she wanted Francis's captain to think so. It was doubtful that a man with a history of desertion would be getting a furlough at the height of summertime fighting, wheat or no wheat; but, Martha may have figured, it was worth a shot.[44]

The other letter Francis found in Martha's envelope was written on a leaf torn from a ruled ledger book. This one was for his eyes alone. It was not entirely free from worry, but mostly it described the causes for hope she would not want the captain to know about. Someone named Thomas was helping her get in a corn crop. "We hav this side the Creek to hoe My Neighbors says that if nothing hapens I will Make a heap of Corn." Flowing from topic to topic, Martha reached for those connections that, if no furlough came, would be all she and Francis had. She imagined them sharing a meal together: "The sweet potatoes is very pretty today and the irish potateos is the pretyest I ever seen I hav a mess today I wish y [paper torn] was hear to eat some with me I would be so glad I would not know how to behave." She wanted them to name their newest child together: "My ᵇᵃᵇʸ will be 4 weeks old satur^day Night she was born the 21 of May write to Me what to name her I had the best time I ever had and I hav bin the stoutest ever sens I haint lay in bed in day time in two Weeks today." She reported some news of a neighbor— "Dickson run away and got to Camp Vance"—and then, as if by accident reminded of Zebulon Vance, her governor, made the only comment about electoral politics she ever did in her letters: "I dont want you to vote for vance vote for Holden." This too was an expression of hope. William W. Holden was a fierce critic of the war, and he ran for governor of North Carolina in 1864 promising to sue for peace. In Holden's candidacy, Southern leaders saw the greatest internal threat the Confederate States had yet faced. Martha saw an end to the war.[45]

The third item Francis found with the two letters was the cutout of the baby's hand. Unmentioned in Martha's letter, this tiny artifact presumably required no explanation. People have outlined the hands and feet of their children for essentially all of human history. Handprints of juvenile prehistoric humans are abundant among cave paintings dating to the Upper Paleolithic period, some twenty thousand years ago. In the modern era, representations of tiny hands—in everything from paper to bronze—have served as mementoes after an infant's death.[46] This baby girl, though unnamed, was perfectly healthy, and Martha— having the easiest postpartum recovery she could recall, of at least nine so far—may have found this one easier to delight in. For Francis receiving it, and doubtless, too, for Martha creating it, the hand registered the movement of the Poteets' family life onto paper. Alvis died with the whole family gathered near him; this baby was not so born.

In sending her husband this particular representation of their daughter's body—not the outline of a foot, not a lock of any hair with

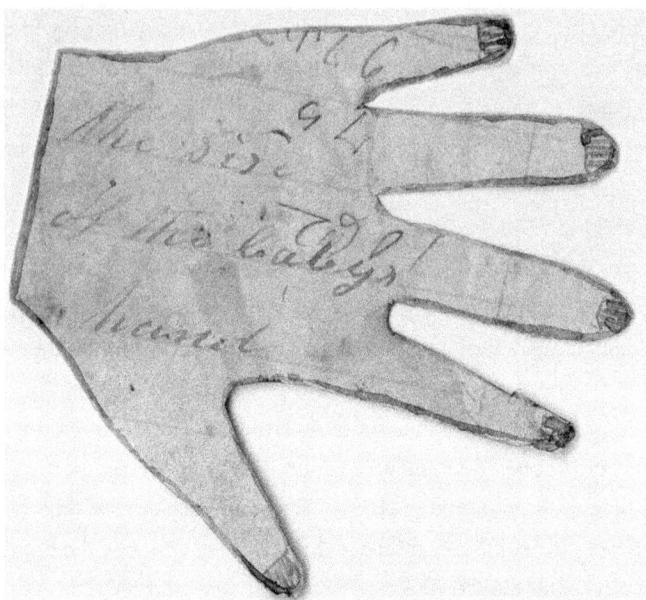

"the sise of the babys hand," enclosure in Martha Poteet to Francis
Marion Poteet, 16 June 1864

which she may have been born—Martha invoked one of Americans'
most cherished conceits about letter writing. Clasping a letter, one
clasped a beloved's hand. Martha and Francis both liked to begin their
letters with prayers that "these few lines may Reach your kind hands,"
as if it were hands in which kindness is invested.[47] Probably few if any
of the Poteet children could write to their father as Thomas Greene
Alford and Mary Creath could, and this baby certainly could not. On
her behalf, Martha created another sort of hand whose kindness Francis
could clasp.

By venturing such inventive turns of epistolary contact as this,
Martha seemed resolved to endure this paper chapter of their
marriage—to believe, and to help her husband believe, in the prospect of their family's ultimate renewal. The new baby was not Alvis,

and the paper representation of the hand was not the new baby. But Martha's three-part letter unmistakably pointed toward a future of possibility. Maybe Francis will get a furlough to cut wheat, maybe not. Maybe they will face months more of separation, but if they must, these letters will preserve them. Each one from Francis "dos me a heep of good," Martha said, and Martha, with a heap of good on her side, could preserve the family. "I cant work another year as hard as I hav this," she worried, but the envelope she mailed on June 16, despite the many signs of hardship among its contents, more than anything testified to her adeptness. If Francis did get a furlough, it would owe at least partly to Martha's thinking to write a separate letter for his captain's eyes. If he did not, he might at least take comfort from Martha's resourcefulness. He may never have viewed his wife as a woman of letters, but now he might picture her deftly orchestrating papers on her table—sheets from blank ledger books, old letters from Francis, the odds and ends of household business.[48]

The scrap of paper Martha chose to set open beneath her four-week-old daughter's hand, on which to trace her fingers, bore some penciled calculations in Martha's writing. On the front, it appears, she was subtracting 75 from 1062, borrowed a one for the ones column but then forgot to deduct it from the tens column, and was about to arrive at 997 when she abandoned it. On the back, she divided 777 by 2 and came up (correctly, rounding down) with 388. The large numbers that Confederate inflation pushed into daily life—"thread is 100 dollars," she had told Francis in the enclosed letter—made for a lot of math that couldn't be done in people's heads. Among poor mountain folk in western North Carolina, there could scarcely have been any ciphering done that was not the arithmetic of desperation. Whatever Martha had been accounting, she surely was figuring against the threat of zero. Of her worry she created this palimpsest: family renewal atop household management.[49]

When winter came to the Petersburg trenches, Francis was treading through mud that was "shoes mouth deep" and drawing "five littel Crackers for one day Rations." In a letter that today is torn and water damaged (and may have been when Martha received it), he confessed he had had it: "I dremp last night that you come down hear to see me I thought that I was the gladest fellow that ever was in the world I thought that I seen my littel sweete baby I thought it was the best Child that we had I am afraid that I never will git to [damaged] still live [damaged] hope and trust [damaged] will live to [damaged] the balance of them [damaged] I would Rather see you now than to have A bushel of gold."[50]

That final sentiment echoed something Martha had already said: "I would rather know that peace was Made than to own Mcdowell County." Not trivially, her wish was not to see each other again; it was for peace. Martha knew there would be no reunion without peace. "If you was to start home a foot you never would get home," she told Francis in February. "The Mc dowell Melisha is at home now and they are after run aways evry day." But signs of peace were proliferating. Even as she wrote this, her last surviving letter, a flag of truce had just gone up at the Petersburg lines. It allowed three Confederate commissioners to pass through Union forces and meet with Abraham Lincoln and William Seward aboard a steamboat at Hampton Roads, some sixty miles down the James River from Francis. Martha could not have known this, and Francis may have known it only as a rumor. But even up in the western mountains, she could sense the end was near. "The sesesh men dos hate to own that we are whiped," she wrote. "They wont talk about it if they can help it it dos me good to tell [it] to them but they hav to own it."[51] The feistiness Martha displayed here—it *does her good* to rub the Confederacy's fall in secessionist men's faces—may have always been a feature of her personality, only now peeking through because she had become a more confident writer. Perhaps the expressive practice of letters had helped it to emerge.

VIRTUAL TOUCHES OF the hand, little newspapers and travelogues, threads of social network, channels of tension and worry, marble-like monuments to the dead: letters could play many roles. At their best, they were like living things—their sentences and pages the seeds and shoots of thought and feeling. Their cultivation took time and patience.

Lydia Watkins was eminently patient. Her correspondence with her son, Benton Lewis, struggled to take root, but it would, after months of effort, bear fruit. It got off to a rough start when Benton, barely nineteen, ran off from the family farm in Cannon Township, outside Grand Rapids, to join a newly formed cavalry regiment, the Eighth Michigan—without telling his mother where he was going. By the time Lydia had a letter from him, he had ridden south across Ohio and sent his greetings from away "down south in dixy" (though he was as yet only in the Cincinnati suburbs of northern Kentucky). Riding off across Kentucky, Benton sent home his reports of new sights—"on our march from Covington to here I saw some of the handsomest farms I ever saw in my life"—and his nascent observations of slavery: "men in Kentucky dont think they have a farm unless they have from 1000 to 20000 acres & just as many darkies as they can get. we see about 10 darkies to ^{one} white person."[52]

His letters from home had a different character. Less inquisitive about Benton's impressions of the South than many mothers, who got to send off their sons with a kiss and extra socks, Lydia had to use letters to say what she may have said at Benton's departure, if he had given her the chance. "We were surprised to hear that you had inlisted," Lydia's first letter said, scolding yet reserved, "but I mistrusted you would when you left. I hope you considerd what you were doing when you took that step you could not have done it ignorantly."[53] For several months, Lydia filled her letters with nagging and reprimand. "I hope you will never allow yourself to be tempted to do wrong such as drinking swearing gambling," she wrote straight off, "or any of those vices so prevelent in the army." When Benton reported having a bad cough, she replied: "it is just as I expected I always told you you would not answer for a soldier." She told him his letters were not long enough: "you see I have filld this better than you did." She reminded him that he must prepare himself spiritually in case he "should get kill,d there among strangers." Her letters were stiff, addressed simply "Benton," and signed only "good by," or "good night, Lydia Watkins."[54]

Benton seemed a maladroit reader of Lydia's relatively muted tones of disapproval (he may have been reading her writing for the first time), and he showed little sign of trying to understand Lydia's perspective. When Benton, not very gracefully, asked her to send him twenty-five dollars—"in as large bills as you can get & send nothing but green backs"—Lydia sent back a detailed accounting of the low prices the family was getting for its crops of wool and wheat. Without explicitly acknowledging his request, she concluded coldly, "so you see how we are situated." Benton failed even to register that she was saying no. A few weeks later he wrote, "now ma I want know if sent that money too me that I sent for if you have I have not seen any thing of it yet."[55]

In the beginning, the lines of Benton and Lydia's correspondence frequently crossed with those of Benton's older sister, Helen, and her husband, Maynard. Benton's brother-in-law had enlisted in the same regiment. When Maynard wrote letters to Helen, she shared them with her mother. This alternate channel of communications bedeviled Benton's already strained relations with Lydia. Her letters, replete from the beginning with remonstrations, soon began throwing back at Benton the news she had of him from other sources. Helen said Maynard lent you money. Maynard said you haven't been mustered in yet (which would have delayed payment of an enlistment bounty). "Thier seems to be something conflicting in your and Maynards letters," Lydia wrote, in what Benton doubtless took for a euphemistic accusation that he was lying. "You say they wont muster you in till they see fit and he says you can be muster,d at any time you are a mind to." Benton's replies became consumed with debunking the hearsay his mother seemed to be taking as truth: "You said that Main said I went in the place of a drafted man but that is not so." "I have let him have more money than I have ever had from him." "You said in your letter that Maynard said that Mr Calkins & Baird agreed to pay me $50 out of their own pockets to make up their No so that they could get their offices this is as big a lie as I ever heard tell of."[56]

Their family life was complicated and may have been tense to begin with. Benton's father, from whom he inherited the surname Lewis, died when Benton was nine. Lydia married John Watkins a few years later. During a year's worth of letters, Benton never spoke of his stepfather, and Lydia referred to him only using the unreferenced pronoun "he." Against this backdrop it is hardly surprising that when a son, who had been in his mother's life longer than her husband, went off to war without telling her, the result might be months of passive aggression. Nor is it surprising that the members of a modest farming family like this one—Lydia had had only three months of formal schooling in her life—were not quite adept enough at writing letters to resolve hurt feelings through the mail. And it shows, painfully, in the mother and son's months of letters that do little except repetitively complain that the other isn't writing frequently enough and volley Maynard's hearsay back and forth.[57]

The tenor of their letters began to shift after Maynard left the regiment and returned home. The men were going into action, joining General Ambrose Burnside's Army of the Ohio for a march over the Cumberland Mountains toward Knoxville. "We intend to sweep Tenn. from one end to the other," Benton wrote. Initially Maynard's reappearance in Michigan seemed like a terrible turn of events for Benton: now his brother-in-law could slander him in person. In time, though, it became clear to the folks back home that Maynard did not intend to go back to his regiment—that he was a deserter. His credibility crumbled, and a door opened for Lydia and Benton to commiserate. Lydia wrote in the late winter of 1864, "I feel so provoked when I think what a fool Main has made of himself I do not know what to do his father wanted we should come over to thier house to see him but I shant go one step. . . . [Helen] said she had rather he would stay ten years than come home that way. . . . she tells him he has disgraced himself and all his folks by his meanness and I say so too."[58]

No doubt relieved that he could stop defending himself against his brother-in-law, Benton began to speak his mind, gently at first—"he is a little worse fellow than I ever thought he was"—and then more strenuously: "I have heard a great deal of blowing about Nate Gilman but [Maynard] is as much worse than Nate as Nate is worse the best of them do not let every one see this part of it." "You said in your letter that Main left the 13th [regiment] owing Crandle a few dollars if he was the only one he owed I will miss my guess I dare say he was owing a dozen in our Compan & tryed to borrow more just before he left." Sometimes Benton's anger was so pitched he quailed from letting his mother see it—but couldn't quite help himself. "I will now write you some in a little diffrent language," he wrote at one point, before handing the pen over to one of his immigrant comrades. The next lines, composed in a different hand, said in German what Benton evidently instructed the man to write: "I wish that he will be caught and justly beaten, hard. I think poorly to my sister."[59]

Benton and Lydia's correspondence became irregular during the winter of 1863–64. He was on the move and hard at work in Burnside's Knoxville Campaign, working to achieve Abraham Lincoln's long-cherished hope of liberating the Unionists in East Tennessee. Like many Northerners, he sent home little artifacts of his travels in the

South, including some pumpkin seeds for his mother's vegetable garden. Back in Michigan, spring was coming, and Lydia's mood brightened. Her renewed connection with her son—at least partly forged by their mutual exasperation with Maynard—colored warmer, more intimate letters. "Now ma," Benton reassured her, "you need not be afraid of my ever deserting I spoke in my other letter of going into the Navy but did not intend to Desert by any means if I go I shall get transfered." Seeing her son now, in heightened contrast with Maynard, as an upright defender of her nation's flag, Lydia began to write to Benton in the way one writes to an adult. She began to profess belief in what he was fighting for.[60]

Her once stiff letters now regularly began "Dear Son"—even, on one occasion, "To My Soldier Boy"—and she signed them "from your mother" and "I remain ever yours."[61] In writing she began to conjure her physical presence and invoke the intimacy of home. "I am seated by the north window in the square room," she would write at the beginnings of letters, as if cozying up for a quiet conversation: "I have just got the children off to Sabath school and I will now improve the time in writing to you." The surprise and hurt of Benton's enlistment may have faded with time. Now she contemplated his military service as part of something larger and invited Benton into those contemplations through her letters. In late April, she attended the funeral of another young man from their town: "you cannot think what feelings I had while listning to that sermon and seeing the parents mourning for thier boy he had been dead five weeks and they could not see him I could imagine my self in thier stead and think I did not know how soon I might have to pass through the same." But she was not debilitated by worry. By midsummer she was "busy taking care of the cherries"— harvesting them by the bushel and "drying all we can so we can have some to send to the soldiers."[62]

She had more to report from the farm that summer: "You remember sending me seven sweet pumpkin seeds last winter from

East Tennessee," she asked Benton. "I was very choice of them and planted them in the lower end of the garden five of them come up and the worms cut off two so I have three left and they look very nice and will soon blossom." This resembled thousands of little dispatches from the home front that soldiers received—ordinary updates on the height of the corn, the fattening hogs, the turns in the weather. But Lydia's pumpkin vines meant something special to her, and she could, through them, express to Benton more than many letters ever contained: "I have to look at them almost every day I think so much of them that I am afraid some thing will happen to them yet I shall feel very proud if I can raise but one because you sent them so far to me." In her horticultural attentions she reproduced the emotional balancing act she performed for Benton: fear that "some thing will happen"; devotion to a "dayly prayer to my Heavenly father that your life may be spared and that you may Come home a wiser and a better man"; hope in the pride she yet will feel in her genuine Tennessee pumpkins, her grown and "better" son.[63]

By the time the pumpkins were ripening, it was election season, and Lydia emerged in her letters as a bold partisan of the Union cause. She sent Benton copies of their local Republican newspaper, the Grand Rapids *Daily Eagle*. "I hope you will get it," she wrote of one issue in particular, "for thier is a great deal for them little Mac men"—that is, supporters of the Democratic challenger George McClellan—"to keep them *chawing* from now till Election if they know enough to sense it." No longer worried that Benton would succumb to army life's temptations of drinking, swearing, and gambling, she charged him to become a political organizer: "I want you to stick to them like a brother and try to convert them to the truth." She had recently bought and read a book on "the life and public doings of Abraham Lincoln" and intended to send it to Benton. Their little town of Cannon, Michigan, was "going for old Abe . . . head and ears," she predicted, and "if it did not I would move out of the town."[64]

Benton had been sick, and the army judged (as Lydia had from the beginning) that he would not answer for a soldier. They transferred him to the Invalid Corps and assigned him to garrison duty at Camp Douglas, a prisoner-of-war camp in Chicago. He was out of harm's way for good. He had more time to write, to cultivate what he and Lydia had planted. He had grown up—through the martial exploits that most boys believed would make them men, of course, but also through writing. Corresponding with Lydia had been such practice that, although his letters displayed lazy penmanship and sloping lines back in 1863, he now was offered a place as clerk to the camp surgeon. A tetchy teenager when he enlisted, by the war's end he was a good-humored young man capable of warm epistolary embraces with his mother.[65]

Exactly three years after Harriet Creath wrote her final letter to Owen while a battle raged in Tennessee, Lydia Watkins seated herself in the quiet back room of her Michigan farmhouse. It had been a good day. "We are having glorious news at preasant," Lydia wrote. "Last Tuesday night we could hear cannon in every direction from us and the good news still keeps coming and I hope it will come till we hear that Jeff is captured or killed." Northern cities and towns had erupted in jubilation after federal forces captured Richmond on April 3, 1865. African American troops led the march into the Confederate capital. The secessionist government had evacuated, and the city's black population, now all free, was in the streets celebrating. One old woman found among the men in blue uniforms the son who had been sold away from her twenty years before. Abraham Lincoln, who was visiting Ulysses S. Grant in the field, came into the city, entered the former executive mansion, and sat down at Jefferson Davis's desk. Back in Washington, D.C., a journalist reported, "the atmosphere was full of the intoxication of joy." Artillerymen fired off a nine hundred gun salute. Public buildings were illuminated that night; in front of the Patent Office, gas jets spelled out "UNION" in flaming letters. From Delaware to California, flags flew and bells rang.[66]

Down in Kinston, North Carolina, where William Tecumseh Sherman had recently passed by on his northward drive, Henry Thompson's and Hiram Blaisdell's regiments both were encamped. Henry wrote to Lucretia, "I have not received a letter in 10 days but it is not Your fault I expect. I hear that they have got old Jeff Davis & family that is the report here." Hiram wrote to Betsy, "O Bet wee hear good news every day Richmond and Petersberg is ours at last with 25,000 prisoners that is a good hall. . . . they say Lee is falling back on dans ville whare sheridan is. . . . Bet I had a real good dream last I am agoing to tell it to you for I believe it will come to pass I thought I was home with you and had a l good hug and kiss and that we ware agoing round a visiting the folks thare O Bet I ~~thought wee was~~ was a taking sollid comfort." Meanwhile, in upstate New York, Betsy was writing to Hiram, "the papers is ful of news Richmond and Peters berg is in our ~~possestion~~ poessecssion Fry day they fired guns in the Afternoon till Bed time." And Lydia Watkins, that quiet Thursday night, with the cannon salutes all done, remembered Benton's twenty-first birthday was coming up. She amiably began filling her page to her son: "Well Benton as they have all gone to bed I thought I would set up long enough to write to you so as to send it out to morrow and I hope you will get it on Monday as you are of age on that day."[67]

When Benton's reply came to her hand, it harbored a little inside expression of thanks for her birthday wishes: "I received yours of the 6th last Tuesday the next day after my birth-day, monday was celebrated here by fireing 100 guns. I told them that it was done on account of my being of age that day." Lydia would have appreciated this joke—invitation to a proud imagining that Union artillerymen were acting at her command when they saluted the tenth of April: the day she gave birth to Benton in 1844, and the day in 1865 that Camp Douglas received word of Robert E. Lee's surrender to Ulysses S. Grant at Appomattox Courthouse, Virginia.[68]

Conclusion: Futures

In any future great national trial, compared with the men of this, we shall
have as weak, and as strong; as silly and as wise; as bad and good. Let us,
therefore, study the incidents of this, as philosophy to learn wisdom from,
and none of them as wrongs to be avenged.

—Abraham Lincoln

D URING THE first winter after the war, a young woman in South
Carolina wrote to her aunt, a long-ago migrant to the West. They had
not corresponded in some time. Finding themselves on opposing sides,
they may have been unable, or felt it improper, to exchange letters prior
to the cessation of hostilities. Perhaps they simply had been too busy
writing to their male relations in the armies. Now, Miss E. Thomas,
having recently received a letter from Aunt Jane, took up her pen and
let loose the pent-up family news of an epoch. She began ordinarily
enough: "Dear Aunt ~~we~~ your kind letter came to hand in deu time we
were very glad to heare frome you once more it ~~is~~ ^{has} been a long time
since we had aleter frome you we as a Familey in usual health at this
time but"—and with this *but* the generic letter became particular—
"this war has prove a cruel war to us." Thus did Miss Thomas open
an unrelenting litany of the conflict's costs:

two of my Brothers are numbered with the dead that s what secession done Joseph was wounded at the battle of the wilderness
in ^{may of} 64 and died in June ~~of~~ his arm was broken amputated but

he never got home Brother Thaddeus was wounded the 25th of last March and died within 24 hours after he recieved the wound he fell in to the hands of ^{the} yankees) ~~till some time in~~ and we never heard any thing about him untill October last and then it was ~~w~~ ^{very} sad news yes our youngest Brother the babe ^{is} dead he was at home on furlow and left for camps on the 14th of march he only lived eleven days after he left home he was ~~t~~ wounded in the charge at ~~fourt~~ ^{fort} stedman near petersburg and his remains are ~~luy~~ laid in yankees soldiers luying ground one and half miles direct east of Petersburg I never expect to se the graves of my brothers I had three brothers the second one is at home he was wounded the 29 of march last and he still walks ~~wit~~ ^{wich} with cruches yet his wound is not heald up yet Franklin was shot through the thigh the letter that the yankees wrote us about Thaddeus said he was wounded in hip oh death has left a wide track behind it uncle Alexander Bradley lost his second and third sons in this war uncle Joseph Bradley two youngest sons was in camps but both back safe his ~~2d~~ second son is dead but he never was in ^{camps} uncle J M Bradley is dead I think he died more than a year a go he was liveing in Louisiana when he died his wife is ~~dead~~ ^{dead} and his daughter is married also his oldest ~~son~~ ^{son} his other two sons was in the war ^{and} I dont know ~~whe~~ ^{wether} they came through safe or not father and mother ~~and~~ ^{are} failing very fast ~~but~~ but the this war was enough to brake the harts of all honest ~~people~~ people

She tried to revert to more customary topics—crops, prices, and the weather—but this effort was short-lived. After a few newsy lines, she remembered more casualties to report: "Esquire Holland familey is all dead but ~~two~~ ^{four} girls and one boy Col Hollan familey is all de^ad but his wife." The letter's complete body count runs into the double digits and perhaps by a large margin, depending on the original size of these families that are "all dead."

Hardly destined to be a Daughter of the Confederacy, Miss Thomas seemed to blame the South's rashness for its sufferings. The many deaths in her family and her neighborhood are, to her, "what secession done," and secession did its damage impartially, to those who supported it and those who did not. Another branch of her family, Aunt Rebecca Bradley's, "was death on secssion but her sons had to fall ~~at~~ at the surine [shrine] of of secession." If such sacrifices were injustices in her eyes, she nevertheless beheld just deserts among the slaveholders who brought on the war: "the negros are all free and agrate many of thier owners have died frome the affect of loosing thier negros and I hope the ballance of them will soon go up the pump."

Having exercised her ire to Aunt Jane for three pages, Miss Thomas turned finally to the back of her letter folio and described one more casualty of war:

> when Brother Franklin came home he had gangreen in his wound and I was his nurs and I got gangreen in ^{my} fore finger on my left hand causein it to be amputated at the nuckel Joint I lost my finger on the 7th of Aug last it is well but tender yet I hateed secession bad enough before I lost my finger but now I cant look upon them with the least of allowance[1]

She expresses her most extreme emotion—the one that exceeds even the hate she felt for secession before—in ambiguous terms. Is it her own hands she "cant look upon . . . with the least of allowance"? Is it secessionists? Is it every single thing around her, as if grief and anger redden her whole field of vision? While she forms these words for Aunt Jane, her mutilated left hand must rest somewhere near the edge of her vision, as it will every time she writes a letter anymore. The loss of her finger, as precisely dated as the deaths of her brothers, is her own inescapable reminder of the war.

Returning veterans, even victorious Northerners, had such reminders in spades. Tens of thousands lost quite a bit more than half a finger. If the war made them writers it also damaged their writing bodies. More than twenty thousand men in the Union army alone survived an amputation. New York newspaper editor William Oland Bourne sponsored a left-handed penmanship contest for men who lost their right arms. Cash prizes were meant to motivate wounded veterans to adapt themselves for productive, independent postwar lives—"to fit themselves for lucrative and honorable positions" as clerks and professionals. The contest drew hundreds of entries and culminated in an 1866 public exhibition attended by Ulysses S. Grant. The reassuring spectacle of this contest, though, could not heal the many scars of war less visible than empty sleeves or even Miss Thomas's knuckle joint. The young man who claimed first prize for his left-handed essay, a former private from Pennsylvania named Franklin Durrah, did not take up any clerkships. He spent the next decade moving between hospitals and his mother's home until, in 1876, he was committed to the insane asylum where he died. No contests or therapies existed to alleviate what would come to be called posttraumatic stress disorder.[2]

The legacies of wartime letter writing are hard to know. Many literary histories of the United States concern themselves with differences between American culture before and after the Civil War. Edmund Wilson attributed to the war a "chastening of American prose style." Like most scholars, he looked for explanations in the works of the famous and highly literate. If writing in the later nineteenth century had become more "direct" and "economical" in its language, "firmer and quicker" in its pace, it was because men like Lincoln and Grant "had no time in which to waste words," Mark Twain popularized the colloquialisms of the West, and newspaper editors pressed for brevity. More attention should yet be paid to the influence of authors whose work was plucked from knapsacks on battlefields, pinned to doorposts for neighbors to read, and pored over in later years by curious children.[3]

The correspondences born of military service made ordinary Americans' inner lives dimly visible, for a time, through stale conventions and poor spelling. Afterwards, that emotional history became dimmer still. For most people, even the fortunate survivors, the end of the rebellion meant falling silent awhile, at least as far as written records show. Homecomings produced few letters. Unforgettable moments of long-anticipated reunion with loved ones in 1865 left fewer records than 1862's petty arguments over how long letters were, how frequently they came, and how much money was forthcoming. Whatever letters people did write amid the workaday rebuilding of their families' lives were less likely to be preserved than those obviously historic dispatches from the battlefront. The histories of the Creaths, Poteets, and Blaisdells, intimate and full in their wartime letters, return to being—as they are for ordinary people most of the time—the spare outlines of births, marriages, and deaths, occasionally punctuated by some surviving official document, a letter or two written during a temporary separation. There is little evidence of their scars, of the ways the Civil War reshaped their bodies and their minds, for good or for ill.

DANIEL REVIS GOT away from the North Carolina militia somehow and made it home, although he probably had to remain in hiding nearly two years. No evidence of his whereabouts exists from the time of his desertion in August 1863 until the summer of 1865. Probably soon after his return, Sarepta showed him where their first-born child, Slocum, was buried. He may or may not have met their second child, the one born during Daniel's first winter in the war, about whom his brother-in-law wrote (feigning to be Sarepta), "the baby is not well." If he ever was well again, he was not still living at the time of the 1870 census. But it could not have been long before Sarepta was pregnant again. Their third son, Daniel Jr., was born in the first year after Daniel Sr. came home, and in 1865 the couple welcomed a daughter,

Eliza. Little else can be deduced. It is unknown whether Daniel ever told Sarepta, or Clint, or anyone, what he had been witness to—what he, perhaps, had perpetrated—at the Shelton Laurel massacre.[4]

He rippled recorded history's surface again when, with the war over and the Confederate government defunct, he could emerge from the shadows safe from punishment or reprisal for his desertion. During a single week in August 1865, he made two important appearances in public: he came before a federal authority to swear the Oath of Allegiance to the United States, and he was admitted to the ministry of the Baptist Church. "Thear follows the Res lution by thes presents," the paper read, "you are there fore authorised to conduct the public worshop of god to expound his word and to do whatever is assigned to the christian ministry." Daniel Revis was now Clint Ward's preacher, and his sister Ellen's, and everyone's on the mountain—part of a lineage stretching back to the Mountain Page Baptist Church's establishment in 1787, when the first white settlers arrived in Henderson County. Sarepta makes no appearance in the spare postwar record, but she reportedly bore another eight children.[5]

Francis Poteet was paroled at Appomattox, made his way south and west to McDowell County, North Carolina, and at last touched the now-larger hand whose paper form he had held in a trench outside Petersburg. The baby was now almost a year old. Francis and Martha named her Eliza. Almost nothing is known about more than two decades of their postwar lives. At some point the family moved about twenty miles, into the next county. Apparently Francis carried on some carpentry and milling, and Martha kept a small store. By the late 1880s, one of their grown daughters, Celenia, was married and living far enough away that Francis and Martha occasionally sent her letters. These always were signed with both their names, but it was Martha, the more expressive correspondent during the war, who composed them.[6]

She was a little cheekier in these letters than she had been with Francis back in the 1860s. "I have writen a time or two and got no answer," she scolded Celenia, "Have you lost the use of your fingers or eye sight or what is the reason you dont ^write^ to me." In a letter written shortly after Christmas, she wrote about how "still and peacible" the holiday had been. During summer months she would report, "your pa has just come in from picking some black buryes." In troubled times, she reported family news unflinchingly. After a visit to Celenia's youngest sister, Isabella, Martha wrote: "she was very bad off with flux and is threatened with miscarriage she suffered dreadfull she sayes she nev er will get well I dont expect to see her any moor I havent heard from her sins I left there I wouldent left her but your pa was ent well when I left and I couldent stay any longer with her I looked for a letter yesterday but got none I expect she is dead with ^out^ she got better."[7]

Celenia evidently became custodian of Francis and Martha's Civil War letters. She bequeathed them to her own daughter, who also stewarded a story she had heard growing up about her grandparents' passing. In springtime 1902, Francis and Martha both were seventy-five years old and had been married almost fifty-five years. Martha fell down in her garden on the evening of April 2, struck dead of an apparent stroke. Francis laid himself down to sleep later that night and never woke up. His death was recorded as a heart attack about four o'clock in the morning on April 3.[8]

Nancy Clark never got to hear the "great many things" Thornton had said he wanted to tell her. By the time he sent that final letter, he had been in Andersonville long enough to see the prison's population of Union soldiers grow from a few thousand to well above twenty-five thousand. It was the fifth-largest human settlement in the Confederate States and the deadliest place a prisoner of war could end up. Men were crowded into the camp about one to every twenty square feet. They were provided with no shelter in any season of the year, received even less food than the famously hungry Confederate army, and could drink only from a single stream that also was their sewer. Desperate men tried tunneling their way out. The same week Thornton wrote his last letter home, there was a spike in the number of prisoners being diagnosed with "nostalgia" and "mental depression." One in every three men sent to Andersonville died there.[9]

Thornton Clark's Civil War was a drama in two acts, each almost exactly a year long—one in active service, one in prison. In September 1862 he took the train up to Indianapolis where he squinted through cinder-burned eyes at unprecedented throngs of men in Camp Morton, stripped naked for a medical exam, and formally joined Uncle Sam's army. In September 1863 he was captured at Chickamauga. During the intervening year he had visited churches and fought battles, been ill and healthy, endured the ups and downs and starts and stops of correspondence with Nancy. He carved her a brooch out of a Stones River mussel shell.

Of his second year at war, virtually nothing is known. September 1864 began with the fall of Atlanta, and officials at Andersonville, who expected the Yankees to come there soon and liberate prisoners, began evacuating. Trainload after trainload of gaunt men who had endured the horrific summer left the prison grounds under the impression they would be exchanged and returned to the North. (In fact, they were being transferred to other Confederate prisons farther from the front.) By early October, the prison population had fallen to barely six thousand, but Thornton Clark was still among them. His much thinner body had come again, at least briefly, beneath a doctor's eyes. In mid-September he was admitted to the prison hospital—a place almost no one left alive—and he died there on October 10, 1864, three days shy of the anniversary of his departure from Camp Morton, which by now had become a prisoner-of-war camp for Confederates. The cause of death was recorded as scurvy—another way of saying that Thornton, like thousands of Union men at Andersonville, starved to death. His body is believed to have been interred on the prison grounds, but its location is unmarked.[10]

Nancy filed for a widow's pension in September 1865, marking another complete year. The trial of Henry Wirz, the former commander of Andersonville, would have been in the papers at the time. (Wirz was the only Confederate official to be convicted of war crimes.) Did she read about it? As she gathered what she needed for the pension application—proof of Thornton's death, their nearly fifteen-year-old marriage certificate—did she also open up Thornton's letters and reread them? What did she do with her own? (Thornton had sent some back to her when she asked to see how her writing was improving. They have not survived.) Had she become a capable enough writer to feel confident doing it now? Did she ever write again? Her 1916 petition for a pension increase, when she was eighty-two years old, is written in a hand that doesn't match her signature. Did she have a pin put in the carved mussel shell as Thornton intended? What did she do with the woodworking tools he had wanted her to take out and oil?[11]

She never left Dale, Indiana. She raised her children and lived to see the youngest, Annie—who was not quite a year old when Thornton last saw her—marry a neighbor named Thomas Medcalf, also an infant when the war started. It was Thomas's father, Cyrus W. Medcalf, who had recruited Thornton in the Forty-Second Indiana, was his captain in Company B, and once lent him five dollars to send home to Nancy. Annie and Thomas had three sons grow up and join the armed forces during World War I. A 1917 feature in the *Dale Reporter* highlighted this "patriotic family"—the three young servicemen whose grandfathers had fought together in the Civil War. A year later, not long after the armistice, the same newspaper carried a death notice for Nancy Clark, "a well known and highly respected pioneer citizen." Her obituary ran alongside a "soldier letter" from a Hoosier private writing home from aboard ship on the Atlantic.[12]

THE BARE OUTLINE of individuals' lives may be reconstructed, but, lacking their written words, we come to understand them less for what they felt and thought than for where they fit in the bigger structures and narratives we can document—to understand them as a class. Some of the people featured in this book became middle class after the war; most became what was called working class. They were not likely to be known for what they wrote. Many better-educated veterans went on to write histories of their regiments and memoirs of their own tours of duty; few men of Daniel Revis's or Hiram Blaisdell's station did.[13]

Fred Hooker, childless and unmarried, foresaw a future as a yeoman farmer back in Connecticut. A great deal of what he laboriously scratched out to his mother, in barely legible cursive and errant block letters, concerned a piece of land he wanted to buy and live on when he came home. "Has old conner Bought the Whitman Land down the Bank or is it sold Yet," he asked his mother in one of the first letters he wrote himself; "Wright & let me know For i am anxious to know iF i ever Live to come home I dont mean to Live in Farmington i mean to By some Place out Back some where where i can keep FowLes & so Forth." So strong was this dream that he would revert to it nearly every time chickens crossed his mind. "How does the chickens get along," he asked his mother later; "Are you going to raise some chickens this sumer or not i think it would Be a good pLan has the soLL whitman Farm Been sold Yet or the Land down the Bank Yet."[14]

Fred survived the Army of the Potomac's brutal summer of 1864 only to die of disease that fall.[15] He did not know that the placid agrarian future he anticipated would not be a reality for most people like him. The majority of farming families who endured the Civil War remained farmers only a generation or two more, if that. The meteoric industrial growth that the Union war effort accelerated was already apparent in the northern states before the war. The workforce shifted from agriculture to manufacturing; population shifted from rural areas to cities. Many farmers would become the working class of what we now call the Rust Belt. Hiram Blaisdell returned safely from the war, to Betsy's infinite relief, and at thirty-seven years of age she bore their only surviving child, Willis, who became a farmer, as his parents had been. Betsy and Hiram lived to see the dawn of the twentieth century and the arrival of a grandchild, Clayton. They may or may not have glimpsed signs of the much-altered world this new century was ushering in. Clayton went to work as a machinist for Continental Can Company in Syracuse.[16]

Improved literacy would not by itself have steered many people toward particular social and economic destinies—farming or factory work or the first steps toward white-collar jobs. With demand for its rifles falling off after the war, the firm of E. Remington & Sons directed its competency in precision metal parts toward a new product: the typewriter. The move was appealingly symbolic of a peacetime society replete with prolific writers—but working-class families were not buying these hundred-dollar machines. The effects wartime letter writing is likeliest to have had on their later lives are nearly impossible to gauge. Did they and their families write letters more often than they otherwise would have? Were they more avid readers? Even if reading and writing faded from their daily lives, had four years of epistolary practice made them more apt to mentally sort the world around them into pleasantries and "particulars"? To repeat phrases of assurance and comfort? To be careful of words that might upset or worry their spouses? To meditate on their own feelings in relation to another's?[17]

If war letters paved anyone's way toward a literate future, it would be soldiers' daughters most of all—the young women who became writers a little sooner and faster because of this war. Alice Clark was almost ten years old when Thornton wrote her a letter detailing some of the features of good writing. She was just shy of her nineteenth birthday when she married a carpenter named Albert F. Brown. (Maybe Thornton's tools, if Nancy indeed kept them oiled and shiny, were a kind of dowry.) By the time her four children were mostly grown, Alice had become a family archivist. In 1907 she received a letter from David C. Smith, treasurer of Indiana's Andersonville Monument

Commission. An error on a muster roll cast some doubt on whether Thornton Clark had died and was buried at Andersonville prison, and Alice was asked if she could produce evidence to settle the matter. She went at this task with a passion. The first great wave of Civil War monument building was past, but the fiftieth anniversary of the conflict was approaching, and Alice was apparently intent upon ensuring that her father would be included.[18]

She apparently had become the de facto bookkeeper of her husband's business, which by then had grown into A. F. Brown & Sons Lumber. On company receipt blanks, Alice copied over by hand several official communications between her mother and the Bureau of Pensions, apparently to preserve the records she was forwarding to the monument commission. She also dispatched an inquiry to John Scammahorn, a son of the family with whom Nancy Clark had migrated from Ohio to Indiana in the 1840s. John now lived in Nebraska, but he had served in the Forty-Second Indiana with Thornton. Alice must have known he had been a prisoner of war, too. Detective-like, she asked him for information about Thornton's time at Andersonville. (His reply detailed a lengthy history in Confederate prisons, but none of them was Andersonville. In conclusion, John said, he "did not know your Father in prison he was in some other prison.") He wanted to be remembered to the folks back in Indiana, "especialy your mother." To Nancy Clark he wished to convey something particular: "ask her if she remember the first night we spent on the old home when we moved from Ohio to us those were shining times." Alice's campaign was successful. About four months before the official dedication of Indiana's monument at Andersonville, David Smith wrote her again to say that her father would be listed among those he called "Indiana's noble dead." Her ability to write served her in a pinch to speak up for her family's place in history.[19]

Other young women relied on their literacy even more. Hellen Alford, the rising scribe of her large southern Indiana family, would become after the war one of its most literate members. All three of her older brothers were dead by the end of 1862, when Hellen was still thirteen years old. Along with her surviving siblings, George and little Thomas Green, Hellen persuaded their father to alter the vision of the future he had held until the war brutally reshaped their family. Rather than shares of Franklin Alford's landholdings in and around Alfordsville, the surviving younger children wanted education. The family left its homestead in the town that bore its name and moved fifty miles north to Bloomington, home of Indiana University, which began admitting women in 1867. Hellen enrolled and graduated in 1871. She became a teacher.[20]

Kate Creath became a teacher, too. The writing lessons she gave her younger sister Mary in their cold Iowa house in 1862 were only the first of those she would give to many children. After Owen's death at Shiloh, Harriet moved the family back to Mount Sterling, Ohio—her birthplace, where her father still lived. She had wanted to do this from the start. She raised the idea about a month after Owen enlisted, when he was only as far away as Jefferson City, Missouri. Owen said no. He had been born and raised in Ohio, too, but—probably mindful of the work it had taken to move to a distant town and establish his business there, perhaps considering their new home a symbol of his own status as an independent head of household—he was reluctant to see their Iowa home fall dormant. He wrote back:

Harriet I dont want you to gow to Ohio and leave your home for Harriet you now how our place was abused when we was away from it and I do think you had better stay at home and take care of our home and Harriet if I never get back it will be for you to do what ever you think best to do but Harriet it will be time enough to think of this when it happens. but Harriet I still feel like I will get home safe at sometime and Harriet I think if I do and can rais one hundred dollars we will gow to Ohio on a visit

for I sould like to have you to see your father and your sisters I
have been thinking vary strong of this and think we will gow and
visit our friends if posable when I get home.

During the two months to come, as Owen made extra money black-
smithing in camp and foresaw earning a regimental farrier's salary, he
probably indulged many such visions of a postwar future: a roast
chicken dinner on the Fourth of July in 1862, and then, once enough
money was saved, a family vacation, a reunion for Harriet with her
father and sisters. After Owen died, with his workshop permanently
shuttered and five children to support, it was time for Harriet, as Owen
had predicted, "to do what ever you think best to do." She evidently
wasted little time.[21]

It is not known exactly how Harriet and the children made the
trip, or when, or where she got the cash, but they were in Madison
County, Ohio, by the fall of 1863, when Harriet filed for a widow's
pension. Her father and older sister, Urana, went with her to the
courthouse and served as witnesses. By the following spring she had
been approved for a pension of eight dollars per month, payable from
the day Owen died almost a year before. Harriet's application documented only four minor children dependent on her support. The
baby Lizzie, whom Owen had never met—"most delicate babe we
ever had," as Harriet wrote on the morning of Shiloh—had not
survived.[22]

What would have been Harriet and Owen's twentieth wedding anniversary passed in December 1864, and the next fall their oldest child
enrolled at Mount Sterling High School. Shortly after Kate graduated,
she took her first teaching position in a school not far outside Mount
Sterling, in Pleasant Township. Over the next several years, until she
married at age twenty-six, she taught in schools across two counties.
On occasion, she used free moments in her schoolroom to write home
to her mother. Letter writing had become effortless for Kate, compared

with that first wartime winter when she turned ten—though this did not make her a zealot for literacy education. If her devotions to teaching her younger sister to write had been tempered by a little disgruntlement when Mary seemed to show her up, her generosity toward her students likewise had its limits. Sitting down in the schoolhouse one morning and confiding to Harriet about her homesickness, Kate wrote, "I am almost tempted to pronounce school teaching a humbug especialy such a school a I have. there is nobody comes but a pack of the very lowest class of pᵉople." Late one January day, she reported, "I have a class of five scholars that I kept in for disobeying my rules. They think it right funny but I think they will change their minds for I intend to keep them till just time to get home by dark, and then if they don't do better I will give them a little oil of some kind." Then she wrapped up her letter, saying "I guess I will close as my class are getting very restless."[23]

For the most part, Kate's letters home weren't about her students at all. They resembled the kinds of conversations she would have with her mother. When Aunt Urana invited her to visit for a week around the Fourth of July, Kate wrote home: "They are going to have a big picnic there and they are expecting to have a nice time, but I am not prepared to go, if I go I shall want a new white dress a new hat and a lace collar and I have not either."[24]

If the war could become as distant a recollection for eighteen-year-old Kate as it seemed on that summer day, she might be the happier for it. But the family plainly did not leave Owen's memory in Iowa. Mary, the slightly younger sister to whom Owen had said, "I think you Can write as good as Kate," named her second son after her father. Owen Lohr lived until 1966. His brother Albert got a degree in engineering at the Ohio State University and had a daughter, Ellen, who went to Kent State, became director of Christian education at several churches, got married, and worked for twenty-six years at a hospital. It was she who stewarded her great-grandparents' Civil War letters. She donated them to the Ohio Historical Society in 1995 and died, aged ninety-two years, while this book was being written.[25]

MARY CATHERINE KENDRICK was called upon to use her letter-writing abilities sooner than she probably expected after her husband returned home. It had been on cold winter nights in the first year of the war that Larkin composed his sweeping invocations of their bond across space: "Oh yes I am some times made To wander as the western Horizon Slides ore the Western hill toward my much loved home when I too can Sail towords you and often ask the silver moon as It So Brillently Shines If It too shines upon my loved ones at home and I often look forward to the end my year." One year after that, he again wrote to Catherine on a cold night—"the whole Earth is covered with snow it comminced falling Tuesday night and continued until last night which was some twenty four or five hours it fell as fast as I ever saw"—but this time his view was from a hospital window.[26]

He had been shot on picket duty along the Rappahannock River in the weeks following the Battle of Fredericksburg. Catherine traveled to Richmond to find him. As winter turned to spring, instead of exchanging letters with each other, they sat together reading letters addressed to both of them from their siblings and parents back in Cleveland County, North Carolina. The couple was briefly separated again when Catherine had to return home and Larkin awaited a furlough or discharge. He wrote few letters during this separation, owing, as he put it, to "the los of my rite arm." In the late summer of 1863 he went before a medical examining board in Raleigh and before long was home to stay. Perhaps facing harassment by home guards late in the war, he secured additional written proof of his exemption from field service. His empty sleeve would have seemed proof enough, but for some reason nonetheless Larkin went into Shelby, the county seat, to get a small scrap of paper signed by two doctors.[27]

No letters document what Larkin Kendrick did during the final months of the war or the first years after. But in the early 1870s, Mary Catherine Kendrick produced a flurry of correspondence. As with Alice Clark Brown, she now had a pressing need to apply the writing skills she had practiced during the war. Catherine was not trying to get her husband on any monuments. She was trying to find out where he had gone.

At first to Tennessee—she knew that. But from there, where? He sent a letter in June 1872 from Memphis. It was written in a strange and shaky penmanship that may have reflected Larkin's adjustments to his disability, or that he asked someone else to write for him.

> By the time this comes to hand i will be out of the united Sates i cannot beare the thought of being brought be fore a court and do that which i swore that i woLd not Do i no that pople will thinck that i Dont care fore My famaly but I will then beter than theat fore I will come to than cathron Dont greave fore me for i think that am Doing just right to Leave the united Sates fore the presant i think that it woLde not greave us enoch fore Me to Leave as it fore me to go to prison i bring My short Leter to a close for the presant asking you to forgive Me Dont right to me any more untell you heare from me[28]

Catherine first sent an inquiry to an aunt in Waynesville, up in the mountains on the way to Tennessee. Larkin had indeed gone through there, Aunt Hettie replied. He said he was on his way to join her brother in Texas, but there was no sign he ever got there. "He promised us when he left here that he would be sure to write back to us," Aunt Hettie said, "but has never done it." Years passed and there continued to be no letters from Larkin, but Catherine persisted. In 1874 she wrote to another cousin up in Haywood County—apparently not for the first time. Cousin Ruth wrote back, "He left here as we have told you to go to Tennessee and perhaps to Texas, but he never went to Texas." The letter went on in much the same way women wrote letters of condolence to Civil War widows: "It is sad indeed to be deprived of a tender companion the way in which you have been deprived of yours. But remember, dear cousin, that is the dealings of an allwise Providence, and I trust He will be your support in this heart-rending affliction. Trust in Him. Rely upon His faithful promises and He will support you. May His guardian angels ever be around you." Another Haywood County relation was more direct in urging Catherine to accept what the whole extended family apparently now believed: "You desired to know what I think about him. I hope he is all right somewhere. But, I really think he is dead." Larkin had borrowed a pistol and a pair of boots, John explained, and insisted he would send back the money to pay for them as soon as he could. That would have been two years ago. "Confident he is an honest man," he wrote, "this impresses the conviction on my mind that he is dead."[29]

The evidence is circumstantial but persuasive: Larkin Kendrick had been riding with the Ku Klux Klan. Cleveland County was, during the war, "one of the strongest secession counties in the state," and during Reconstruction it saw one of the fiercest backlashes. Klan membership there has been estimated as high as one thousand men, at a time when the total number of men, women, and children in the county was fewer than thirteen thousand. One observer said, "I think nine-tenths of the Democrats in that county are Ku Klux." And the Cleveland County Klan was as virulent as any such group across the South. "There is scarcely a night," a local official reported, "but that some person is whipped or scourged by the Ku Klux." Involvement in the Klan incurred little scorn from the people of the county. A friendly letter to Larkin and Mary Catherine in 1868, from Catherine's sister and her husband, included the remark, "The Kau Kauk Klan has done more good than any thing else that ever hapend."[30]

Congress passed the Second Enforcement Act in 1871, empowering federal troops to apprehend Klan members and federal courts to prosecute them. Cleveland County was among the first places to which President Grant dispatched U.S. marshals and army units. A detachment came to Shelby in April; hundreds of men were apprehended and tried. Thus did Larkin Kendrick calculate it would be better for him to leave the state, and then the country, and forever his family, than to stay, face trial, and assuredly go to prison. It was from this—one of the last major federal efforts to secure African Americans' civil rights until the 1960s—that Larkin Kendrick fled.

Federal suppression of the Klan was more or less successful, for the time—it did away with Larkin Kendrick—but it certainly did not put an end to lynching, and the Klan would resurge decades later. By then, though white supremacists in the South were still waging rebellion against the Constitution, the wider world had changed dramatically. The United States, parts of it at least, had become a place of automobiles, airplanes, skyscrapers, and moving pictures. A city dweller could observe the fiftieth anniversary of Appomattox by going to see the blockbuster movie playing in theaters that month—a three-hour melodrama about the Civil War and Reconstruction called *The Birth of a Nation*. It was a reactionary film, steeped in nostalgia for the tyrannical social order the Civil War had been fought to destroy. It deplored the freedom of southern blacks and glorified the Ku Klux Klan's reign of terror over them. The president of the United States had it screened in the White House.

The film was based on a novel called *The Clansman*, written by a southerner named Thomas Dixon, who was born in Shelby, North Carolina, during the Civil War. He was the nephew of a Confederate colonel who became the leader of the Cleveland County Ku Klux Klan. As a boy of six, young Thomas watched a 1500-man band of vigilantes, led by his uncle, lynch a black man for allegedly raping a white woman. They hanged him in the Shelby town square and riddled him with bullets. Thomas remembered that scene, recreated it, and helped bring it before the eyes of millions of white Americans who had not endured the Civil War, who were all too ready to forget its meaning and purpose, to believe someone else's freedom threatened their own, to discard black lives. Very likely, one of the masked riders young Thomas Dixon had watched on that night in 1870—in a white robe with one empty sleeve—was Larkin Kendrick.[31]

In that sense, he had not disappeared. He never has. Surprising residues of our history well up in the turgid currents of American culture—what we write and read, what we remember, what we suffer and stand up for. To find that Larkin Kendrick, beneath the vestments of one of the most virulent hatreds ever known, was a man who could gaze skyward and meditate on his love for his wife, "as costant as the Wheales of time," may seem discordant, but it should not be very surprising. Tenderness and viciousness may abide in the same soul and be parceled out unequally, for terrible reasons. Larkin could, on occasion, rise to the challenge letter writing presents us: with nerves abuzz from brain to hand, form words that would alight in another human mind; reach across what, from our usual, earth-bound perspective, looks like distance, and forge bonds with people united beneath the same sky. He could not or would not see that, when the sun "was a setting behin the western Horising, it was shedding its brite Rays" on black families, too, or he did not care that it was. Probably no amount of letter writing would have changed this about him. No amount of reading and studying his Civil War letters will reveal the origin of intolerance, or a recipe for its destruction. But we ought not look away. Abraham Lincoln said on the Gettysburg battlefield, "It is for us the living, rather, to be dedicated here to the unfinished work which they who fought here have thus far so nobly advanced." Here among the

Civil War's more distant lineage, that unfinished work includes taking seriously the words, however apparently inarticulate, of distant people—distant in time or space, skin color or creed, education or accent. It includes listening to "every American," as a later president said, "whose story is not yet written."[32]

Appendix: Biographies

Hellen Alford (b. 1849) was the only girl among six siblings whose grandfather settled the town of Alfordsville, Indiana. Her three older brothers, Warren, Wayne, and Lafayette, all enlisted in Union regiments. All three were dead by the end of 1862.

Betsy Eldridge Blaisdell (b. 1833) and Hiram Blaisdell (b. 1835) lived in Martville in Cayuga County, New York. They lost a child shortly before Hiram joined (just ahead of being drafted into) the Third New York Artillery in September 1864. He served primarily in North Carolina.

Thornton Clark (b. 1826) and Nancy Phipps Clark (b. 1833) were married in 1851. They lived in the town of Dale in Spencer County, Indiana, and had four children. Thornton was a farmer and a carpenter. He enlisted in the Forty-Second Indiana Infantry in August 1862, and his army service took him to Camp Joe Reynolds (later Camp Morton) in Indianapolis; Louisville, Kentucky; and locations in Tennessee, Alabama, and Georgia.

Owen Creath (b. 1826) and Harriet Loofbourrow Creath (b. 1827) were married in 1844 in Ohio. They migrated to Washington, Iowa, where Owen worked as a blacksmith. He enlisted in the Thirteenth Iowa Infantry in October 1861 and served in Missouri and Tennessee. Their two oldest children were Sarah Catherine (whom they called Kate) and Mary Jane, who were nine and seven at the beginning of the war.

Rebecca Pitchford Davis (b. 1812) lived in Warren County, North Carolina, in the Piedmont near the Virginia border. Four of her sons fought in the Confederate army. Burwell and George survived the war; Weldon and Tom did not.

Frederick Hooker (b. 1844) enrolled in the Second Connecticut Heavy Artillery in late 1863 and was mustered in early in 1864. His mother, Jeannette Sweet Hooker (b. 1808), married Frederick's father, James Hooker, in 1840, following the death of her first husband. James Hooker died when Frederick was an infant. Jeannette lived in Farmington, Connecticut. Fred was stationed at Fort Ellsworth in Virginia and then joined the Army of the Potomac during Grant's Overland Campaign. He was largely illiterate at the start of his enlistment but soon learned to write his own letters.

Larkin Kendrick (b. 1837) and Mary Catherine Putnam Kendrick (b. 1837) were married in 1855. They lived in Cleveland County, North Carolina. He joined the Thirty-Fourth North Carolina Infantry in September 1861. One of their children died while Larkin was hospitalized after being shot in the arm in Virginia in 1862. He was discharged from duty and returned home sometime in late 1863.

Sarepta Ward Revis (b. 1844) married Daniel Webster Revis (b. 1835) in January 1861. They lived on Corbin Mountain in Henderson County, North Carolina. After Daniel enlisted in the Sixty-Fourth North Carolina Infantry, Sarepta resided with her brother, Hezekiah C. "Clint" Ward, and Clint's wife, Ellen Revis Ward, who was also Daniel's sister. Clint wrote most letters for Sarepta, who was apparently illiterate. Two of the couple's children died during Daniel's army service, which was concentrated in western North Carolina and eastern Tennessee. He deserted in the summer of 1863.

Henry J. H. Thompson (b. 1832) was a musician in the Fifteenth Connecticut Infantry. He enlisted in August 1862 and served on the Washington defenses and in Virginia and North Carolina. His wife, Lucretia, remained at their home in Fair Haven, Connecticut. Henry passed through New York City en route home from the war on July 4, 1865 and their only child was born on July 4, 1866.

Martha Warrick (b. ca. 1830s) and Thomas Warrick (b. ca. 1833) lived in Coosa County, Alabama. Thomas served in the Thirty-Fourth Alabama Infantry, primarily in Alabama, Tennessee, and Georgia. Both relied on amanuenses to write many of their letters, but Martha sometimes wrote by herself.

Notes

Introduction

1. Quoted as reproduced in Henry S. Burrage, *Brown University in the Civil War: A Memorial* (Providence, RI: Providence Press Co., 1868), 106–107.

2. Michael E. Ruane, "Civil War Soldier's Heartbreaking Farewell Letter Was Written before Death at Bull Run," *Washington Post*, 20 July 2011.

3. Larkin Kendrick to Mary Catherine Kendrick, 20 Jan. 1862, PC.1921, Larkin S. Kendrick Papers, State Archives of North Carolina, Raleigh. Stephen Berry also juxtaposed a poor North Carolinian's letter with Sullivan Ballou's in his foreword to Michael Ellis's *North Carolina English, 1861–1865: A Guide and Glossary* (Knoxville: University of Tennessee Press, 2013), as I discovered after writing this introduction.

4. Edmund Wilson, *Patriotic Gore: Studies in the Literature of the American Civil War* (New York: Oxford University Press, 1962), xi; Daniel Aaron, *The Unwritten War: American Writers and the Civil War* (New York: Random House, 1973); Walt Whitman, "Specimen Days," in *Complete Poetry and Collected Prose*, ed. Justin Kaplan (New York: Library of America, 1982), 779. For examples of the scholarly study of Civil War literature, see esp. Coleman Hutchison, ed., *A History of American Civil War Literature* (New York: Cambridge University Press, 2015), and Timothy Sweet, ed., *Literary Cultures of the Civil War* (Athens: University of Georgia Press, 2016).

5. Mary Livermore, *My Story of the War: A Woman's Narrative of Four Years Personal Experience* (Hartford, CT: A. D. Worthington and Co., 1890), 141. The calculations based on the New York regiment are Gary Gallagher's in *The Union War* (Cambridge, MA: Harvard University Press, 2011), 57–58.

6. David M. Henkin, *The Postal Age: The Emergence of Modern Communications in Nineteenth-Century America* (Chicago: University of Chicago Press, 2006), 3, 31. For studies of Civil War letter writing generally, see Henkin, 137–147; Rebecca Weir, "'An Oblique Place': Letters in the Civil War," in *The Edinburgh Companion to Nineteenth-Century American Letters and Letter-Writing*, ed. Celeste-Marie Bernier, Judie Newman, and Matthew Pethers (Edinburgh: Edinburgh University Press, 2016); and L. Bao Bui, "'I Feel Impelled to Write': Male Intimacy, Epistolary Privacy, and the Culture of Letter Writing during the American Civil War" (Ph.D. diss., University of Illinois at Urbana-Champaign, 2016).

7. For vivid accounts of the physical act of letter writing by ordinary Americans in the antebellum and Civil War eras, see Martha Hodes, *The Sea Captain's Wife: A True Story of Love, Race, and War in the Nineteenth Century* (New York: Norton, 2006), 22–34, and Theresa Strouth Gaul, introduction to *To Marry an Indian: The Marriage of Harriet Gold and Elias Boudinot in Letters, 1823–1839* (Chapel Hill: University of North Carolina Press, 2005), 23–48.

8. Grant Taylor to Malinda Taylor, 22 Sept. 1862, and Malinda Taylor to Grant Taylor, 29 Sept. 1862, in *This Cruel War: The Civil War Letters of Grant and Malinda Taylor, 1862–1865*, ed. Ann K. Blomquist and Robert A. Taylor (Macon, GA: Mercer University Press, 2000), 95, 98.

9. Harvey Reid, *Uncommon Soldiers: Harvey Reid and the 22nd Wisconsin March with Sherman*, ed. Frank L. Byrne (Knoxville: University of Tennessee Press, 2001), xv. When Stephen Ambrose edited a Union soldier's letters, he went further: to "avoid repetition," he omitted the soldier's many "references to his health" as well as "personal or family matters of little interest to the general reader." James K. Newton, *A Wisconsin Boy in Dixie: Civil War Letters of James K. Newton*, ed. Stephen A. Ambrose (Madison: University of Wisconsin Press, 1961), v.

10. Mary Franklin to C. J. Brandon, 9 Apr. 1865, Confederate Memorial Literary Society Collection, under the management of the Virginia Historical Society, Richmond; William A. Neal, from Camp Velasco, to his wife in Navarro County, TX, 18 July 1864, Civil War Miscellany, box 2C447, Briscoe Center for American History, University of Texas at Austin; Margret Box and Frances Box to

William Box, 20 May 1862, in Box Family Papers, 1857–1864, South Caroliniana Library, University of South Carolina, Columbia, SC. On letter writing as "a fulfillment of form," see William Merrill Decker, *Epistolary Practices: Letter Writing in America before Telecommunications* (Chapel Hill: University of North Carolina Press, 1998), 26, as well as Henkin, *Postal Age*, 111–117.

11. Important studies of epistolary culture, mainly in other contexts and time periods, include Konstantin Dierks, *In My Power: Letter Writing and Communications in Early America* (Philadelphia: University of Pennsylvania Press, 2009); Susan E. Whyman, *The Pen and the People: English Letter Writers, 1660–1880* (New York: Oxford University Press, 2009); Lindsay O'Neill, *The Opened Letter: Networking in the Early Modern British World* (Philadelphia: University of Pennsylvania Press, 2014); and Eve Tavor Bannet, *Empire of Letters: Letter Manuals and Transatlantic Correspondence, 1680–1820* (New York: Cambridge University Press, 2005). For studies of highly literate writers' letters in the nineteenth-century United States, see Decker, *Epistolary Practices*; Elizabeth Hewitt, *Correspondence and American Literature, 1770–1865* (Cambridge: Cambridge University Press, 2004); Theresa Strouth Gaul and Sharon Harris, eds., *Letters and Cultural Transformations in the United States, 1760–1860* (Burlington, VT: Ashgate, 2009); and Ronald J. Zboray, *A Fictive People: Antebellum Economic Development and the American Reading Public* (New York: Oxford University Press, 1993), 110–121. Books focused, like the present one, on relative outsiders or newcomers to epistolary culture include David Gerber, *Authors of Their Lives: The Personal Correspondence of British Immigrants to North America in the Nineteenth Century* (New York: New York University Press, 2006), and Martyn Lyons, *The Writing Culture of Ordinary People in Europe, c. 1860–1920* (New York: Cambridge University Press, 2013).

12. In this respect, ordinary Civil War letters resemble folk art and working-class literature. "Working-class art," writes a leading scholar of the subject, "like other elements of working-class life, is highly traditional . . . , often built around repeated elements—refrains, formulas, and commonly accepted assumptions about characters." Paul Lauter, "Working-Class Women's Literature: An Introduction to Study" (1980); repr., *Radical Teacher* 100 (Fall 2014): 62–76, quotation on 64.

13. See, among others, Bell Irvin Wiley, *The Life of Johnny Reb: The Common Soldier of the Confederacy* (1943; repr., Baton Rouge: Louisiana State University Press, 2008), and *The Life of Billy Yank: The Common Soldier of the Union* (1952;

repr., Baton Rouge: Louisiana State University Press, 2008); Reid Mitchell, *Civil War Soldiers: Their Expectations and Their Experiences* (New York: Simon & Schuster, 1988); James McPherson, *For Cause and Comrades: Why Men Fought in the Civil War* (New York: Oxford University Press, 1997); and Chandra Manning, *What This Cruel War Was Over: Soldiers, Slavery, and the Civil War* (New York: Alfred A. Knopf, 2007).

14. On methodological problems in the use of Civil War soldiers' letters, see Jason Phillips, "Battling Stereotypes: A Taxonomy of Common Soldiers in Civil War History," *History Compass* 6 (2008): 1407–1425; Michael Barton, "Studying Civil War Soldiers: The State of the Art and Science," Soldier Studies, Spring 2009, http://www.soldierstudies.org/index.php?action=barton; Ian Delahanty, "Soldiers' Letters and Diaries," Essential Civil War Curriculum (Virginia Center for Civil War Studies), June 2015, http://www.essentialcivilwarcurriculum.com /soldiers-diaries-and-letters.html; Thomas E. Rodgers, "Civil War Letters as Historical Sources," *Indiana Magazine of History* 93 (1997): 105–110; and John E. Hallwas, "Civil War Accounts as Literature: Illinois Letters, Diaries, and Personal Narratives," *Western Illinois Regional Studies* 13 (Spring 1990): 46–60.

15. See McPherson, *For Cause and Comrades*, ix. Tellingly, in Randall Jimerson's *The Private Civil War: Popular Thought during the Sectional Conflict* (Baton Rouge: Louisiana State University Press, 1988), based largely on soldiers' letters, the literacy level of quotations is markedly higher in the chapter on ideological conceptions of the war than in the rest of the book.

16. Robert E. Bonner's *The Soldier's Pen: Firsthand Impressions of the Civil War* (New York: Hill & Wang, 2006) is the exceptional book that favors "gradual evolutions of ideas and images" over "snippets and choice quotes." *I Remain Yours* takes up Bonner's call for attention to Civil War soldiers' letters as a form of "American literary expression" and extends that attention to soldiers' families. Another methodological innovation appears in Robert L. Bee's comparison of one soldier's letters with the same man's retrospective journal writings on the same wartime experiences. *The Boys from Rockville: Civil War Narratives of Sgt. Benjamin Hirst, Company D, 14th Connecticut Volunteers* (Knoxville: University of Tennessee Press, 1998).

17. Mine is an old definition of literature—something any literate person can produce. Only in the nineteenth century and after did a more specialized sensibility emerge in which one piece of writing might be "merely literate" while another was "literary." See Raymond Williams, *Keywords: A Vocabulary of Culture*

and Society, rev. ed. (New York: Oxford University Press, 1985), 183–88; Hayden White, "The Suppression of Rhetoric in the Nineteenth Century," in *The Rhetoric Canon*, ed. Brenda Deen Shildgen (Detroit: Wayne State University Press, 1997), 21–31; and Sandra M. Gustafson, "Literature," in *Keywords for American Cultural Studies*, ed. Bruce Burgett and Glenn Hendler, 2nd ed. (New York: New York University Press, 2014), 158–161. Also see Christopher Hager, *Word by Word: Emancipation and the Act of Writing* (Cambridge, MA: Harvard University Press, 2013).

18. On problems in the historical interpretation of emotional expression, see Barbara H. Rosenwein, "Worrying about Emotions in History," *American Historical Review* 107 (2002): 821–845; and William M. Reddy, *The Navigation of Feeling: A Framework for the History of Emotions* (New York: Cambridge University Press, 2001). For a brief overview of emotional life in the wartime North, see J. Matthew Gallman, *The North Fights the Civil War: The Home Front* (Chicago: Ivan R. Dee, 1994), 74–83.

19. David Johnson to Eliza Ann Johnson, 15 Sept. 1862, in " 'I Take My Pen in Hand': Civil War Letters from Owen County, Indiana, Soldiers," ed. Vivian Zollinger, *Indiana Magazine of History* 93 (1997): 111–196, quotation on 134.

20. Tilmon Baggarly to Margaret Baggarly, 6 Feb. 1863, Tilmon F. Baggarly Papers, 1860–1879, David M. Rubenstein Rare Book & Manuscript Library, Duke University, Durham, NC (hereafter Rubenstein Library-DU).

21. Anne Ruggles Gere, "Kitchen Tables and Rented Rooms: The Extracurriculum of Composition," *College Composition and Communication* 45 (1994): 75–92. Also see Susan Miller, *Assuming the Positions: Cultural Pedagogy and the Politics of Commonplace Writing* (Pittsburgh, PA: University of Pittsburgh Press, 1998). On the pedagogical functions of letter writing also see Henkin, *Postal Age*, 23–24.

22. Class, education, and literacy did have a sectional dimension, though. In the South, 35 percent of the school-age population attended school in 1860, and they had 80 school days per year. In the North, 72 percent of children attended school, for an average of 175 days per year. James B. McPherson and James K. Hogue, *Ordeal by Fire: The Civil War and Reconstruction*, 4th ed. (New York: McGraw Hill, 2009), 28. It is not coincidental that the majority of Northern letter writers featured in this book are from places like southern Indiana and eastern Iowa, which had lower literacy rates than, say, Boston and Philadelphia.

23. On a similar phenomenon, the development of literacy among European soldiers during World War I, see Lyons, *Writing Culture of Ordinary People in Europe*, esp. 34–52.

24. Lucretia Thompson to Henry Thompson, 4 Nov. 1863, and Henry to Lucretia, 8 Nov. 1863, Henry J. H. Thompson Papers, Rubenstein Library-DU.

25. David W. Blight, "Introduction," *When This Cruel War Is Over: The Civil War Letters of Charles Harvey Brewster* (Amherst: University of Massachusetts Press, 1992), 8. As Paul A. Cimbala and Randall M. Miller put it, "the home front was no more quarantined from the battlefield and camp experiences of Union soldiers than the soldiers' wartime experiences were from their own home life" (introduction to *An Uncommon Time: The Civil War and the Northern Home Front* [New York: Fordham University Press, 2002], xv). Important books that likewise consider the interrelationship of women's experiences and military conflict include Jane Schultz, *Women at the Front: Hospital Workers in Civil War America* (Chapel Hill: University of North Carolina Press, 2004), and Stephanie McCurry, *Confederate Reckoning: Power and Politics in the Civil War South* (Cambridge, MA: Harvard University Press, 2010). On connections between soldiers and the home front, also see Reid Mitchell, *The Vacant Chair: The Northern Soldier Leaves Home* (New York: Oxford University Press, 1993), 19–37.

26. On Civil War letters written to public figures by people without formal education, see Christopher Hager, " 'if we Ever Expect to be a Pepple': The Epistolary Culture of African American Soldiers," in *Literary Cultures of the Civil War*, ed. Timothy Sweet (Athens: University of Georgia Press, 2016), 23–38, and Stephanie McCurry, *Confederate Reckoning*, 133–177.

27. On women and gender during the Civil War, see especially the essays in Catherine Clinton and Nina Silber, eds., *Divided Houses: Gender and the Civil War* (New York: Oxford University Press, 1992). On women's farm labor, see R. Douglas Hurt, *Food and Agriculture during the Civil War* (Santa Barbara, CA: Praeger, 2016). On conceptions of manhood during the Civil War, see Gerald F. Linderman, *Embattled Courage: The Experience of Combat in the American Civil War* (New York: Free Press, 1987); Mitchell, *Vacant Chair*; and Stephen W. Berry II, *All That Makes a Man: Love and Ambition in the Civil War South* (New York: Oxford University Press, 2003). On the historical gendering of literacy education, see E. Jennifer Monaghan, *Learning to Read and Write in Colonial America* (Amherst: University of Massachusetts Press, 2005), and Tamara Plakins Thornton, *Handwriting in America: A Cultural History* (New Haven, CT: Yale University Press, 1996), 42–71.

28. Ronald J. Zboray and Mary Saracino Zboray's extensive research on literacy and literary culture suggests that educated people's diary keeping and other literacy activities waned during the Civil War, while "letter writing, by contrast, became more copious." "Cannonballs and Books: Reading and the Disruption of Social Ties on the New England Home Front," in *The War Was You and Me: Civilians in the American Civil War*, ed. Joan E. Cashin (Princeton, NJ: Princeton University Press, 2002), 237–261, quotation on 245.

1. Letters

1. Edward Hooker, *The Descendants of Rev. Thomas Hooker* (Rochester, NY: Margaret Huntington Hooker, 1909); Dudley Prentice, "50 High Street," in "Prentice Papers: History of Farmington Houses," vol. 3 (1974), Farmington Public Library, Farmington, CT.

2. This spate of deaths may indicate a tuberculosis epidemic in the neighborhood.

3. Frederick Hooker to Jeannette Hooker, 4 Feb. 1864, Frederick Hooker Letters, MS 57315, Connecticut Historical Society, Hartford.

4. Frederick Douglass, *Narrative of the Life of Frederick Douglass, an American Slave, Written by Himself* (Boston: Anti-Slavery Office, 1845). On literacy among the enslaved and formerly enslaved, see Christopher Hager, *Word by Word: Emancipation and the Act of Writing* (Cambridge, MA: Harvard University Press, 2013).

5. Hooker, *Descendants*, 246, and Gideon Welles, "Appointment from the Secretary of the Navy to Acting Volunteer Lieutenant Hooker," in *Official Records of the Union and Confederate Navies in the War of the Rebellion* ser. 1, vol. 8 (Washington, DC: Government Printing Office, 1899), 8.

6. Fred mentions the three exams a few months later, in his letter of 3 Apr. 1864, Frederick Hooker Letters.

7. Scott Nelson and Carol Sheriff, *A People at War: Civilians and Soldiers in America's Civil War, 1854–1877* (New York: Oxford University Press, 2008), 176 and 182n51. Heavy-artillery regiments such as the one Fred joined were generally thought less dangerous than the infantry, too.

8. Frederick Hooker to Jeannette Hooker, 11 Feb. 1864, Frederick Hooker Letters.

9. Frederick Hooker to Jeannette Hooker, [3?] Mar. 1864, Frederick Hooker Letters. A fellow New Englander, Thomas Nickerson, sent a condolence letter to

the mother of a member of Thomas's company who had recently died: "i myself has roat him a great may letters to send to you. and he used to bring me his letters which he recived from you and have me to read them, and by the letters which i have seen that came from you i take you to bee a very nice Woman." Thomas O. Nickerson to Ellen Bullock, 19 Jan. 1862, in *Yankee Correspondence: Civil War Letters between New England Soldiers and the Home Front*, ed. Nina Silber and Mary Beth Sievens (Charlottesville: University of Virginia Press, 1996), 28.

10. Larkin Kendrick to Mary Catherine Kendrick, 20 Jan. 1862 and 28 Jan. 1863, PC.1921, Larkin S. Kendrick Papers, State Archives of North Carolina, Raleigh (hereafter SANC); Charley Futch to John Futch, 16 Oct. 1861, PC. 507, Futch Letters, 1861–1863, SANC.

11. U.S. Census Office, *A Compendium of the Ninth Census (1870)* (Washington, DC: U.S. Government Printing Office, 1872), 458. Measures of literacy are not scientific. Frederick Hooker, who could not write but evidently had some ability to read, may or may not have been numbered among those two percent.

12. William Cline to Mary Cline, 14 Apr. 1862, Cline Papers, SANC (quoted in Michael Ellis, *North Carolina English, 1861–1865: A Guide and Glossary* [Knoxville: University of Tennessee Press, 2013], xxxi).

13. Thomas Warrick to Martha Warrick, 30 Apr. 1862, Thomas Warrick Papers, Alabama Department of Archives and History, Montgomery (hereafter ADAH).

14. Thomas Warrick to Martha Warrick, 2 and 18 Apr. 1863, Thomas Warrick Papers.

15. Thomas Warrick to Martha Warrick, 8 Apr. 1863, Thomas Warrick Papers.

16. Entry for 5 Sept. 1862, Margaret Ann Meta Morris Grimball Diary #975-z, Southern Historical Collection, The Wilson Library, University of North Carolina at Chapel Hill (hereafter SHC).

17. Sarepta Revis to Daniel Revis, 12 Oct. 1862, PC.1914, Daniel W. Revis Letters, SANC.

18. Sarepta Revis and John Morgan to Daniel Revis, 22 Oct. 1862, Daniel W. Revis Letters.

19. Ibid.

20. Sarepta Revis to Daniel Revis, 3 Nov. 1862; H. C. Ward to Daniel Revis, 17 Dec. 1862; H. C. Ward to John Morgan, 17 May 1863; and Sarepta Revis to Daniel Revis, 23 June and 21 July 1863, Daniel W. Revis Letters. Incidentally, the

added *I* in "strange" is unmistakably present in the letters for Sarepta but not in Clint's own.

21. See entry for "nothing strange" in Ellis, *North Carolina English*.

22. *Congressional Globe*, Thirty-Seventh Cong., Third Sess., 1152 (1863). Simon Hulbert quoted in Bell Irvin Wiley, *The Life of Billy Yank: The Common Soldier of the Union* (1952; repr., Baton Rouge: Louisiana University Press, 2008), 183. "Walt Whitman's Letter for a Dying Soldier Discovered," NPR .org, http://www.npr.org/2016/03/12/470214579/walt-whitmans-letter-for -a-dying-soldier-to-his-wife-discovered. Some soldiers even reported that prostitutes sometimes (presumably for a fee) penned illiterate men's letters home. See L. Bao Bui, " 'I Feel Impelled to Write': Male Intimacy, Epistolary Privacy, and the Culture of Letter Writing during the American Civil War" (Ph.D. diss., University of Illinois at Urbana-Champaign, 2016), 76–77 and 102–103.

23. David W. Blight, ed., *When This Cruel War Is Over: The Civil War Letters of Charles Harvey Brewster* (Amherst: University of Massachusetts Press, 1992), 22; Elizabeth Hyde Botume, *First Days amongst the Contrabands* (Boston: Lee and Shepard, 1893), 145, 143.

24. Alonzo Reed to "My Dear Mother," 9 July 1865, Alonzo Reed Letters, David M. Rubenstein Rare Book & Manuscript Library, Duke University, Durham, NC (hereafter Rubenstein Library-DU).

25. Kenneth A. Lockridge, *Literacy in Colonial New England: An Enquiry into the Social Context of Literacy in the Early Modern West* (New York: Norton, 1974); E. Jennifer Monaghan, *Learning to Read and Write in Colonial America* (Amherst: University of Massachusetts Press, 2005).

26. Michael Warner, *The Letters of the Republic: Publication and the Public Sphere in Eighteenth-Century America* (Cambridge, MA: Harvard University Press, 1990), 18. St. George Tucker, *Blackstone's Commentaries, with Notes of Reference to the Constitution and Laws of the Federal Government of the United States, and of the Commonwealth of Virginia*, vol. 3 (Philadelphia: William Young Birch and Abraham Small, 1803), 305.

27. "Given that the vast majority of the earliest cuneiform texts are administrative—detailing transactions involving property, materials, and labor— it is indeed difficult not to see the invention of writing as a solution to the practical bureaucratic problems posed by an increasingly complex economy." This was less obviously the case in China and Mesoamerica, the other places where writing

appears to have been invented independently, but it is the ancient Near East's writing systems, and social uses for writing, that are the direct (if distant) antecedents of the English language and early American literate culture. Christopher Woods, "Visible Language: The Earliest Writing Systems," introduction to *Inventions of Writing in the Ancient Middle East and Beyond*, ed. Woods with Emily Teeter and Geoff Emberling (Chicago: Oriental Institute of the University of Chicago, 2010), 17.

28. Konstantin Dierks, *In My Power: Letter Writing and Communications in Early America* (Philadelphia: University of Pennsylvania Press, 2009), 21, and David Randall, "Epistolary Rhetoric, the Newspaper, and the Public Sphere," *Past & Present* 198 (2008): 3–32; see esp. 10–12.

29. On the relationship among the emergence of the middle class, rising literacy, and the advent of the novel, see Ian Watt's classic account, *The Rise of the Novel: Studies in Defoe, Richardson, and Fielding* (1957; repr., Berkeley: University of California Press, 2001). On letter-writing manuals see Dierks, *In My Power*, esp. 142–155; Elizabeth Hewitt, *Correspondence and American Literature, 1770–1865* (Cambridge: Cambridge University Press, 2004), 10–12; and Carol Poster, ed., *Letter-Writing Manuals and Instruction from Antiquity to the Present: Historical and Bibliographic Studies* (Columbia: University of South Carolina Press, 2007). Also see Lucille M. Schultz, "Letter-Writing Instruction in Nineteenth-Century Schools in the United States," in *Letter Writing as a Social Practice*, ed. David Barton and Nigel Hall (Philadelphia: John Benjamins, 2000), 109–130; Ronald J. Zboray, "The Letter and the Fiction Reading Public in Antebellum America," *Journal of American Culture* 10 (Spring 1987): 29; David M. Henkin, *The Postal Age: The Emergence of Modern Communications in Nineteenth-Century America* (Chicago: University of Chicago Press, 2006), 111–116. Samuel Richardson's *Clarissa* and *Pamela*—and the tradition of epistolary novels that followed from them, into the first decade of the nineteenth century—also functioned as letter-writing manuals of a sort, providing additional model letters (some to be avoided rather than copied).

30. Samuel Richardson, "Preface" and "Contents of the Letters," *Letters Written to and for Particular Friends, on the Most Important Occasions* (London: C. Rivington, 1741), ECCO, http://name.umdl.umich.edu/004845953.0001 .000. Also see Victoria Myers, "Model Letters, Moral Living: Letter-Writing Manuals by Daniel Defoe and Samuel Richardson," *Huntington Library Quarterly* 66 (2003): 373–391.

31. *Encyclopedia Britannica*, 7th ed., s.v. "Letter." The cookbook entry is *The Young Woman's Companion; or, Frugal Housewife, Containing the Most Approved Methods of Pickling, Preserving, Potting, Collaring, Confectionary* (Manchester, Eng.: Russell and Allen, 1813), 387–388. The quotation appears in multiple editions of the ubiquitous *Complete Letter-Writer, or Polite English Secretary* (London: Stanley Crowder, 1772) and its North American spin-offs, among other manuals. This sense of exposure has not gone away, either: as a writer in the *New York Times Magazine* put it in 2008, "in the heavily text-based media that require people constantly to type words to one another, it's your diction by which you're judged, rather than your accent, your appearance, your bearing or your handwriting, as in other eras." Virginia Heffernan, "Lexicographical Longing," *New York Times Magazine*, 11 May 2008, pp. 18–19.

32. *Young Secretary's Guide* quoted in Dierks, *In My Power*, 72; *The Complete Letter-Writer*, 5th ed. (Edinburgh: David Paterson, 1776), 44–46; Jonathan Gibson, "Significant Space in Manuscript Letters," *Seventeenth Century* 12 (1997): 1–10.

33. *The New Universal Letter-Writer; or, Complete Art of Polite Correspondence* (Philadelphia: Lippincott, 1856), 34; compare with the English antecedent, *Complete Letter-Writer*, 5th ed., 47. Also see Hewitt, *Correspondence and American Literature*, 11.

34. Charles Morley, *A Practical Guide to Composition* (Hartford, CT: R. White, 1838), 41.

35. Dierks refers to the "prescriptive force of letter writing," meaning that "social practices accrued into cultural standards, even more so because people read more personal letters than letter manuals" (*In My Power*, 5). Also see Henkin, *Postal Age*, 109–117.

36. Sarepta Revis to Daniel Revis, 3 Nov. 1862, Daniel W. Revis Letters.

37. Possibly Sarepta withheld these "maney thinges" less from Clint than from people (besides Daniel) she feared might read the letter. Either way, the line plainly reflects a concern Sarepta asked Clint to write down, not anything he would have suggested or supplied.

38. Daniel Revis to Sarepta Revis, 8 Nov. 1862 and undated, Daniel W. Revis Letters. An archivist conjectures that the undated letter is from mid-November 1862, but it had to have been earlier, before John Morgan joined the Sixty-Fourth North Carolina, since it is in this letter that Daniel says, "tel John morgan to rite for you." Whenever it was written, it's impossible to know when

it arrived on Corbin Mountain and therefore impossible to know whether it, Daniel's first letter, was at hand when Sarepta first asked Clint to write for her. In short, Daniel's first letter may have been available as a model for Clint's first, but it may not have.

39. Quoted in Allen Walker Read, "Could Andrew Jackson Spell?," *American Speech* 38 (1963): 188–195.

40. Preface to *Complete Letter-Writer* (1758), A2; *The New Universal Letter-Writer; or, Complete Art of Polite Correspondence* (Philadelphia: Lippincott, 1856), 25, 21. Also see Beth Barton Schweiger, "A Social History of English Grammar in the Early United States," *Journal of the Early Republic* 30 (2010): 533–555.

41. "Ogresses—One in Particular," *Vanity Fair*, 26 Apr. 1862, p. 206. Lindley Murray was a leading American grammarian of the late eighteenth century.

42. George H. Ewing to "Dear Parents," 19 Feb. 1863, in John T. Greene, ed., *The Ewing Family Civil War Letters* (East Lansing: Michigan State University Press, 1994), 45; [Harriet Farley], "Evening before Pay-Day," *Lowell Offering* (1841), reprinted in *The Lowell Offering: Writings by New England Mill Women*, ed. Benita Eisler (New York: Norton, 1998), 167–168. Also see Christopher Hager, "Lowell Mill Girls: Literacy, Letter-Writing, and Literary Production in the Early Nineteenth-Century Factory," in *A History of American Working-Class Literature*, ed. Paul Lauter and Nicholas Coles (New York: Cambridge University Press, 2017), 60-75.

43. Lister Asquith to Thomas Jefferson, 7 Sept. 1785, in *The Papers of Thomas Jefferson*, vol. 8, *25 February–31 October 1785*, ed. Julian P. Boyd (Princeton, NJ: Princeton University Press, 1953), 500–501; Jakie L. Pruett and Scott Black, eds. *Civil War Letters, 1861–1865: A Glimpse of the War between the States* (Austin, TX: Eakin Press, 1985), 63.

44. Abram Hayne Young to "Dear Sister," 11 Aug. 1862, in Mary Wyche Burgess, ed., "Civil War Letters of Abram Hayne Young," *South Carolina Historical Magazine* 78 (1977): 59, editor's quotation on 56. Often, apologies such as these appear to refer only to the quality of the penmanship—"bad writing" was illegible, not necessarily inarticulate. A Pennsylvania soldier wrote, "Please excuse bad writing and mistaks and also the abruptness with which I end one subject and begin another." Orlando Gray to Juliana Reynolds, 26 May 1862, Papers of Tilton C. Reynolds, Manuscript Division, Library of Congress, http://www.loc.gov/item/mreynolds000056/. As mentioned above, Konstantin Dierks makes a persuasive case that letter writers themselves did more to influence letters than

manuals did. For the most part, I agree, but these frequently voiced notions about composition—that one ought not abruptly "end one subject and begin another"—raise an objection to that analysis. Such notions are difficult to trace to any source other than prescriptive manuals, which almost uniformly extolled the virtues of "fluid" composition. I have never seen a letter registering complaint about the "flow" of a letter received. Many ordinary letter writers worried that their letters weren't fluid, but there is little evidence that letter readers minded.

45. Ab Wideman to Martha Warrick, 19 May 1864, Thomas Warrick Papers, ADAH; Fred H. Rogers to "Dear Mother," 11 Oct. 1861, Frederick Rogers Civil War Collection, Bangor Historical Society, Bangor, ME, https://www .mainememory.net/artifact/31888.

46. Marti Skipper and Jane Taylor, eds., *A Handful of Providence: The Civil War Letters of Lt. Richard Goldwaite, New York Volunteers, and Ellen Goldwaite* (Jefferson, NC: McFarland, 2004), 39, 54, 64–65; Marian H. Blair, "Civil War Letters of Henry W. Barrow to John W. Fries," *North Carolina Historical Review* 34 (1957): 77; Olivia to "My dear [Lelia?]," 1 Apr. 1865, Confederate Memorial Literary Society Collection, under the management of the Virginia Historical Society, Richmond.

47. Mauriel Phillips Joslyn, *Charlotte's Boys: Civil War Letters of the Branch Family of Savannah* (Gretna, LA: Pelican Publishing Company, 2010), 226; George H. Randall to his wife, 8 Nov. 1861, in *A War of the People: Vermont Civil War Letters*, ed. Jeffrey D. Marshall (Hanover, NH: University Press of New England, 1999), 50–51. For more on the physical situation of soldiers' letter writing, see Bell Irvin Wiley, *The Life of Johnny Reb: The Common Soldier of the Confederacy* (1943; repr., Baton Rouge: Louisiana State University Press, 2008), 192–216; and *The Life of Billy Yank: The Common Soldier of the Union* (1952; repr., Baton Rouge: Louisiana State University Press, 2008), 183–189.

48. Margaret Black Tatum, ed., "'Please Send Stamps': The Civil War Letters of William Allen Clark," parts 1–4, *Indiana Magazine of History* 91 (1995): 432, 213, 415–416, 431, 426, 434.

49. So fervently did Victorian-era Americans believe this that some schoolmasters for the well-to-do employed a baroque implement called the talantograph, which bound the hand in the most proper position for penmanship. Tamara Plakins Thornton, *Handwriting in America: A Cultural History* (New Haven, CT: Yale University Press, 1996), 54.

50. George Worden to Fannie Worden, 14 Feb. 1864, George E. Worden Civil War Letters, Indiana Historical Society, Indianapolis (hereafter IHS). Journalist quoted in David Henkin, *Postal Age*, 55. On associations of handwriting and handwritten letters with physical presence, see Thornton, *Handwriting in America*, 41, 52–53; William Merrill Decker, *Epistolary Practices: Letter Writing in America before Telecommunications* (Chapel Hill: University of North Carolina Press, 1998), 15, 40, and 249n33; and Henkin, *Postal Age*, 55.

51. J. H. Hundley to "Dear Wife," 16 June 1863, Hundley Family Papers #4971-z, SHC; also quoted in Ellis, *North Carolina English*, 163. "Your Dear nece Cora" to "Dear Uncle," undated, Confederate Memorial Literary Society Collection; Lucinda Silk to Thomas Poe, 12 Apr. [1863?], Thomas Bueford Poe Civil War Letters, IHS.

52. Perry Leonard to John Leonard, 28 Sept. 1862, John F. Leonard Papers, #3585-z, SHC.

53. "Cousin Amanda" to James Mead, 24 Dec. 1862, Mead Family Papers, University of Iowa Libraries, Iowa City, IA.

54. He had spoken of this possibility: "the reasond i did not write before i was exspectting to come home all tim but i have not got there yet but if nothing happens i mean to Come home and stay a day or so." Frederick Hooker to Jeannette Hooker, [2?] Mar. 1864, Frederick Hooker Letters. It is not known whether he did in fact return home before his regiment left Connecticut.

55. Sarah Robbins, *Managing Literacy, Mothering America: Women's Narratives on Reading and Writing in the Nineteenth Century* (Pittsburgh, PA: University of Pittsburgh Press, 2004), 20-25.

56. Frederick Hooker to Jeannette Hooker, 26 Mar., 1, 3, and 5 Apr. 1864, Frederick Hooker Letters.

57. Frederick Hooker to Jeannette Hooker, 11 Apr. 1864, Frederick Hooker Letters.

58. Perkins to "Dear Miss," 22 Apr. 1865, Confederate Memorial Literary Society Collection; Sara E. Fales to Edmund Fales, 4 May 1862, in *Yankee Correspondence: Civil War Letters between New England Soldiers and the Home Front*, ed. Nina Silber and Mary Beth Sievens (Charlottesville: University of Virginia Press, 1996), 135; S. Gantz to J. and E. Gantz, 26 July 1863, in *Civil War Letters of the Gantz Family*, ed. Lucille H. Lussenden (Baltimore: Gateway Press, 2002), 67; George Parker to "Dear Parents" (Ammon and Frances Parker), 3 Dec. 1861, Robert W. Parker Papers #5261, SHC; Joseph Sherman Diltz to Mary

Diltz, 24 Jan. 1862, and Mary to Joseph, 6 May 1863, Joseph Sherman Diltz Papers, Rubenstein Library-DU.

59. On coming of age as a theme of Northern soldiers' writings, see Reid Mitchell, *The Vacant Chair* (New York: Oxford University Press, 1993), 3–18.

60. Frederick Hooker to Jeannette Hooker, 11 Apr. 1864, Frederick Hooker Letters.

61. Daniel Revis to Sarepta Revis, 7 Dec. 1862, Daniel W. Revis Letters.

62. H. C. Ward to Daniel Revis, and Sarepta Revis to Daniel Revis, 17 Dec. 1862, Daniel W. Revis Letters.

63. The arrival of Sarepta's second child is hitherto unannounced, as far as the surviving letters show.

64. Daniel Revis to Sarepta Revis, 12 Jan. 1863, Daniel W. Revis Letters.

65. Daniel Revis to Sarepta Revis, 13 Apr. 1863, Daniel W. Revis Letters.

2. Impressions

1. Fred Dally to "My dearest Mother," 25 June–ca. 12 July 1862, W. S. Hoole Special Collections Library, University of Alabama, Tuscaloosa (hereafter Hoole Library-UA).

2. Daniel Revis to Sarepta Revis, 12 Jan. and 10 Feb. 1863, PC.1914, Daniel W. Revis Letters, State Archives of North Carolina, Raleigh (hereafter SANC).

3. Harriet Henderson to "Dear Uncle," 24 Apr. 1863, HM 74520, Huntington Library, San Marino, CA; Louisa Cook to "Dear Mother & sisters" and to "Dear Sister Emma," 9 June and 12 Oct. 1862, in *Covered Wagon Women: Diaries and Letters from the Western Trails, 1862–1865*, ed. Kenneth L. Holmes, vol. 8 (Lincoln: University of Nebraska Press, 1989), 32, 53.

4. On the Civil War as an event of human mobility, especially in the South, see Yael A. Sternhell, *Routes of War: The World of Movement in the Confederate South* (Cambridge, MA: Harvard University Press, 2012).

5. *The Journals and Miscellaneous Notebooks of Ralph Waldo Emerson*, ed. Linda Allardt and David W. Hill, vol. 15, *1860–1866* (Cambridge, MA: Harvard University Press, 1982), 64; Dolph Damuth to "Dear Friends," 15 Apr. 1863, in *The Soldier's Pen: Firsthand Impressions of the Civil War*, by Robert E. Bonner (New York: Hill and Wang, 2006), 38; Henry L. Burnell to "Dear Father," 24 Mar. 1862, Henry L. Burnell Papers, 1861–1903, South Caroliniana Library,

University of South Carolina, Columbia; George Patten to Sarah S. Patten, 31 Mar. 1864, Papers of George D. Patten, HM 59975–60012, Huntington Library; undated archival envelope, folder 3 (1864), Henry J. H. Thompson Papers, David M. Rubenstein Rare Book & Manuscript Library, Duke University, Durham, NC (hereafter Rubenstein Library-DU); Elijah Barker to George and Elizabeth Johnston, 7 Jan. 1862, in " 'I Take My Pen in Hand': Civil War Letters from Owen County, Indiana, Soldiers," ed. Vivian Zollinger, *Indiana Magazine of History* 93 (1997): 134; George H. Ewing to "Dear Parents," 4 Nov. 1862, in *The Ewing Family Civil War Letters*, ed. John T. Greene (East Lansing: Michigan State University Press, 1994), 25.

6. Iowa Royster to "Dear Ma," 29 June 1863, Royster Family Papers #4183, Southern Historical Collection, The Wilson Library, University of North Carolina at Chapel Hill (hereafter SHC); children's names from the finding aid.

7. Benjamin Barrett to "Dear Broth ann Sister," 18 Nov. 1861, in *The Confederacy Is on Her Way Up the Spout: Letters to South Carolina, 1861–1864*, ed. J. Roderick Heller III and Carolynn Ayres Heller (Athens: University of Georgia Press, 1992), 39.

8. John Jefcoat to Rachel Jefcoat, 9 Sept. 1862, John J. Jefcoat Papers, Rubenstein Library-DU; Letter to "My dear Husband," 10–11 Jan. 1863, Oxford (MS), HM 58079, Huntington Library; Martha Poteet to Francis Poteet, PC.1825, Poteet-Dickson Letters, 1861–1902 and undated, SANC; Unknown to "My Very Dear Son," 7 Apr. 1865, Confederate Memorial Literary Society Collection, under the management of the Virginia Historical Society, Richmond. For an exhaustive treatment of the subject, see Ella Lonn, *Salt as a Factor in the Confederacy* (1933; repr., Tuscaloosa: University of Alabama Press, 1965). Henderson letter, 24 Apr. 1863, Huntington Library.

9. For the history of the Shelton Laurel massacre, I have relied on Phillip Shaw Paludan's searching study of those events, *Victims: A True Story of the Civil War* (Knoxville: University of Tennessee Press, 1981), as well as the regimental history of the Sixty-Fourth North Carolina by B. T. Morris, in *Histories of the Several Regiments and Battalions from North Carolina in the Great War, 1861–1865*, ed. Walter Clark, vol. 3 (Goldsboro, NC: Nash Brothers, 1901), 659–671. For the Shelton Laurel massacre in the larger context of women's roles in deserter networks and retributive violence against them by Confederate forces, see Stephanie McCurry, *Confederate Reckoning: Power and Politics in the Civil War South* (Cambridge, MA: Harvard University Press, 2010), 124–132.

10. Daniel Revis to Sarepta Revis, 10 Feb. 1863, Daniel W. Revis Letters.

11. "An Address before the Literary Societies of Dartmouth College, Hanover, New Hampshire, on July 22, 1863," in *The Later Lectures of Ralph Waldo Emerson, 1843–1871*, ed. Ronald A. Bosco and Joel Myerson, vol. 2, *1855–1871* (Athens: University of Georgia Press, 2001), 317.

12. Daniel Revis to Sarepta Revis, 8 Nov. 1862, H. C. (Clint) Ward to John Morgan, 17 May 1863, and Sarepta to Daniel, 17 June 1863, Daniel W. Revis Letters.

13. In this respect, the private letters of the Civil War partake of a tension between ideas about the conflict—as either impervious to representation in language, or so abundantly documented as to defy comprehension—that have characterized the memory and literary historiography of the Civil War for decades. See Christopher Hager and Cody Marrs, "Afterword: Archiving the War," in *A History of American Civil War Literature*, ed. Coleman Hutchison (New York: Cambridge University Press, 2016), 331–342.

14. Today the most influential web designers counsel rigid conformity in the layout of websites, which "must tone down their individual appearance and distinct design." Jakob Nielsen, "End of Web Design," 23 July 2000, Nielsen Norman Group, https://www.nngroup.com/articles/end-of-web-design/.

15. Thornton's occupation is recorded on his volunteer enlistment form as "farmer" and in the 1860 census as "carpenter." He wrote home to Nancy at one point, "Levi Kemp owes 40 ct balance on a small Chair tell him that you want it." Thornton Clark to Nancy Clark, 17 Nov. 1862, Thornton Clark Papers, M 0436, Indiana Historical Society, Indianapolis (hereafter IHS). The children's ages are extrapolated from the 1860 U.S. census, Spencer County, Indiana, population schedule, Carter Township, p. 118 (penned), dwelling 855, family 848, Thornton Clark; digital image, *Ancestry.com* (www.ancestry.com); citing NARA microfilm publication M653, roll 297. Thornton's military records are in a separate collection from the letters: Thornton Clark Civil War Papers, SC 3020, IHS.

16. Julia Ward Howe, "Battle Hymn of the Republic," *Atlantic Monthly*, Feb. 1862, p. 145; James Sloan Gibbons, "Three Hundred Thousand More" (1862), reprinted in *Words for the Hour: A New Anthology of Civil War Poetry*, ed. Faith Barrett and Cristanne Miller (Amherst: University of Massachusetts Press, 2005), 92–93; George Frederick Root's "Battle Cry of Freedom," one of the most successful patriotic songs of the time, also was composed in response to Lincoln's July 1, 1862, call for three hundred thousand troops. On patriotic songs during the

early part of the war, see Christian McWhirter, *Battle Hymns: The Power and Popularity of Music in the Civil War* (Chapel Hill: University of North Carolina Press, 2012), 50–57. Also see Judith Giesberg, *Army at Home: Women and the Civil War on the Northern Home Front* (Chapel Hill: University of North Carolina Press, 2012), 8

17. Cuyler Reynolds, *Albany Chronicles* (Albany: J. B. Lyon, 1906), 627; Thomas H. O'Connor, *Civil War Boston: Home Front and Battlefield* (Boston: Northeastern University Press, 1997), 102; W. H. H. Terrell, *Indiana in the War of the Rebellion* (Indianapolis: Douglass & Conner, 1869), 40–41; Thornton Clark volunteer enlistment form, Thornton Clark Civil War Papers. On recruitment in 1862, also see Giesberg, *Army at Home,* 49–50.

18. W. T. Sherman to Gen. H. W. Slocum, 24 July 1864, in *Official Records of the War of the Rebellion,* ser. 1, vol. 38, part 5 (Washington, DC: Government Printing Office, 1891), 246; W. T. Sherman to Gen. John A. Logan, 21 Dec. 1863, in *Official Records,* ser. 1, vol. 31, part 3 (Washington, DC: Government Printing Office, 1890), 459. On the economic and symbolic importance of Mississippi River navigation to the states of the Old Northwest, see Earl J. Hess, *The Civil War in the West: Victory and Defeat from the Appalachians to the Mississippi* (Chapel Hill: University of North Carolina Press, 2012), 2–7, and R. Douglas Hurt, *Food and Agriculture during the Civil War* (Santa Barbara, CA: Praeger, 2016), 4–5.

19. Morton quoted in Walter Rice Sharp, "Henry S. Lane and the Formation of the Republican Party in Indiana," *Mississippi Valley Historical Review* 7 (1920): 94n4; Charles H. Coleman, "The Use of the Term 'Copperhead' during the Civil War," *Mississippi Valley Historical Review* 25 (1938): 263–264.

20. Joseph Collingwood to Rebecca Collingwood, 12 Aug. 1862 (misdated 12 Mar.), Collingwood Papers, Huntington Library (quoted in James McPherson, *For Cause and Comrades: Why Men Fought in the Civil War* [New York: Oxford University Press, 1997], 135). Calculations from "Population at the Military Ages," in *Population of the United States in 1860; Compiled from the Original Returns of the Eighth Census,* by Joseph C. G. Kennedy (Washington, DC: Government Printing Office, 1864), xvii; and "Summary of Troops Furnished," in *A Compendium of the War of the Rebellion,* by Frederick H. Dyer (Des Moines, IA: Dyer Publishing Company, 1908), 11.

21. Isaac Mark Abbot to "Dear folks at Home," 5 and 8 Sept. 1862, Isaac Mark Abbott Collection, Manuscripts Record Group 34, Concordia College Archives,

Moorehead, MN, available at http://digitalhorizonsonline.org/cdm/landingpage
/collection/cord-dfah.

22. Thornton Clark to Nancy Clark, 19 Sept. 1862, Thornton Clark Papers.

23. David Randall, "Epistolary Rhetoric, the Newspaper, and the Public
Sphere," *Past & Present* 198 (Feb. 2008): 3–32, see esp. 16–23.

24. [Orville J. Victor], *Beadle's Dime Letter-Writer, a Perfect Guide to All Kinds
of Correspondence* (New York: Beadle and Co., 1863), 22; Franklin Alford to
Warren Alford, 31 Oct. 1861, Alford Family Papers, IHS; Lucretia Thompson to
Henry Thompson, 4 June [1865?], Henry J. H. Thompson Papers; Betsy Blaisdell
to Hiram Blaisdell, 15 Nov. 1864, Civil War Manuscripts Collection (MS 619), series 1, box 6, Manuscripts and Archives, Yale University Library, New Haven,
CT. Peter Stallybrass has argued that there is a tradition among letter writers
dating back to the sixteenth century of trying to write as little as possible while
still meeting the expectation of filling blank space ("What Is a Letter?" lecture
delivered at Yale University, 7 Dec. 2016).

25. Lindsay O'Neill, *The Opened Letter: Networking in the Early Modern British
World* (Philadelphia: University of Pennsylvania Press, 2014), 53–54; Milton Barrett to J. and C. McMahan and friends, 11 Aug. 1861, in *The Confederacy Is on Her
Way up the Spout: Letters to South Carolina, 1861–1864*, ed. J. Roderick Heller III
and Carolynn Ayres Heller (Athens: University of Georgia Press, 1992), 24–25.

26. O'Neill, *Opened Letter*, 170–171; Elijah Barker to George and Elizabeth
Barker Johnston, 4 Dec. 1861 (quoted in Zollinger, " 'I Take My Pen in Hand,' "
132); Charley Johnson to Mary Johnson, 25 Oct. 1861, in *The Civil War Letters of
Colonel Charles F. Johnson, Invalid Corps*, ed. Fred Pelka (Amherst: University of
Massachusetts Press, 2004), 49.

27. Joseph Hollis to Thomas Hollis, 12 May 1863, "Hollis Correspondence,"
Indiana Magazine of History 36 (1940): 278; J. F. Hei to "My Dear Sons," 17
Mar. 1865, Confederate Memorial Literary Society Collection; Larkin Kendrick
to Mary Catherine Kendrick, 2 Oct. 1862, PC.1921, Larkin S. Kendrick Papers,
SANC. It is in soldiers' letters about battle that the trope of the Civil War's fundamental *inexpressibility* arguably originated. McPherson makes a related point
in *For Cause and Comrades*, 12, 141.

28. Ronald J. Zboray and Mary Saracino Zboray note the same tendency in
letters by New England civilians: "while away from home near battle fronts, [they]
cherished hearing about everyday family life and fancying nothing had changed,
asked their correspondents to write about their literary reading among other

details of home life—and not their concerns about the war." "Cannonballs and Books: Reading and the Disruption of Social Ties on the New England Home Front," in *The War Was You and Me: Civilians in the American Civil War*, ed. Joan Cashin (Princeton, NJ: Princeton University Press, 2002), 246.

29. Lists of staple commodity prices, incidentally, were in fact a version of "the news," and both soldiers and folks at home seemed to relish the fact that they *could* report this, so very ubiquitous are such inventories as Thomas Warrick's (at a time of Confederate inflation): "evry thing is so hy her that ther is no use of talking about it water millons is worth from ten to twenty dollars a pies peaches and apples one dollar and a half a dozen and evry thing is in proportion." Thomas Warrick to Martha Warrick, 2 Aug. 1863, Thomas Warrick Papers, Alabama Department of Archives and History, Montgomery. These recitations in private letters closely mimicked the commercial columns and advertisements in newspapers, including variants of the stock phrase "everything else in proportion."

30. Isaac Mann to John Deaver, 27 Feb. 1862, and Isaac Mann to Susan Mann, 28 Mar. 1862, Letters from Isaac Mann to Susan Deaver Mann, 1862–1864, HM 21882–21908, Huntington Library.

31. This is in fact an influential tenet of information theory. Communication occurs most effectively, Claude Shannon proposed, by combining "information" (what is new and unpredictable, original) and "redundancy" (what is prescribed by custom or rules of syntax) in about equal measure. Claude E. Shannon and Warren Weaver, *The Mathematical Theory of Communication* (1949; repr., Urbana and Chicago: University of Illinois Press, 1998).

32. Frederick Hooker to Jeannette Hooker, 1 Apr. 1864, Frederick Hooker Letters, MS 57315, Connecticut Historical Society, Hartford; Sarah Dooley to Rufus Dooley, 12 Mar. 1863, IHS. For representative examples of drawings in soldiers' letters, see Frederick Hooker to Jeannette Hooker, 23 Mar. and 3 Apr. 1864, Frederick Hooker Letters; James Woodbury to "Dear Friends," 14 Oct. 1861, Rubenstein Library-DU; Eldridge Platt to Adelah Platt, 23 Apr. 1863, Eldridge B. Platt Papers #4767, SHC; Frederick Rogers to Hannah Rogers, 11 Oct. 1861, Frederick Rogers Civil War Collection, Bangor Historical Society, Bangor, ME; and William Edgerton to Dorothy Edgerton, 18 Nov. 1863, William W. Edgerton Civil War Letters, Special Collections, University of Houston Libraries.

33. Steven R. Boyd, *Patriotic Envelopes of the Civil War: The Iconography of Union and Confederate Covers* (Baton Rouge: Louisiana State University Press, 2010).

34. Isaac Mann to Susan Mann, 28 Mar. 1862, Letters from Isaac Mann to Susan Deaver Mann; for the full song, see George Stuyvesant Jackson, *Early Songs of Uncle Sam* (Boston: Bruce Humphries, 1933), 98.

35. Lafayette Alford to Mary Alford, 24 Nov. 1861, Alford Family Papers. The passage from Ellsworth's letter runs: "I am perfectly content to accept whatever my fortune may be, confident that He who noteth even the fall of a sparrow, will have some purpose even in the fate of one like me. My darling and ever loved parents, good-bye. God bless, protect, and care for you.—Elmer." By a certain definition, Ellsworth was the first combat fatality of the war. Adam Stauffer, "'The Fall of a Sparrow': The (Un)timely Death of Elmer Ellsworth and the Coming of the Civil War," *Gettysburg College Journal of the Civil War Era* 1 (2010): 44–52.

36. For educated Americans earlier in the nineteenth century, the back of the folio stayed blank and served as the outer covering of the letter, which was folded, sealed, and addressed on the back. By the time of the Civil War, envelopes had become standard equipment for letter writing.

37. Caleb Phillips to Caroline Phillips, 9 Sept. [1864], Caleb Henry Phillips Collection, Hoole Library-UA.

38. Caleb's regiment, the Sixtieth Massachusetts—a militia unit of men enrolled only for one hundred days—had been on the East Coast until mid-August, when they were sent to Indianapolis to garrison Camp Morton, which by now housed more Confederate prisoners than new Union recruits. Civil War Soldiers and Sailors System, National Park Service, www.nps.gov/civilwar/soldiers -and-sailors-database.htm.

39. *The Things They Carried* is Tim O'Brien's 1990 story collection based on his military experience in Vietnam.

40. Thornton Clark to Nancy Clark, undated (from "Camp Jo Rheynolds") and 15 Oct. 1862, Thornton Clark Papers.

41. S. F. Horrall, *History of the Forty-Second Indiana Volunteer Infantry* (Chicago: Donohue & Henneberry, 1892), 153.

42. 1850 U.S. census, Jefferson County, Kentucky, population schedule, 2nd district, City of Louisville, p. 170 (stamped), dwelling 373, family 430, Will H. Bulkley; digital image, *Ancestry.com* (www.ancestry.com); citing NARA microfilm publication M432, roll 206. *Twenty-Ninth Annual Report of the American Tract Society* (New York: American Tract Society, 1854), 191. Bulkley's shop was at 313 Fourth Street, on the site of the current Hyatt Regency. Thornton Clark to Nancy Clark, 21 Oct. 1862, Thornton Clark Papers.

43. Thornton Clark to Nancy Clark, 21 Oct. 1862, Thornton Clark Papers.

44. U.S. Bureau of the Census, "Population of Civil Divisions Less Than Counties; Table III State of Indiana," *Eighth Census of the United States, 1860* (Washington, DC: U.S. Census Office, 1862), 1:124; "Early Black Settlements: Spencer County," Indiana Historical Society, http://www.indianahistory.org /our-collections/reference/early-black-settlements/spencer-county.

45. Thornton Clark to Nancy Clark, 21 Oct. 1862, Thornton Clark Papers.

46. Ibid. The page break is between "enchanted" and "fairy."

47. "A Good Woman Gone" (Nancy Clark obituary), *Dale Reporter*, 3 Jan. 1919, p. 1; *History of Warrick, Spencer, and Perry Counties, Indiana* (Chicago: Goodspeed & Bros, 1885), 426.

48. Thornton Clark to Nancy Clark, 9 Nov. 1862, Thornton Clark Papers.

49. Ibid.

3. Bonds

Epigraph: Helen M. Noye Hoyt Papers, Clements Library, University of Michigan, Ann Arbor. I am grateful to Ian Finseth for this quotation.

1. "Married men, $366 bounty! Single men, $222!! Now is the time! To rally round the flag of the country!" Civil War Posters, 1861–1865, New-York Historical Society, New York, available at http://cdm16694.contentdm.oclc.org/cdm /ref/collection/p16694coll47/id/2807; James Jackson Davis to Betty Davis, 28 Aug. 1862, James Jackson Davis Papers, David M. Rubenstein Rare Book & Manuscript Library, Duke University, Durham, NC.

2. Channing quoted in David Henkin, *The Postal Age: The Emergence of Modern Communications in Nineteenth-Century America* (Chicago: University of Chicago Press, 2006), 51. [Orville J. Victor], *Beadle's Dime Letter-Writer, a Perfect Guide to All Kinds of Correspondence* (New York: Beadle and Co., 1863), 11, 13, 53; italics in original. On the popularity of Beadle's publications among both soldiers and civilians, see Alice Fahs, *The Imagined Civil War: Popular Literature of the North and South, 1861–1865* (Chapel Hill: University of North Carolina Press, 2001), 228–230.

3. Thornton Clark to Nancy Clark, 14 and 17 Nov. 1862 and 17 Mar. 1863, Thornton Clark Papers, M 0436, Indiana Historical Society, Indianapolis (hereafter IHS).

4. Thornton Clark to Nancy Clark, 9 Nov. 1862, Thornton Clark Papers.

5. Ronald J. Zboray and Mary Saracino Zboray, "Cannonballs and Books: Reading and the Disruption of Social Ties on the New England Home Front," in

The War Was You and Me: Civilians in the American Civil War, ed. Joan Cashin (Princeton, NJ: Princeton University Press, 2002), 249; Frank Morse to Ellen Morse, 12 Oct. 1862, Frank C. Morse Papers, Massachusetts Historical Society, Boston (quoted in Zboray and Zboray, 250). L. Bao Bui considers the "social networks" and "privacy settings" of Civil War soldiers' letters in " 'I Feel Impelled to Write': Male Intimacy, Epistolary Privacy, and the Culture of Letter Writing during the American Civil War" (Ph.D. diss., University of Illinois at Urbana-Champaign, 2016), quotations on 8 and 18.

6. Joan D. Hedrick has given a compelling account of how privately circulating manuscripts underlie and inform printed literature in "Parlor Literature: Harriet Beecher Stowe and the Question of 'Great Women Artists,' " *Signs* 17 (1992): 275–303. "Communications circuit" is from Robert Darnton, "What Is the History of Books?" in *Reading in America: Literature & Social History*, ed. Cathy Davidson (Baltimore: Johns Hopkins University Press, 1989), 30. See Ronald J. Zboray and Mary Saracino Zboray, "The Bonds of Print: Reading on Home Front and Battlefield," in *Massachusetts and the Civil War: The Commonwealth and National Disunion*, ed. Matthew Mason, Katheryn P. Viens, and Conrad Edick Wright (Amherst: University of Massachusetts Press, 2015), 195–223. On letters and networks, see Lindsay O'Neill, *The Opened Letter: Networking in the Early Modern British World* (Philadelphia: University of Pennsylvania Press, 2014), and Bui, " 'I Feel Impelled to Write.' "

7. For an even broader conception of letters' role in the formation of social bonds, at the level of the nation, see Elizabeth Hewitt, *Correspondence and American Literature, 1770–1865* (New York: Cambridge University Press), 16–51. Experiments with sorting mail on railcars began in the summer of 1862, and the U.S. Postal Service established the Railway Mail Service two years later. The sorting of mail en route aboard specially equipped train cars improved delivery time by almost a full day for many Northerners. Nancy Pope, "150th Anniversary of Railway Mail Service," Smithsonian National Postal Museum blog, 28 Aug. 2014, http://postalmuseumblog.si.edu/railway-post-office/.

8. Harriet Newby to Dangerfield Newby, 22 Apr. 1859, in "Appendix to Message 1: Documents Relative to the Harpers Ferry Invasion," *Governor's Message and Reports of the Public Officers of the State, of the Boards of Directors, and of the Visitors, Superintendents, and Other Agents of Public Instruction or Interests of Virginia* (Richmond, VA: William P. Ritchie, 1859), 116–117.

9. Some captured letters were not made public during the war but came to light later, including some that are quoted throughout this book. A "Soldier Letters"

Collection (inaptly named, since many were written by civilians), formerly held by the Confederate Memorial Literary Society and now housed at the Virginia Historical Society, came from a large haul of Confederate mail destroyed in Washington—of which a Michigan congressman saved more than three hundred letters. See John M. Coski, "Captured Mail Provides Kaleidoscope of the South in the Last Months of the War," *Museum of the Confederacy Magazine* (Summer 2010): 7–13; and Joshua Shaffer and John M. Coski, "War Correspondence," *Civil War Monitor* 5 (Spring 2015): 50–57, 75. Selections from a batch of undelivered Northern home front letters appear in Edward G. Longacre, " 'Come Home Soon and Dont Delay': Letters from the Home Front, July, 1861," *Pennsylvania Magazine of History and Biography* 11 (1976): 395–413.

10. Julia Wilbur, diary entry for 24 June 1862, Julia Wilbur Papers (MC #1158), Special Collections, Haverford College, Haverford, PA; Charles Henry Snedeker Civil War Diary (typescript), entry for 3 Aug. 1863, Auburn University Special Collections & Archives Department, Auburn, AL; diary entry for 15 Feb. 1862, Jesse Calvin Spaulding Papers, Albert and Shirley Small Special Collections Library, University of Virginia, Charlottesville; Rutherford B. Hayes to Lucy Hayes, 30 June 1862, in *The Diary and Letters of Rutherford B. Hayes, Nineteenth President of the United States*, ed. Charles Richard Williams, vol. 2 (Columbus: Ohio State Archeological and Historical Society, 1922), 294; Harmon Marton to his sister, 25 Aug. 1863 (typescript), Georgia Archives, Morrow, GA; quoted in Bell Irvin Wiley, *The Life of Johnny Reb: The Common Soldier of the Confederacy* (1943; repr., Baton Rouge: Louisiana State University Press, 2008), 75; Civil War Soldiers and Sailors System, National Park Service, www.nps.gov/civilwar/soldiers-and-sailors-database .htm (hereafter CWSS).

11. "Yankee Letters," *Macon (GA) Daily Telegraph*, 1 June 1863, p. 1; "An Unusual Sight," *Atlanta Daily Intelligencer*, 6 Sept. 1862, p. 3; "From the 116th Regiment," Civil War Newspaper Clippings file, Unit History Project, New York State Military Museum, Saratoga Springs, available at https://dmna.ny .gov/historic/reghist/civil/infantry/116thInf/116thInfCWN.htm.

12. Mary Chesnut, diary entry of 2 June 1862, in *Mary Chesnut's Civil War*, ed. C. Vann Woodward (New Haven, CT: Yale University Press, 1981), 358; William Thompson Lusk to Cousin Lou, 1 Aug. 1861, in *War Letters of William Thompson Lusk*, ed. William Chittenden Lusk (New York: privately printed, 1911), 66; "Patriot War Correspondence; From the Eleventh Regiment," *Wisconsin Patriot*, 7

June 1862, p. 4; "The Yankee and the Almighty Dollar," *Richmond Examiner*, 12 July 1862, p. 1; "Yankee Letters," reprinted from the *Richmond Whig* in the *Macon (GA) Daily Telegraph*, 6 Aug. 1861, p. 3. On Southern newspapers' characterizations of the North generally, including using "published extracts from enemy letters picked up on the battlefield to depict the moral depravity of 'Billy Yank' and his feminine correspondents," see J. Cutler Andrews, "The Confederate Press and Public Morale," *Journal of Southern History* 32 (1966): 445–465, quotation on 451.

13. *Daily Missouri Republican*, 7 Sept. 1862, p. 3, and 9 Sept. 1862, p. 3; *Daily Missouri Democrat*, 10 Sept. 1862, p. 1. For more on this episode, see LeeAnn Whites, "'Corresponding with the Enemy': Mobilizing the Relational Field of Battle in St. Louis," in *Occupied Women: Gender, Military Occupation, and the American Civil War*, ed. LeeAnn Whites and Alecia P. Long (Baton Rouge: Louisiana State University Press, 2009), 103–116; and Wiley, *Life of Johnny Reb*, 200 and 389n35.

14. Jos. Cross, *Camp and Field: Papers from the Portfolio of an Army Chaplain*, vol. 1 (Macon, GA: Burke, Boykin, 1864), 96; Elvira Powers, *Hospital Pencillings* (Boston: Edward L. Mitchell, 1866), 147–152.

15. "A Yankee Love Letter," *Macon (GA) Daily Telegraph*, 15 Jan. 1863, p. 2. In fact, this "Yankee love letter" is based on a parody that had circulated for some time, having appeared at least as early as 1841 as "A Western Love Letter" supposedly written by a woman in "Suspendersburg, Away in the Ill-yen-noise" (*New Orleans Times-Picayune*, 18 June 1839, p. 2). On dialect, see Michael Ellis, *North Carolina English, 1861–1865: A Guide and Glossary* (Knoxville: University of Tennessee Press, 2013).

16. William Lusk to Elizabeth Lusk, 10 Apr. 1862, in *War Letters of William Thompson Lusk*, 136; Mary Chesnut, diary entry of 24 July 1861, in Woodward, *Mary Chesnut's Civil War*, 108; Oliver Wendell Holmes Sr., "My Hunt after 'The Captain,'" *Atlantic Monthly*, December 1862, p. 749.

17. *Gallipolis (OH) Journal*, 7 Aug. 1862, p. 1.

18. Louisa May Alcott, *The Annotated Little Women*, ed. John Matteson (New York: Norton, 2016), 7; Josiah Athey to Emily Athey, 18 May 1863, Athey Family Papers, Alabama Department of Archives and History, Montgomery (hereafter ADAH); Thomas Warrick to Martha Warrick, 9 July 1864, Thomas Warrick Papers, ADAH; Abram Young to Mary Jane Boozer (sister), 8 Mar. 1864, in "Civil War Letters of Abram Hayne Young," ed. Mary Wyche Burgess,

South Carolina Historical Magazine 78 (1977): 56–70, quotation on 62; Thornton Clark to Nancy Clark, 8 May 1863, Thornton Clark Papers.

19. In the antebellum United States, women tended to have more richly developed conceptions of friendship than men and to rely heavily on their female friends. See Carroll Smith-Rosenberg, "The Female World of Love and Ritual: Relations between Women in Nineteenth-Century America," in *Disorderly Conduct: Visions of Gender in Victorian America* (New York: Oxford University Press, 1985), 53–76. Women's culture of friendship seems to have been a useful model for men in need of sentimental connections to home during the Civil War.

20. Harvey Hightower to Martha Hightower (sister), 8 Aug. 1862, in "Letters from H. J. Hightower, A Confederate Soldier, 1862–1864," ed. Dewey W. Grantham Jr., *Georgia Historical Quarterly* 40 (1956): 174–189, quotation on 176; Mattie J to "Absent Friend," 1 Apr. 1865, Confederate Memorial Literary Society Collection, under the management of the Virginia Historical Society, Richmond. Young, unmarried soldiers often addressed letters to their entire household— "Dear ones at home," or "Dear family." Married men rarely did this, instead addressing their wives and asking them to relay messages to others—although in some cases, as when the older generation dwelled in the same household, a married man would address letters jointly to his wife and to his or her parents.

21. Isaac Mann to Susan Mann, 1 Jan. 1862, Letters from Isaac Mann to Susan Deaver Mann, Huntington Library, San Marino, CA. More than one writer had this habit of surrounding names with dots, for reasons I can only conjecture in any given instance.

22. On women's letter writing generally, see Carolyn Steedman, "A Woman Writing a Letter," in *Epistolary Selves: Letters and Letter-Writers, 1600–1945*, ed. Rebecca Earle (Brookfield, VT: Ashgate, 1999), 111–133. On letters between husbands and wives in the Civil War South, and the "new frankness" and "unprecedented intimacy" those letters could spark, see Drew Gilpin Faust, *Mothers of Invention: Women of the Slaveholding South in the American Civil War* (Chapel Hill: University of North Carolina Press, 1996), 114–123; quotation on 162.

23. See, e.g., Rebecca Davis to Burwell Davis, 2 May 1863, and Matthew Davis to Burwell Davis, 22 May 1864, Rebecca Pitchford Davis Letters, #3328-z, Southern Historical Collection, The Wilson Library, University of North Carolina at Chapel Hill (hereafter SHC).

24. Rebecca Davis to Weldon Davis, 10 July 1861, and to Burwell Davis, 21 Aug. and 18 July 1861, and 2 May 1863, Rebecca Pitchford Davis Letters.

25. Rebecca Davis to Burwell Davis, 20 Jan. and 12 Sept. 1864, 17 May 1863, and Weldon Davis to Rebecca Davis, 28 June and 14 May 1863, Rebecca Pitchford Davis Letters.

26. Frances Parker to Joseph Burroughs, 10 Aug. 1861, and Frances Parker to Robert Parker, 12 July 1861, and to Joseph Burroughs, 10 Aug. 1861, Robert W. Parker Papers #5261, SHC. This and the other Parker family letters cited below also appear (though somewhat regularized in transcription) in Catherine M. Wright, *Lee's Last Casualty: The Life and Letters of Sgt. Robert W. Parker, Second Virginia Cavalry* (Knoxville: University of Tennessee Press, 2008). Biographical details about the Parker family are drawn from Wright's introduction and endnotes.

27. Robert Parker to Rebecca Parker, 19 June 1861, and Frances Parker to Robert Parker, 26 July 1861, Robert W. Parker Papers.

28. Robert Parker to Rebecca Parker, 17 May 1863, and Rebecca Parker to Robert Parker, undated scrap, on verso of note dated 20 May 1864, Robert W. Parker Papers.

29. Margaret Ross to Robert Ross, 14 Dec. 1863, and Robert Ross to Margaret Ross, 3 Jan. 1864, box 2C447, Civil War Miscellany, Briscoe Center for American History, University of Texas at Austin.

30. Ann Butler to William Butler, 30 Jan. 1865, C. Ann Butler letter, MS 114, Georgia Historical Society, Savannah; CWSS. On Gardner being Jewish, see Daniel R. Weinfeld, "A Certain Ambivalence: Florida's Jews and the Civil War," *Southern Jewish History* 17 (2014): 91–129.

31. The vast archive of Civil War soldiers' letters bears the marks of many an amateur historian's or editor's attentions. Jason Phillips contends that the interventions of families long after the war may in some instances have elided relatively unflattering parts of epistolary records. See "Battling Stereotypes: A Taxonomy of Common Soldiers in Civil War History," *History Compass* 6 (2008): 1407–1425. While this is impossible to know with certainty, it is plainly visible that many descendants of Civil War soldiers toiled assiduously over the documents—sometimes helpfully, sometimes not. More than one individual seated at a typewriter in the early to mid-twentieth century, trying to transcribe nearly century-old letters, overwrote in blue ink the pale, hard-to-read words of an original letter (see, for instance, the James W. Watkins Papers, Stuart A. Rose Manuscript, Archives, and Rare Book Library, Emory University, Atlanta, GA). Women's letters rarely have received such treatment. Collections in which women's

letters survive typically appear to have lain untouched for many years—no one having separated what looked to them like wheat from what looked like chaff.

32. Owen Creath to Harriet Creath and children, 15 Dec. 1861, Owen M. Creath Papers, MSS 1532, Ohio Historical Society, Columbus.

33. Sarah (Kate) Creath to Owen Creath, 4 Feb. 1862, and Owen Creath to Harriet Creath and children, 27 Jan. 1862, Owen M. Creath Papers.

34. Owen Creath to Harriet Creath and children, 2 Mar. 1862, and Sarah (Kate) Creath to Owen Creath, 23 Feb. 1862, Owen M. Creath Papers.

35. Harriet Creath to Owen Creath, 23 Feb. 1862, Owen M. Creath Papers.

36. Harriet Creath to Owen Creath, 23 Feb., 16 Feb., and 2 Mar. 1862, Owen to Harriet, 10 Feb. and 12 Mar. 1862, Owen M. Creath Papers

37. Hellen Alford to Warren Alford, 9 Mar. 1862, Alford Family Papers, IHS. Many of the Alford family's letters appear (though not quite perfectly transcribed) in Richard S. Skidmore, ed., *The Alford Brothers: "We All Myst Dye Sooner or Later"* (Hanover, IN: Nugget Publishers, 1995). Elizabeth Kellams was admitted to the Indiana Hospital for the Insane on 19 March 1862 displaying mania and homicidal propensities. The Civil War was not explicitly cited as an "exciting cause" (it was for some other patients at the same asylum); her admission record does note she was born in South Carolina. Central State Hospital Records, Indiana State Archives, Indianapolis.

38. Mary Alford to Warren Alford, 12 Jan. 1862. On Mary's learning to write, also see Warren to Mary, 25 Jan. 1862. These two letters are not among the Alford Family Papers at the Indiana Historical Society; they appear in Skidmore, *Alford Brothers*, 193 and 199.

39. Clem reports, "he drawed a chair on me and I took from him knocked him down and whiped hime." Clem Reily to Warren Alford, 20 Aug. 1861, Alford Family Papers.

40. Warren Alford to Lafayette Alford, 22 Sept. 1861, and Franklin Alford to Warren Alford, 27 Jan. 1862, Alford Family Papers.

41. Hellen Alford to Warren Alford, 9 Feb. 1862, and J. L. Laverty to Franklin Alford, 30 Jan. 1862, Alford Family Papers.

42. Thomas Augst, *The Clerk's Tale: Young Men and Moral Life in Nineteenth-Century America* (Chicago: University of Chicago Press, 2003), esp. 14–15; Hellen Alford to Warren Alford, 9 Feb. 1862, Alford Family Papers.

43. Harriet Creath to Owen Creath, 16 Feb. 1862, Owen M. Creath Papers; Ulysses S. Grant to Simon Bolivar Buckner, 16 Feb. 1862, transcribed from

digitized original, Armed Forces History, Division of History of Technology, National Museum of American History, Washington, DC, http://amhistory.si .edu/militaryhistory/collection/object.asp?ID=466. For Johnston's movements, see John R. Lundberg, "'I Must Save This Army': Albert Sidney Johnston and the Shiloh Campaign," in *The Shiloh Campaign*, ed. Steven E. Woodworth (Carbondale: Southern Illinois University Press, 2009), 12; Steven E. Woodworth, *Shiloh: Confederate High Tide in the Heartland* (Santa Barbara, CA: Praeger, 2013), 19–20; and T. M. Hurst, "Battle of Shiloh," *American Historical Magazine* 7 (1902): 22–37.

44. Owen Creath to Harriet Creath and children, 2 and 9 Mar. 1862, Owen M. Creath Papers. On steamboat transport during the Civil War in general, see James A. Huston, *The Sinews of War: Army Logistics, 1775–1953* (Washington, DC: Center of Military History, 1966), 211–214; on the concentration of forces that would fight at Shiloh, see O. Edward Cunningham, *Shiloh and the Western Campaign of 1862*, ed. Gary D. Joiner and Timothy B. Smith (New York: Savas Beatie, 2009), 77–79.

45. William Warren to "My Dear Wife," 11 Mar. 1862, William H. Warren Letters, BL 349, State Historical Society of Iowa, Iowa City; Owen Creath to Harriet Creath and children, 6 and 9 Mar. 1862, Owen M. Creath Papers; Hurst, "Battle of Shiloh," 31; Owen Creath to Harriet Creath and children, 12 Mar. 1862, Owen M. Creath Papers.

46. Owen Creath to Harriet Creath and children, 9 and 15 Mar. 1862, Owen M. Creath Papers. Other soldiers moving via steamer to Tennessee reported similar mail stoppages. Oliver Boardman, also of Iowa, wrote to his brother from well up the Tennessee River, "for certain reasons they will not let us send letters back for afew days." Oliver Boardman to Henry, 12 Mar. 1862, Oliver Boardman Correspondence and Journals, Special Collections Department MsL B6621, University of Iowa, Iowa City.

47. Owen Creath to Harriet Creath and children, 5, 8, and 29 Jan., 16 Feb., 27 Jan., and 6 Mar. 1862, Owen M. Creath Papers.

48. Owen Creath to Harriet Creath and children, 24 Mar. 1862, Owen M. Creath Papers.

49. Owen Creath to Harriet Creath and children, 15 and 16 Mar. 1862, Owen M. Creath Papers.

50. Owen Creath to Harriet Creath and children, 16 Mar. 1862, Harriet to Owen, 2 Mar. 1862, Owen to Harriet, 24 Mar. 1862, Owen M. Creath Papers;

William Warren to "My Dear Wife," 22 Mar. 1862, William H. Warren Letters; Leander Stillwell, "In the Ranks at Shiloh," *Journal of the Illinois State Historical Society* 15 (April–July 1922): 460–476, quotation on 463–464; Owen Creath to Harriet Creath, 24 and 15 Mar. 1862, Owen M. Creath Papers.

51. Owen Creath to Harriet Creath and children, 16 Mar. 2862, Owen M. Creath Papers; Larry J. Daniel, *Shiloh: The Battle That Changed the Civil War* (New York: Simon and Schuster, 1997), 77; William Warren to "My dear Wife," 25 Mar. 1862, and to "My Dear Wife and family," 4 Apr. 1862, William H. Warren Letters; Owen to Harriet, 24 and 28 Mar. and 2 Apr. 1862, Owen M. Creath Papers; William Warren to "My Dear Wife," 4 Apr. 1862; Owen to Harriet, 2 Apr. 1862, Owen M. Creath Papers.

52. Owen Creath to Harriet Creath and children, 20 Mar., 9 Mar., and 20 Mar. 1862, Owen M. Creath Papers.

53. William Warren to "My Dear Wife," 11 Mar. 1862, William H. Warren Letters; Owen Creath to Harriet Creath and children, 12 Mar. 1862, Owen M. Creath Papers.

54. Owen Creath to Harriet Creath and children, 28 Mar. 1862, Owen M. Creath Papers.

55. Harriet Creath to Owen Creath, 6 Apr. 1862, Owen M. Creath Papers.

56. For troop positions and movements at Shiloh, see Daniel, *Shiloh*, esp. 177–181 and 286–287, and S. H. M. Byers, *Iowa in War Times* (Des Moines, IA: W. D. Condit, 1888), 140–141. Also see Wayne and Lafayette Alford to Franklin Alford, 16 Apr. 1862, Alford Family Papers.

4. Strains

1. Charles Sedgwick to Katharine Sedgwick (daughter), 2 May 1848, and to Elizabeth Buckminster Dwight Sedgwick (wife), 3 May 1848, in *Letters from Charles Sedgwick to His Family and Friends* (Boston: privately printed, 1870), 277, 278. Charles Sedgwick was the brother of the novelist and abolitionist Catharine Maria Sedgwick, who edited the collection of his letters here cited. "The Dead Letter Office," *Living Age* 9 (1846): 23–24; Courtney Fullilove, "'Dead Letters—By a Resurrectionist': Liberty and Surveillance in the Tombs of the U.S. Post Office," *Common-Place* 12 (Jan. 2012), http://www.common-place-archives.org/vol-12/no-02/tales/.

2. Richard R. John, "The Lost World of Bartleby, the Ex-Officeholder: Variations on a Venerable Literary Form," *New England Quarterly* 70 (1997): 631–641; Richard R. John, *Spreading the News: The American Postal System from Franklin to Morse* (Cambridge, MA: Harvard University Press, 1995), 77–78; Winifred Gallagher, *How the Post Office Created America* (New York: Penguin, 2016), 143–146. For the many mid-nineteenth century treatments of the Dead Letter Office in the periodical press, see the more than twenty contemporary articles cited in Matthew Pethers, "Dead Letters and the Secret Life of the State in Nineteenth-Century America," in *The Edinburgh Companion to Nineteenth-Century American Letters and Letter-Writing*, ed. Celeste-Marie Bernier, Judie Newman, and Matthew Pethers (Edinburgh: Edinburgh University Press, 2016), 136–151.

3. Francis Copcutt, "A Day in the Dead-Letter Office," *Knickerbocker*, Feb. 1860, p. 203.

4. Herman Melville, "Bartleby, the Scrivener," in *The Piazza Tales and Other Prose Pieces, 1839–1860*, ed. Harrison Hayford, Alma A. MacDougall, G. Thomas Tanselle, et al. (Evanston, IL: Northwestern University Press, 1987), 45.

5. Henry Thompson to Lucretia Thompson, 25 Sept., 5 Oct., and 11 Nov. 1862, Henry J. H. Thompson Papers, David M. Rubenstein Rare Book & Manuscript Library, Duke University, Durham, NC. Henry was not unique in claiming it a burden to preserve home letters. See L. Bao Bui, "'I Feel Impelled to Write': Male Intimacy, Epistolary Privacy, and the Culture of Letter Writing during the American Civil War" (Ph.D. diss., University of Illinois at Urbana-Champaign, 2016), 175–176.

6. Henry Thompson to Lucretia Thompson, 19 Sept. and 16 Nov. 1862, Henry J. H. Thompson Papers.

7. Henry Thompson to Lucretia Thompson, 11 Nov. and 14 and 25 Sept. 1862, Henry J. H. Thompson Papers.

8. Henry Thompson to Lucretia Thompson, 25 Sept., 5 Oct., 7 Sept., 10 Oct., and 9 Nov. 1862, Henry J. H. Thompson Papers.

9. Lucretia Thompson to Henry Thompson, 21 and 15 Apr. 1863, and Henry Thompson to Lucretia Thompson, undated, on envelope addressed to Henry postmarked 1 Aug. 1863, Fair Haven, CT, and 8 Aug. 1863, Washington, DC, Henry J. H. Thompson Papers.

10. Lucretia Thompson to Henry Thompson, 4 Dec. 1863, and Henry to Lucretia, 7 Dec. 1863 (same sheet), Henry J. H. Thompson Papers.

11. Isaac Mann to Susan Mann, 28 Mar. 1862, Letters from Isaac Mann to Susan Deaver Mann, 1862–1864, HM 21882–21908, Huntington Library.

12. Lafayette Alford to Mary Alford, 24 Nov. 1861, Alford Family Papers, Indiana Historical Society, Indianapolis (hereafter IHS); John Lehman to Johann Adam Lehmann, 5 Sept. 1863, Lehman Family Papers, Bentley Historical Library, University of Michigan, Ann Arbor.

13. Sarah Myers to Joel Myers, 3 July 1861, in " 'Come Home Soon and Dont Delay' ": Letters from the Home Front, July, 1861," ed. Edward G. Longacre *Pennsylvania Magazine of History and Biography* 11 (1976): 395–413. One historian has found localized evidence that the Civil War caused an uptick in divorces; see David Silkenat, *Moments of Despair: Suicide, Divorce, and Debt in Civil War Era North Carolina* (Chapel Hill: University of North Carolina Press, 2011), 101–105.

14. "The advantages and disadvantages of the two methods are well known: [synchronous communication] is more costly, because it requires the partners to synchronize to establish the communication, but then, once established, it is more effective." Catuscia Palamidessi, "Comparing the Expressive Power of the Synchronous and Asynchronous *Pi*-Calculi," *Mathematical Structures in Computer Science* 13 (2003): 685–719. Google "when not to use email" and you will find an array of corporate consultants advising business people never to write e-mails "to give bad or negative news" or "to express feelings"—among numerous other things Civil War families had no choice but to do in letters.

15. Awareness of the telegraph permeated American society, but access to it did not. "The telegraph was so expensive, observed one commentator in 1856, that its use was necessarily restricted to the 'wealthier classes'. . . . Fewer than 2 percent of the American people, in the estimation of [Western Union] company president Norvin Green, would ever have the occasion to send a telegram at all." Richard R. John, "Letters, Telegrams, News," in Bernier, Newman, and Pethers, eds., *Edinburgh Companion*, 121.

16. Konstantin Dierks, *In My Power: Letter Writing and Communications in Early America* (Philadelphia: University of Pennsylvania Press, 2009), 83.

17. Malachy Postlethwayt, *The Universal Dictionary of Trade and Commerce*, vol. 2 (London: W. Strahan, 1774), s.v. "Mercantile Accountantship" (quoted in Dierks, *In My Power*, 82).

18. See, for instance, the letter by African American soldier Prince Albert, who used "the 28th Ult." and "the 28th inst." interchangeably to refer to the same

day. Ira Berlin, ed., *Freedom: A Documentary History of Emancipation, 1861–1867*, ser. 2, *The Black Military Experience* (Cambridge: Cambridge University Press, 1982), 428–429.

19. Caroline Kirkland, *A New Home—Who'll Follow? Or, Glimpses of Western Life* (New York: C. S. Francis, 1839). See Ronald J. Zboray, *A Fictive People: Antebellum Economic Development and the American Reading Public* (New York: Oxford University Press, 1993), 118.

20. Grant Taylor to Malinda Taylor, 4 and 13 Mar., 19 Apr., and 9 Oct. 1864, in *This Cruel War: The Civil War Letters of Grant and Malinda Taylor, 1862–1865*, ed. Ann K. Blomquist and Robert A. Taylor (Macon, GA: Mercer University Press, 2000), 228, 232, 240, and 292.

21. Larkin Kendrick to Mary Catherine Kendrick, 20 Jan., 3 and 16 Mar., and 8 May 1862, Larkin S. Kendrick Papers, State Archives of North Carolina, Raleigh (hereafter SANC).

22. Thornton Clark to Nancy Clark, 14 Nov. 1862, Thornton Clark Papers, M 0436, IHS.

23. Ibid.

24. Thornton Clark to Nancy Clark, 17 Nov. and 11 and 13 Dec. 1862, Thornton Clark Papers.

25. Thornton Clark to Nancy Clark, 22 Dec. 1862, Thornton Clark Papers; *Official Records of the War of the Rebellion*, ser. 1, vol. 20, part 1 (Washington, DC: Government Printing Office, 1887), 245.

26. Larry J. Daniel, *Battle of Stones River: The Forgotten Conflict between the Confederate Army of Tennessee and the Union Army of the Cumberland* (Baton Rouge: Louisiana State University Press, 2012), 140–141. James McPherson, *Battle Cry of Freedom: The Civil War Era* (New York: Oxford University Press, 1988), 580. Hoosier soldier quoted in Daniel, 197. The casualty rate at Stones River was the highest of the war as a percentage of men engaged (Williamson Murry and Wayne Wei-siang Hsieh, *A Savage War: A Military History of the Civil War* [Princeton, NJ: Princeton University Press, 2016], 298).

27. Thornton Clark to Nancy Clark, 8 Jan. 1863, Thornton Clark Papers.

28. Larkin Kendrick to Mary Catherine Kendrick, 17 May 1862, Larkin S. Kendrick Papers. On the inescapable orientation toward the future in epistolary writing, see Christopher Hager, *Word by Word: Emancipation and the Act of Writing* (Cambridge, MA: Harvard University Press, 2013), 73–78.

29. Beecher quoted in Joan Hedrick, "Parlor Literature: Harriet Beecher Stowe and the Question of 'Great Women Artists,'" *Signs* 17 (1992): 275–303, quoted on 291. Newspapers quoted in Drew Gilpin Faust, "Altars of Sacrifice: Confederate Women and Narratives of the War," *Journal of American History* 76 (1990): 1200–1228, quoted on 1211. Also see Faust, *Mothers of Invention: Women of the Slaveholding South in the American Civil War* (Chapel Hill: University of North Carolina Press, 1996), 116–118.

30. Bell Irvin Wiley, *The Life of Johnny Reb: The Common Soldier of the Confederacy* (1943; repr., Baton Rouge: Louisiana State University Press, 2008), 209. On Southern women's fears of pregnancy, see Faust, *Mothers of Invention*, 123–126. James M. McPherson, *For Cause and Comrades: Why Men Fought in the Civil War* (New York: Oxford University Press, 1997), 133, 139.

31. See Chapter 6.

32. Ronald J. Zboray and Mary Saracino Zboray, "Cannonballs and Books: Reading and the Disruption of Social Ties on the New England Home Front," in *The War Was You and Me: Civilians in the American Civil War*, ed. Joan E. Cashin (Princeton, NJ: Princeton University Press, 2002), 237–261, quotation on 247.

33. Betsy Blaisdell to Hiram Blaisdell, 13 Oct. 1864, series 1, box 6, Civil War Manuscripts Collection (MS 619), Manuscripts and Archives, Yale University Library, New Haven, CT. On Cayuga County's Republican majority, see John W. O'Brien, "The Beginnings of the Republican Party in Cayuga County," *Collections of Cayuga County Historical Society* 10 (1893): 47–49

34. Betsy Blaisdell to Hiram Blaisdell, 13 and 21 Oct. 1864, Civil War Manuscripts Collection.

35. Betsy Blaisdell to Hiram Blaisdell, 21 and 13 Oct. 1864, Civil War Manuscripts Collection.

36. Betsy Blaisdell to Hiram Blaisell, 17 Jan. 1865 and 15 Dec. 1864, Civil War Manuscripts Collection.

37. Hiram Blaisdell to Betsy Blaisdell, 23 Nov., 13 Oct., and 1 Nov. 1864, Civil War Manuscripts Collection.

38. Betsy Blaisdell to Hiram Blaisdell, 26 Nov. 1864, Civil War Manuscripts Collection.

39. Adam Mayers, *Dixie and the Dominion: Canada, the Confederacy, and the War for the Union* (Toronto: Dundurn Press, 2003), 105–116; Cathryn J. Prince, *Burn the Town and Sack the Banks! Confederates Attack Vermont!* (New York: Carroll & Graf, 2006), 139–159; Dennis K. Wilson, *Justice under Pressure: The*

Saint Albans Raid and Its Aftermath (Lanham, MD: University Press of America, 1992), 17–25; Michelle Arnosky Sherburne, *The St. Albans Raid: Confederate Attack on Vermont* (Charleston, SC: The History Press, 2014).

40. Ann Pierce to Marshall, 19 Oct. 1864, in *A War of the People: Vermont Civil War Letters*, ed. Jeffrey D. Marshall (Hanover, NH: University Press of New England, 1999), 267–268; "The Vermont Raid," *New York Herald*, 28 Oct. 1864, p. 1; Ben H. Dewey to Col. William Wells, 5 Nov. 1864, in Marshall, *War of the People*, 277–278; Sherburne, *St. Albans Raid*, 104–105; "The St. Alban's Raid," *Frank Leslie's Illustrated Newspaper*, 12 Nov. 1864, pp. 115–116 and 120–121.

41. Brian Gabrial, "'Alarming Intelligence': Sensationalism in Newspapers after the Raids at Harpers Ferry, Virginia, and St. Albans, Vermont," in *Sensationalism: Murder, Mayhem, Mudslinging, Scandals, and Disasters in 19th-Century Reporting*, ed. David B. Sachsman and David W. Bulla (New Brunswick, NJ: Transaction Publishers, 2013), 19–32, quotations from *New York Times* (6 Nov. 1864) and *Chicago Tribune* (11 Nov. 1864) on 27 and 23; Prince, *Burn the Town and Sack the Banks!*, 178–189; "The Situation," *New York Herald*, 23 Oct. 1864, p. 1. The rumor about the regimental movement is in Hiram Blaisdell to Betsy Blaisdell, 22 Nov. 1864, Civil War Manuscripts Collection. Also see Gabrial, "'Alarming Intelligence,'" 22–25; "Order from Gen. Dix," *New York Times*, 30 Oct. 1864, p. 8.

42. Betsy Blaisdell to Hiram Blaisdell, 21 Oct. and 15, 17, and 20 Nov. 1864, Civil War Manuscripts Collection.

43. Betsy Blaisdell to Hiram Blaisdell, 15 and 17 Nov. 1864, Civil War Manuscripts Collection.

44. For examples of medical records citing the Civil War as an "exciting cause" for admission into insane asylums, see Richard F. Nation and Stephen E. Towne, eds., *Indiana's Civil War: The Civil War in Documents* (Athens: Ohio University Press, 2009), 97–100.

45. Betsy Blaisdell to Hiram Blaisdell, 20 Nov. 1864, Civil War Manuscripts Collection.

46. Betsy Blaisdell to Hiram Blaisdell, 23 Nov. 1864, Civil War Manuscripts Collection.

47. Hiram Blaisdell to Betsy Blaisdell, 30 Nov. 1864, Civil War Manuscripts Collection.

48. Betsy Blaisdell to Hiram Blaisdell, 8 Dec. 1864, Civil War Manuscripts Collection.

49. See Betsy Blaisdell letters to Hiram, 8 Dec. 1864 through 8 Jan. 1865, Civil War Manuscripts Collection.

50. Betsy Blaisdell to Hiram Blaisdell, 11 Dec. 1864, and Hiram to Betsy, 25 and 27 Dec. 1864, Civil War Manuscripts Collection.

51. Betsy Blaisell to Hiram Blaisdell, 8 Dec. 1864, and Hiram to Betsy, 16 Dec. 1864, Civil War Manuscripts Collection.

52. Betsy Blaisell to Hiram Blaisdell, 5 and 8 Jan. 1864, Civil War Manuscripts Collection. Betsy Blaisdell's letters have made a single appearance in the extant historiography of the Civil War: "Betsy Blaisdell declared that if she only had the strength, presumably sapped by the war itself, she would feel 'as if I could raise up and slay every one that upholds this war.' Many reserved their ire for people like Blaisdell herself, whose opposition to the war could seem an even greater betrayal than the secessionists.'" Scott Reynolds Nelson and Carol Sheriff, *A People at War: Civilians and Soldiers in America's Civil War* (New York: Oxford University Press, 2007), 239. As I believe the foregoing pages have demonstrated, to take those fourteen quotable words, from all of Betsy Blaisdell's three dozen surviving letters, and thus to proffer her as an exemplar of Copperhead sentiment, is a profound oversimplification. Though Betsy did desperately want the war to end, the severity of her phrasing surely reflects more about the extremities of her temperament than about her politics. She never wrote a single negative word about the Union cause. Hiram, in fact, upon meeting several former slaves in Virginia, remarked happily: "it is pleasant to hear how thankful they are to be freed they think that old Abe is the man to carry the thing through." Hiram Blaisdell to Betsy Blaisdell, 8 Oct. 1864, Civil War Manuscripts Collection.

53. Sarepta Revis to Daniel Revis, 7 June 1863, and Daniel Revis to Sarepta Revis, 5 June 1863, PC.1914, Daniel W. Revis Letters, SANC.

54. Sarepta Revis to Daniel Revis, 3 Nov. 1862 and 7 and 23 June 1863, Daniel W. Revis Letters.

55. Sarepta Revis to Daniel Revis, 21 July 1863, Daniel to Sarepta, 31 May [1863], and Sarepta to Daniel, 17 June 1863, Daniel W. Revis Letters.

56. Daniel Revis to Sarepta Revis, Ellen Revis Ward, and Joseph Ward, 14 July 1863, Daniel W. Revis Letters.

57. Daniel Revis to Sarepta Revis, 9 July 1863, Daniel W. Revis Letters.

58. Daniel Revis to Sarepta Revis, 15 Aug. [1863], Daniel W. Revis Letters.

5. Breaks

1. Glenn Tucker, *Chickamauga: Bloody Battle in the West* (Indianapolis: Bobbs-Merrill, 1961), 218–232.

2. Tucker, *Chickamauga*, 251–259, and Shelby Foote, *The Civil War: A Narrative*, vol. 2, *Fredericksburg to Meridian* (New York: Random House, 1963), 735–736.

3. Thornton Clark to Nancy Clark, 22 Jan. and 31 May 1863, Thornton Clark Papers, M 0436, Indiana Historical Society, Indianapolis (hereafter IHS); James K. Huhta, "Fortress Rosecrans," *Tennessee Encyclopedia of History and Culture*, 2010, http://tennesseeencyclopedia.net/entry.php?rec=502.

4. Thornton Clark to Nancy Clark, 6 Mar., 26 Apr., 2 and 21 June, 6 July, and 24 Aug. 1863, Thornton Clark Papers.

5. Thornton Clark to Nancy Clark, 1, 18, and 22 Apr., 2 June, and 6 July 1863, Thornton Clark Papers.

6. This letter is not among the Thornton Clark Papers at the Indiana Historical Society. I am grateful to Daryl Lovell, Alice Clark's great-great-grandson, for sharing his transcription from the family collection.

7. Thornton Clark to Nancy Clark, 24 Aug. 1863, Thornton Clark Papers.

8. Thornton Clark to Nancy Clark, 7, 20, and 24 Aug. 1863, and Thornton Clark to Nancy Clark and children, 15 Sept. 1863, Thornton Clark Papers.

9. Thornton Clark to Nancy Clark, 16 June 1864, Thornton Clark Papers. Letters written by men in prisoner-of-war camps were the only ones subject to official censorship during the Civil War. On the postal procedure at Andersonville, see William Marvel, *Andersonville: The Last Depot* (Chapel Hill: University of North Carolina Press, 1994), 80–81.

10. Walt Whitman, "Come Up from the Fields Father," in *Poetry and Prose*, ed. Justin Kaplan (New York: Library of America, 1996), 437–438; italics in original.

11. Drew Gilpin Faust documents the many ways the war unsettled *ars moriendi*, the culture of the "Good Death," in *This Republic of Suffering: Death and the American Civil War* (New York: Alfred A. Knopf, 2008), 3–31. Also see Sean A. Scott, *A Visitation of God: Northern Civilians Interpret the Civil War* (New York: Oxford University Press, 2011), 191–214, and Frances M. Clarke, *War Stories: Suffering and Sacrifice in the Civil War North* (Chicago: University of Chicago Press, 2011), 42–46.

12. Arminda Kite to B. A. Cameron, 1 July 1863, Bluford Alexander Cameron Papers, Briscoe Center for American History, University of Texas at Austin (hereafter Briscoe Center-UTA).

13. See Faust, *This Republic of Suffering*, 14–18, and Ashley Michelle Mays, " 'To Suffer in Silence': Confederate Widows' Grieving Processes after the Civil War" (MA thesis, University of North Carolina-Chapel Hill, 2010).

14. Joseph Trolinger to John Long, 31 Dec. 1863 [1862], Long Family Papers, #3269-z, Southern Historical Collection, The Wilson Library, University of North Carolina at Chapel Hill (hereafter SHC). On battlefield burial, including the importance to families of locating and marking graves, see Faust, *This Republic of Suffering*, 61–101 and 129–130.

15. George Davis to Rebecca Davis, 9 Nov. 1863, Rebecca to Matthew Davis, 14 Nov. 1863, Matthew to Burwell Davis, 17 Nov. 1863, Rebecca to Burwell, 21 Nov. and 7 Dec. 1863, and B. F. Powell to "Uncle Ned," 6 Dec. 1863, Rebecca Pitchford Davis Letters, #3328-z, SHC.

16. Matthew Davis to Burwell Davis, 10 Dec. 1863, and Elizabeth Blount to Rebecca Davis, 8 Dec. 1863, Rebecca Pitchford Davis Letters.

17. Rebecca Davis to Burwell Davis, 20 Dec. 1863, Rebecca Pitchford Davis Letters. Biographical details from notes by Blanche Egerton Baker in the Davis papers.

18. Rebecca Davis to [Burwell Davis?], 15 [Oct. 1864?] (emphasis in original); Rebecca Davis to Burwell Davis, 1 Nov. 1864; and Rebecca Davis to Matthew Davis, 22 May 1864, Rebecca Pitchford Davis Letters.

19. Jane E. Schultz, *Women at the Front: Hospital Workers in Civil War America* (Chapel Hill: University of North Carolina Press, 2004), 37; Henrietta Stratton Jaquette, ed., *Letters of a Civil War Nurse: Cornelia Hancock, 1863–1865* (Lincoln: University of Nebraska Press, 1998), 4; Louisa May Alcott, *Hospital Sketches* (Boston: James Redpath, 1863), 44.

20. Thomas Warrick to Martha Warrick, 17 and 22 Sept. and 6 and 30 Oct. 1862, Thomas Warrick Papers, Alabama Department of Archives and History, Montgomery.

21. Walt Whitman to Mr. and Mrs. Samuel B. Haskell, 27 July 1863, in *The Correspondence*, by Walt Whitman, ed. Edwin Haviland Miller (New York: New York University Press, 1961–1977), 1:119; Whitman, "Our Wounded and Sick Soldiers," *New York Times*, 11 Dec. 1864, p. 1.

22. Kate Kern to Mrs. C. J. Presnell, 2 Oct. 1864, Kate Kern Letters, Library of Virginia, Richmond (quoted in Jane E. Schultz, "Healing the Nation: Condolence and Correspondence in Civil War Hospitals," *Proteus* 17 [Fall 2000]: 35); Thomas B. Barker to Roscoe Barker, 20 July 1861, Thomas Barker Letter, Coll. 2–289, Maine Historical Society, Portland.

23. Larkin Kendrick to Mary Catherine Kendrick, 28 July 1862, PC.1921, Larkin S. Kendrick Papers, State Archives of North Carolina, Raleigh; C. T. Dalton to Oliver Martin and Family, 5 Aug. 1862, William T. Martin Papers, Stuart A. Rose Manuscript, Archives, and Rare Book Library, Emory University, Atlanta, GA. "Over the course of the war, the composition of condolence letters to family at home became something of a stock-in-trade for some soldiers" (Scott, *Visitation of God*, 200).

24. [James] H. Freeman to "Madam," 19 Aug. 1864, enclosed in Rebecca Guy to the Adjutant General of the Army, 11 Mar. 1865, G-42 1865, Letters Received Relating to Recruiting, ser. 366, Colored Troops Division, Record Group 94, National Archives. The letter is transcribed and published in Ira Berlin, ed., *Freedom: A Documentary History of Emancipation, 1861–1867*, ser. 2, *The Black Military Experience* (Cambridge: Cambridge University Press, 1982), 600–601. Also see Christopher Hager, *Word by Word: Emancipation and the Act of Writing* (Cambridge, MA: Harvard University Press, 2013), 116–118.

25. George Worden to Fannie Worden, 26 Feb. 1864, George E. Worden Civil War Letters, IHS.

26. George Worden to Fannie Worden, 1 Feb. 1864, George E. Worden Civil War Letters.

27. George Worden to Fannie Worden, 14 Feb. 1864, George E. Worden Civil War Letters.

28. George Worden to Fannie Worden, 15 Feb. 1864, George E. Worden Civil War Letters.

29. Susan J. Matt, *Homesickness: An American History* (New York: Oxford University Press, 2011), 75–101. Also see Frances Clarke, "So Lonesome I Could Die: Nostalgia and Debates over Emotional Control in the Civil War North," *Journal of Social History* 41.2 (Winter 2007): 253–282.

30. George Worden to Fannie Worden, 1 and 8 Mar. 1864, George E. Worden Civil War Letters.

31. George Worden to Fannie Worden, 28 Feb. and 1 Mar. 1864, George E. Worden Civil War Letters; emphasis in original.

32. George Worden to Fannie Worden, 8 Mar. 1864, George E. Worden Civil War Letters.

33. George Worden to Fannie Worden, 14 Mar. 1864, George E. Worden Civil War Letters.

34. Frank Saltzgiver to Mrs. Worden, 21 Mar. 1864, George E. Worden Civil War Letters.

35. Jefferson Davis in Shelby Foote, *The Civil War: A Narrative*, vol. 3, *Red River to Appomattox* (1974; repr., New York: Vintage, 1986), 140. "Second Inaugural Address," in *The Collected Works of Abraham Lincoln*, vol. 8, ed. Roy P. Basler (New Brunswick, NJ: Rutgers University Press, 1953), 333.

36. William Gilliland to Martha Gilliland, 26 June 1863, MS.54–136, Gilliland Civil War Letters, Mississippi Valley Collection, University of Memphis Library, Memphis, TN; Thomas Warrick to Martha Warrick, 9 Oct. 1862, Thomas Warrick Papers; Heber Hollis to Thomas Hollis, 9 Sept. 1863, in "Hollis Correspondence," *Indiana Magazine of History* 36 (1940): 280.

37. For the Lehman family biography and timeline, I have relied on "The Adam Lehman Family," unpublished typescript, Lehman Family Papers, Bentley Historical Library, University of Michigan, Ann Arbor.

38. John Lehman to family, 9 Oct. 1862, John Lehman to "Dear Parents," 8 Dec. 1862, and John Lehman to "Dear Parents Brothers and sisters," 15 Dec. 1862, Lehman Family Papers.

39. Frederick Lehman to "Dear Sister," 25 Feb. 1863 (typescript), Lehman Family Papers.

40. John Lehman to family, 15 Dec. 1862, Lehman Family Papers. Frederick wrote at least one letter on a sheet of the same bank drafts—a December 29, 1862, letter (in English) to his sister Mary. It appears that some of Fred's letters from December 1862 have not survived, so he may have used more pages of John's purloined checkbook for letters to his parents. There was in fact a long tradition of writing on currency; Joshua R. Greenberg, "Bank Notes and Queries: Writing on Early Republic Paper Money" (Early American Material Texts conference, Philadelphia, 27 May 2016). The logic and rhetoric of "debt" had long characterized correspondents' sense of their mutual obligations; see Rebecca Earle, "Introduction: Letters, Writers, and the Historian," in *Epistolary Selves: Letters and Letter-Writers, 1600–1945*, ed. Earle (Brookfield, VT: Ashgate, 1999), 8.

41. John Lehman to family, 16 Apr. 1863 (typescript), Lehman Family Papers. The transcriber of this letter, the manuscript of which evidently is lost, records

only that "the first twenty lines" of the holograph were in German. It is not known what those lines said.

42. John Lehman to "Dear & beloved Parents," 10 May 1863, Lehman Family Papers.

43. John Lehman to "Dear Parents and Dear Sister Vrona," 13 June 1863, Lehman Family Papers. John had not been in the hottest fighting at Chancellorsville—his was one of the regiments that remained across the Rappahannock from Fredericksburg while Joe Hooker maneuvered around the Confederate rear—but he did cross the river and attack Marye's Heights under heavy shelling.

44. John Lehman to "Dear Parents and Dear Sister Verona," 17 July 1863, and John Lehman to "My Dear Parents and Miss Verona," 13 Nov. 1863, Lehman Family Papers.

45. John Lehman to Verona Lehman, 7 Mar., 16 Apr., and 1 May 1864, Lehman Family Papers.

46. John Lehman to Verona Lehman, undated [1864], Lehman Family Papers.

47. John Lehman to Verona Lehman, 31 Jan. 1864, and John Lehman to Verona Lehman and "Miss Charlotte," 7 Mar. 1864, Lehman Family Papers. Epistolary matchmaking, with fewer romantic overtones than Verona may have used, was not uncommon. Lucinda Silk, writing to her cousin Thomas, a Kentucky-born Union soldier, asked him to "tell your old woman to rit to me" and tried to forge other epistolary relationships, too: "Mary caviness ses that shee wants you to rit to her and she wil rit to you and shee wants isiek to rit to her and shee wil rit to him." Lucinda Silk to Thomas Poe, 12 Apr. [1863?], Thomas Bueford Poe Civil War Letters, IHS.

48. John Lehman to Verona Lehman, 1 May 1864, Lehman Family Papers. On wagons: *Official Records of the War of the Rebellion*, ser. 1, vol. 33 (Washington, DC: Government Printing Office, 1891), 854–855.

49. S. Franklin Schoonmaker to Lehman family, ca. 7 May 1864, in John Lehman pocket diary, Lehman Family papers.

50. Robert Richardson to Martha Dickson, 7 Apr. 1863, PC.1825, Poteet-Dickson Letters, 1861–1902 and undated, State Archives of North Carolina, Raleigh. On the "namelessness" of the Civil War dead, see Ian Finseth, "The Civil War Dead: Realism and the Problem of Anonymity," *American Literary History* 25.3 (Fall 2013): 535–562.

51. William Moxley to George Moxley, 2 Apr. 1862. William M. Moxley Papers, 1854–1901, Briscoe Center-UTA (reprinted in *Oh, What a Loansome Time I Had: The Civil War Letters of Major William Morel Moxley, Eighteenth Alabama Infantry, and Emily Beck Moxley*, ed. Thomas W. Cutrer [Tuscaloosa: University of Alabama Press, 2002], 137).

52. George Collard to Harriet Creath, 16 Apr. 1862, in widow's pension application no. 36,575, certificate no. 19,246; service of Owen M. Creath (Pvt., Co. K, Thirteenth Iowa Inf.), Record Group 15: Civil War Pension Files, National Archives and Records Administration, Washington, DC.

6. Unions

1. Henry Thompson to Lucretia Thompson, undated [1862], 5 Oct. 1862, 19 Mar. and 23 April 1863; Lucretia Thompson to Henry Thompson, 29 May and 1 June 1863, Henry J. H. Thompson Papers, David M. Rubenstein Rare Book & Manuscript Library, Duke University, Durham, NC (hereafter Rubenstein Library-DU).

2. Henry Thompson to Lucretia Thompson, 22 July 1863; "Minnets of a Diary," 19 Apr. 1864; letter to Lucretia Thompson, 4 Aug. 1864 (emphasis in original), Henry J. H. Thompson Papers.

3. Francis Poteet to Martha Poteet, 3 and 23 Nov. 1863, PC.1825, Poteet-Dickson Letters, 1861–1902 and undated, State Archives of North Carolina, Raleigh (hereafter SANC).

4. Francis Poteet to Martha Poteet, 22, 8, and 22 Nov. 1863, Poteet-Dickson Letters. On white Southern soldiers' comparing themselves to slaves, see Randall C. Jimerson, *The Private Civil War: Popular Thought during the Sectional Conflict* (Baton Rouge: Louisiana State University Press, 1988), 206–209.

5. Francis Poteet to Martha Poteet, 23 Nov. 1863, Poteet-Dickson Letters.

6. Sophia Shaw to "My Dear Brother," 9 Feb. 1865, Confederate Memorial Literary Society Collection, under the management of the Virginia Historical Society, Richmond; Daniel Revis to Sarepta Revis, 12 June 1863, PC.1914, Daniel W. Revis Letters, SANC; Margaret Baggarly to Tilmon Baggarly, 17 Dec. 1862, Tilmon F. Baggarly Papers, 1860–1879, Rubenstein Library-DU; Eli Fogelman to Lucy Fogleman, 21 Mar. 1863, Eli Fogleman Letters #5279-z, Southern Historical Collection, The Wilson Library, University of North Carolina at Chapel Hill (hereafter SHC). For more dreams in correspondence

between wives and husbands, see Drew Gilpin Faust, *Mothers of Invention: Women of the Slaveholding South in the American Civil War* (Chapel Hill: University of North Carolina Press, 1996), 114–115.

7. J. C. Pemberton to Jefferson Davis, 17 July 1863, in *Official Records of the War of the Rebellion*, ser. 1, vol. 24, part 3 (Washington, DC: Government Printing Office, 1889), 1010.

8. Ella Lonn, *Desertion during the Civil War* (1928; repr., Lincoln: University of Nebraska Press, 1998), 26, 231–235. On problems in counting deserters from the Southern side, see Mark A. Weitz, *More Damning than Slaughter: Desertion in the Confederate Army* (Lincoln: University of Nebraska Press, 2005), vii–xix. Also see Joan E. Cashin, "Deserters, Civilians, and Draft Resistance in the North," in *The War Was You and Me: Civilians in the American Civil War*, ed. Cashin (Princeton, NJ: Princeton University Press, 2002), 262–285.

9. Betsy Blaisdell to Hiram Blaisdell, 1 Dec. 1864, 5 and 3 Jan. 1865, series 1, box 6, Civil War Manuscripts Collection (MS 619), Manuscripts and Archives, Yale University Library, New Haven, CT.

10. Thomas Kendrick to Larkin and Mary Catherine Kendrick, 20 Sept. 1864, Larkin S. Kendrick Papers, SANC; James Lockmiller to Clarissa Lockmiller, 5 July 1862, Lockmiller Family Papers, 1862–1863 (MSS815), Stuart A. Rose Manuscript, Archives, and Rare Book Library, Emory University, Atlanta, GA; Benjamin Rountree, "Letters of a Confederate Soldier," *Georgia Review* 18 (1964): 280.

11. Patt Divine to "dear Wife," [?] Nov. 1863, Civil War Biographical File, Briscoe Center for American History, University of Texas at Austin; Joseph Diltz to Mary Diltz, 25 June 1862, Joseph Sherman Diltz Papers, Rubenstein Library-DU. On secrecy about desertion in soldiers' letters, see L. Bao Bui, "'I Feel Impelled to Write': Male Intimacy, Epistolary Privacy, and the Culture of Letter Writing during the American Civil War" (Ph.D. diss., University of Illinois at Urbana-Champaign, 2016), 112–114.

12. Hiram Blaisdell to Betsy Blaisdell, 6 Dec. 1864, and Betsy Blaisdell to Hiram Blaisdell, 21 Oct. 1864, Civil War Manuscripts Collection.

13. Hiram Blaisdell to Betsy Blaisdell, 6, 16, and 28 Dec. 1864, Civil War Manuscripts Collection.

14. Melissa Baker to Obadiah Baker, 11 Aug. 1862, box 2, envelope 22, Obadiah Ethelbert Baker Papers, Huntington Library, San Marino, CA; Roseanna McGowan to "Dear Friend," 15 February 1865, Confederate Memorial Literary Society Collection.

15. Betsy Blaisdell to Hiram Blaisdell, 3 Jan. 1865, Civil War Manuscripts Collection; Tilmon Baggarly to Margaret Baggarly, undated, box 6, section A, Tilmon F. Baggarly Papers, 1860–1879, Rubenstein Library-DU; Grant Taylor to Malinda Taylor, 4 Jan. 1865, in *This Cruel War: The Civil War Letters of Grant and Malinda Taylor, 1862–1865*, ed. Ann K. Blomquist and Robert A. Taylor (Macon, GA: Mercer University Press, 2000), 321; Lucy Fogleman to Eli Fogleman, 15 Jan. 1863, Eli Fogleman Letters.

16. Confederate officials quoted in Lonn, *Desertion during the Civil War*, 29; Wiley, *The Life of Billy Yank: The Common Soldier of the Union* (1952; repr., Baton Rouge: Louisiana State University Press, 2008), 449.

17. Frederick Hooker to Jeannette Hooker, 18 May 1864, Frederick Hooker Letters, MS 57315, Connecticut Historical Society, Hartford. Fred may have had his calendar just slightly off. He said he mailed the sixty dollars from Belle Plains on May 16 and dated his letter from Fredericksburg May 18, but the published regimental history suggests Fred would have disembarked at Belle Plains on May 18 and been in Fredericksburg on the evening of May 19. Theodore F. Vaill, *History of the Second Connecticut Volunteer Heavy Artillery* (Winsted, CT: Winsted Printing Company, 1868), 48–50.

18. Stephen Crane, *The Red Badge of Courage* (New York: D. Appleton, 1896), 34; Shelby Foote, *The Civil War: A Narrative*, vol. 3, *Red River to Appomattox* (New York: Random House, 1974), 240.

19. Vaill, *History of the Second Connecticut Volunteer Heavy Artillery*, 52, 58, 62; Gordon C. Rhea, *Cold Harbor: Grant and Lee, May 26–June 3, 1864* (Baton Rouge: Louisiana State University Press, 2002), 240–241. "Dotted line" quoted in Dudley Landon Vaill, *The County Regiment: A Sketch of the Second Regiment of Connecticut Volunteer Heavy Artillery* (Litchfield Co., CT: University Club, 1908), 37–38.

20. Thomas W. Hyde, *Following the Greek Cross; or, Memories of the Sixth Army Corps* (Boston: Houghton Mifflin, 1894), 201; S. Millett Thompson, *Thirteenth Regiment of New Hampshire Volunteer Infantry* (Boston: Houghton Mifflin, 1888), 360; quoted in Matthew Warshauer, *Connecticut in the American Civil War* (Middletown, CT: Wesleyan University Press, 2011), 148.

21. Vaill, *History of the Second Connecticut*, 67.

22. Frederick Hooker to Jeannette Hooker, undated (between 4 and 10 June 1864), Frederick Hooker Letters.

23. Frederick Hooker to Jeannette Hooker, 10 June 1864, Frederick Hooker Letters. On conditions at Cold Harbor, see Kathryn Shively Meier, "I Told Him

to Go On: Enduring Cold Harbor," in *From Cold Harbor to the Crater: The End of the Overland Campaign*, ed. Gary W. Gallagher and Caroline E. Janney (Chapel Hill: University of North Carolina Press, 2015), 73–108.

24. Margaret Black Tatum, "'Please Send Stamps': The Civil War Letters of William Allen Clark, Part II," *Indiana Magazine of History* 41 (1995): 208. For dollar values see Samuel H. Williamson, "Seven Ways to Compute the Relative Value of a U.S. Dollar Amount, 1774 to Present," MeasuringWorth.com, 2016, www.measuringworth.com/uscompare/.

25. Grant Taylor to Malinda Taylor, 9 July 1864, in Blomquist and Taylor, *This Cruel War*, 268.

26. Victoria E. Bynum, *The Free State of Jones: Mississippi's Longest Civil War* (Chapel Hill: University of North Carolina Press, 2001), 100. "The idea that soldiers' wives' desperate letters were driving men to desertion was widely held by the Confederate public and officials alike," writes Stephanie McCurry in *Confederate Reckoning: Power and Politics in the Civil War South* (Cambridge, MA: Harvard University Press, 2010), 192. Kate Cumming, a Confederate nurse, reported the opinion in her hospital that "the women were the cause of nearly all the desertions" (*Kate: The Journal of a Confederate Nurse*, ed. Richard Barksdale Harwell [Baton Rouge: Louisiana State University Press, 1959], 143).

27. McCurry, *Confederate Reckoning*, 133–177.

28. Quoted in Lonn, *Desertion during the Civil War*, 13. According to Lonn, "The court was melted to tears," though Edward Cooper was sentenced to death anyway, in accordance with the law. He later was pardoned by Robert E. Lee.

29. Elizabeth Davis to James Davis, 5 Aug. and 17 July 1862, James Jackson Davis Papers, 1854–1948, Rubenstein Library-DU.

30. Official Union records document fewer than 150 deserters executed. The real number may have been higher and at least matched in the Confederate army. Wiley, *Life of Billy Yank*, 206. Also see James M. McPherson, *For Cause and Comrades: Why Men Fought in the Civil War* (New York: Oxford University Press, 1997), 132–140, and Jimerson, *Private Civil War*, 231–235. I am grateful to Mike Ellis for sharing his compilation of references to execution by firing squad in the Corpus of American Civil War Letters (www.ehistory.org/projects/common-tongues.html).

31. Thomas Warrick to Martha Warrick, 19 Dec. 1862, Thomas Warrick Papers, Alabama Department of Archives and History, Montgomery.

32. Henry Thompson to Lucretia Thompson, 22 Dec. 1862 and 7 Jan. 1863, Lucretia to Henry, 14 Jan. 1863, and Henry to Lucretia, 13 Aug. 1864, Henry J. H. Thompson Papers, Rubenstein Library-DU.

33. Barton A. Meyers, *Rebels against the Confederacy: North Carolina's Unionists* (New York: Cambridge University Press, 2014), 69, 102; John C. Inscoe and Gordon B. McKinney, *The Heart of Confederate Appalachia: Western North Carolina in the Civil War* (Chapel Hill: University of North Carolina Press, 2000), 129–131. Chronology of Francis's movements is deduced from his letter of 12 Jan. 1864 and Martha's of 21 Jan., 4 Feb., and 2 Nov. 1864, Poteet-Dickson Letters.

34. Francis Poteet to Martha Poteet, 12 Jan. 1864, Poteet-Dickson Letters.

35. Martha Poteet to Francis Poteet, 7 Jan. 1864, Poteet-Dickson Letters.

36. Francis Poteet to Martha Poteet, 8 Feb. 1864, and Martha to Francis, 7 Apr. 1864, Poteet-Dickson Letters.

37. Martha Poteet to Francis Poteet, 21 Jan. 1864, Poteet-Dickson Letters.

38. Martha Poteet to Francis Poteet, 4 Feb. 1864, Poteet-Dickson Letters.

39. Ibid. On class tensions in the South, especially as inflamed by the conscription rules, see Jimerson, *Private Civil War*, 192–194.

40. Martha Poteet to Francis Poteet, 4 Feb. 1864, Poteet-Dickson Letters. On poor whites' attitudes toward the Civil War in North Carolina—the state that contributed the most men to the Confederate army but also witnessed some of the fiercest resistance to the war—see Bill Cecil-Fronsman, *Common Whites: Class and Culture in Antebellum North Carolina* (Lexington: University Press of Kentucky, 1992), 203–218. On class resentment in the Confederacy generally, see Steven Hahn, *The Roots of Southern Populism: Yeoman Farmers and the Transformation of the Georgia Upcountry, 1850–1890* (New York: Oxford University Press, 1983), 116–133.

41. Martha Poteet to Francis Poteet, 18 Feb. 1864, Poteet-Dickson Letters.

42. Martha Poteet to Francis Poteet, 7 Apr. 1864, Poteet-Dickson Letters.

43. Francis Poteet to Martha Poteet, 4 May 1864, and enclosure in Martha Poteet to Francis Poteet, 16 June 1864 (folder 20), Poteet-Dickson Letters. For the movements of Francis's regiment, I have relied on W. A. Day, *A True History of Company I, 49th Regiment, North Carolina Troops in the Great Civil War* (Newton, NC: Enterprise Job Office, 1893).

44. Martha Poteet to Francis Poteet, 16 June 1864 (folder 21), Poteet-Dickson Letters.

45. Martha Poteet to Francis Poteet, 16 June 1864 (folder 20), Poteet-Dickson Letters. James M. McPherson, *Battle Cry of Freedom: The Civil War Era* (New York: Oxford University Press, 1988), 695–698.

46. Leslie Van Gelder, "Counting the Children: The Role of Children in the Production of Finger Flutings in Four Upper Paleolithic Caves," *Oxford Journal of Archaeology* 34 (2015): 119–138; Kevin Sharpe and Leslie Van Gelder, "Evidence for Cave Marking by Paleolithic Children," *Antiquity* 80 (2006): 937–947; Linda L. Layne, " 'He Was a Real Baby with Baby Things': A Material Culture Analysis of Personhood, Parenthood, and Pregnancy Loss," *Journal of Material Culture* 5 (2000): 321–345.

47. Francis Poteet to Martha Poteet, 4 Oct. 1864, Poteet-Dickson Letters. This phrase, with only rare and modest variations, appears in more than half the couple's thirty-six surviving letters—though that shouldn't necessarily indicate the emptiness of the gesture. The internal evidence of the letters also suggests they wrote a great number of letters that were never delivered.

48. For a study of another Appalachian woman's growing resourcefulness during the war, see John C. Inscoe, *Race, War, and Remembrance in the Appalachian South* (Lexington: University Press of Kentucky, 2008), 144–174.

49. Enclosure in Martha Poteet to Francis Poteet, 16 June 1864 (folder 20), Poteet-Dickson Letters.

50. Francis Poteet to Martha Poteet, 31 Dec. 1864, 18 Jan. 1865, Poteet-Dickson Letters.

51. Martha Poteet to Francis Poteet, 2 Feb. 1865, Poteet-Dickson Letters.

52. Benton Lewis to Lydia Watkins, 20 May, 13 June 1863, Lydia Watkins Papers, 1863–1865, Bentley Historical Library, University of Michigan, Ann Arbor. (What I have cited as Benton's letter of 20 May, from Covington, Kentucky, bears a penciled indication by an archivist suggesting it is dated "May 4th," but this is not possible—the regiment did not even leave Michigan until May 12. Benton either had written 18 and then changed it to 20, or vice versa.) Transcriptions of selected letters between Lydia and Benton appear in Virginia Everham, "Letters from Home," in *Michigan Women in the Civil War* (Lansing: Michigan Civil War Centennial Observance Commission, 1963), 35–63.

53. Lydia Watkins to Benton Lewis, 26 May 1863, Lydia Watkins Papers.

54. Lydia Watkins to Benton Lewis, 26 May and 17 July 1863, 16 Feb. 1864, Lydia Watkins Papers.

55. Benton Lewis to Lydia Watkins, 4 July 1863, Lydia Watkins to Benton Lewis, 17 July 1863, and Benton Lewis to Lydia Watkins, 3 Aug. 1863, Lydia Watkins Papers.

56. Lydia Watkins to Benton Lewis, 17 July 1863 and 16 Feb. 1864, Benton Lewis to Lydia Watkins, 20 and 4 Mar., 17 Apr. 1864, Lydia Watkins Papers.

57. Biographical sketch in Lydia Watkins Papers. Only after fourteen months of correspondence with Benton did Lydia begin to use her husband's name, calling him "Watkins." Lydia Watkins to Benton Lewis, 31 July 1864, Lydia Watkins Papers.

58. Benton Lewis to Lydia Watkins, 20 Aug. 1863, and Lydia Watkins to Benton Lewis, 16 Feb. 1864, Lydia Watkins Papers.

59. Benton Lewis to Lydia Watkins, 3 Feb., 27 and 12 Mar. 1864, Lydia Watkins Papers. My thanks to Julia Goesser Assaiante for her translation of the lines in German.

60. Benton Lewis to Lydia Watkins, 20 Mar. 1864, Lydia Watkins Papers.

61. Lydia Watkins to Benton Lewis, 8 May, 17 and 31 July 1864, Lydia Watkins Papers.

62. Lydia Watkins to Benton Lewis, 22 May, 24 Apr., 17 July 1864, Lydia Watkins Papers.

63. Lydia Watkins to Benton Lewis, 17 July, 24 Apr. 1864, Lydia Watkins Papers.

64. Lydia Watkins to Benton Lewis, 26 and 20 Sept. 1864, Lydia Watkins Papers; emphasis in original. Multiple Lincoln biographies were published in 1863 and 1864, especially targeting young readers; see Alice Fahs, *The Imagined Civil War: Popular Literature of the North and South, 1861–1865* (Chapel Hill: University of North Carolina Press, 2001), 266–267.

65. For penmanship, see especially last page of Benton Lewis to Lydia Watkins, 20 May 1863, and on clerking, see Benton Lewis to Lydia Watkins, 16 Mar. 1865, Lydia Watkins Papers.

66. Lydia Watkins to Benton Lewis, 6 Apr. 1865, Lydia Watkins Papers; Christopher Hager, *Word by Word: Emancipation and the Act of Writing* (Cambridge, MA: Harvard University Press, 2013), 184–185; Shelby Foote, *The Civil War*, vol. 3, 898–901 (journalist quotation on 900); Noah Andre Trudeau, *Out of the Storm: The End of the Civil War, April–June 1865* (Baton Rouge: Louisiana State University Press, 1994), 82–83; Martha Hodes, *Mourning Lincoln* (New Haven, CT: Yale University Press, 2015), 26–29.

67. Henry Thompson to Lucretia Thompson, 15 Apr. 1865, Henry J. H. Thompson Papers; Hiram Blaisdell to Besty Blaisdell, 8 Apr. 1865, and Betsy Blaisdell to Hiram Blaisdell, 9 Apr. 1865, Civil War Manuscripts Collection; Lydia Watkins to Benton Lewis, 6 Apr. 1865, Lydia Watkins Papers.

68. Benton Lewis to Lydia Watkins, 16 Apr. 1865, Lydia Watkins Papers.

Conclusion

1. E. A. R. Thomas to Aunt Jane McCarver, 17 Jan. 1866, William T. Anderson Papers, Archives of DePauw University and Indiana United Methodism, Greencastle, IN.

2. Frances M. Clark, *War Stories: Suffering and Sacrifice in the Civil War North* (Chicago: University of Chicago Press, 2011), 146–171; Bourne quoted on 148. On the contest also see Brian Matthew Jordan, *Marching Home: Union Veterans and Their Unending Civil War* (New York: Norton, 2014), 105–126; Allison M. Johnson, "'The Scars We Carve': Disruptive Bodies in Civil War Literature" (Ph.D. diss., UCLA, 2013), 186–212; and Colleen Glenney Boggs, "The Civil War's 'Empty Sleeve' and the Cultural Production of Disabled Americans," *J19: The Journal of Nineteenth-Century Americanists* 3 (2015): 54. The twenty thousand figure is almost certainly an underreporting. No reliable statistics exist for Southern amputees; see Brian Craig Miller, *Empty Sleeves: Amputation in the Civil War South* (Athens: University of Georgia Press, 2015), 10–12. On Franklin Durrah, see Jalynn Olsen Padilla, "Army of 'Cripples': Northern Civil War Amputees, Disability, and Manhood in Victorian America" (Ph.D. diss., University of Delaware, 2007), 57–58. On posttraumatic stress among Civil War soldiers, see Jordan, *Marching Home*, 126–130, and Eric T. Dean Jr., *Shook over Hell: Post-Traumatic Stress, Vietnam, and the Civil War* (Cambridge, MA: Harvard University Press, 1997).

3. Edmund Wilson, *Patriotic Gore: Studies in the Literature of the American Civil War* (New York: Oxford University Press, 1962), 635–669; quotations on 638, 648, and 650. For arguments that the Civil War reshaped American culture, see Louis Menand, *The Metaphysical Club* (New York: Farrar, Straus, and Giroux, 2001) and Randall Fuller, *From Battlefields Rising: How the Civil War Transformed American Literature* (New York: Oxford University Press, 2011). For an alternative view, see Cody Marrs, *Nineteenth-Century American Literature and the Long Civil War* (New York: Cambridge University Press, 2015).

4. 1870 U.S. census, Henderson County, North Carolina, population schedule, Green River Township, p. 267a (stamped), dwelling 9, family 9, David [*sic*] Revis; digital image, *Ancestry.com* (www.ancestry.com); citing NARA microfilm publication M593, roll 1143.

5. D. R. Revis Oath of Allegiance, 29 Aug. 1865, and J. C. Pace to Daniel W. Revis (preacher's license), 23 Aug. 1865, PC.1914, Daniel W. Revis Letters, State Archives of North Carolina, Raleigh (hereafter SANC); Jennie Jones Giles, "Settling County History," *Hendersonville Times-News,* 16 April 2006, www .blueridgenow.com/news/20060416/settling-county-history. An unsigned biographical note in the archive's finding aid counts twelve children, including the two who died (Finding Aid of the Daniel W. Revis Letters, SANC).

6. Dan W. Olds, "A John Poteet of Burke and McDowell Counties, NC, and his family" (Spartanburg, SC: n.p., 2001), http://freepages.genealogy.rootsweb .ancestry.com/~dano/poteatbook.pdf.

7. Francis and Martha Poteet to F. M. and Celenia Dickson, 16 Jan. 1889, 4 July 1891, PC.1825, Poteet-Dickson Letters, 1861–1902 and undated, SANC.

8. "Family memorandum written by Rufina Celena Poteet Dickson," Poteet-Dickson Letters; Olds, "A John Poteet."

9. William Marvel, *Andersonville: The Last Depot* (Chapel Hill: University of North Carolina Press, 1994), 63–64, 72–73, 92, 101, 111.

10. Marvel, *Andersonville,* 198–203, 214; "Memorandum from Prisoner of War Records," Thornton Clark Civil War Documents, #SC3020, Indiana Historical Society (hereafter IHS). On scurvy among prisoners, see Alfred Jay Bollet, "Scurvy and Chronic Diarrhea in Civil War Troops: Were They Both Nutritional Deficiency Syndromes?" *Journal of the History of Medicine and Allied Sciences* 47 (1992): 49–67. The reason Thornton's grave was unmarked is likely that, after the September evacuation of most prisoners, Confederate officials forced black men—some slaves, some imprisoned soldiers from the U.S. Colored Troops—to take over burial detail. They were largely illiterate, and few records were kept of interments at Andersonville in fall 1864 (Marvel, *Andersonville,* 203).

11. Nancy Clark, widow's pension application no. 113,843, certificate no. 81,625; service of Thornton Clark (Pvt., Co. B, Forty-Second Indiana Inf.), Record Group 15: Civil War Pension Files, National Archives and Records Administration, Washington, DC.

12. "A Patriotic Family," *Dale (Indiana) Reporter,* 17 Apr 1917, p. 3; "A Good Woman Gone" (Nancy Clark obituary), *Dale Reporter,* 3 Jan. 1919, p. 1.

13. On postwar writings by Civil War veterans, see David W. Blight, *Race and Reunion: The Civil War in American Memory* (Cambridge, MA: Harvard University Press, 2001), especially 172–181.

14. Frederick Hooker to Jeannette Hooker, 3 and 5 Apr. 1864, Frederick Hooker Letters, Connecticut Historical Society, Hartford (hereafter CHS).

15. K. Nolin, Civil War Manuscripts Project, CHS.

16. Clayton W. Blaisdell obituary, *Syracuse (New York) Post-Standard*, 15 Mar. 1950, p. 16; Mark Lause, *Free Labor: The Civil War and the Making of an American Working Class* (Urbana: University of Illinois Press, 2015).

17. On the limitations of literacy as a means of social mobility, see Harvey Graff, *The Literacy Myth: Literacy and Social Structure in the Nineteenth-Century City* (New York: Academic Press, 1979). On Remington, see Anne Trubek, *The History and Uncertain Future of Handwriting* (New York: Bloomsbury, 2016), 85.

18. David C. Smith to Mrs. A. F. Brown, 12 July 1907, private collection. My thanks to Daryl Lovell for sharing an abundance of material related to Thornton and Nancy Clark and their descendants.

19. J. A. Scammahorn to Alice Brown, 18 Dec. 1907, private collection. *Report of the Unveiling and Dedication of Indiana Monument at Andersonville, Georgia, Thursday, November 26, 1908* (Indianapolis: Wm. B. Burford, 1909). David C. Smith to Alice Brown, 29 July 1908, private collection. Brown Brothers Lumber is still open on Medcalf Street in Dale. It's now affiliated with Ace Hardware; see "Brown Brothers Lumber Company," *Historic Business Register*, IHS, www.indianahistory.org/our-services/books-publications/hbr/.

20. Richard S. Skidmore, "Epilogue," in *The Alford Brothers: "We Must All Dye Sooner or Later"* (Hanover, IN: Nugget Publishers, 1995), 333–337.

21. Owen Creath to Harriet Creath and children, 29 Dec. 1861, Owen M. Creath Papers, MSS 1532, Ohio Historical Society, Columbus.

22. Harriet Creath, widow's pension application no. 36,575, certificate no. 19,246; service of Owen M. Creath (Pvt., Co. K, Thirteenth Iowa Inf.), Record Group 15: Civil War Pension Files, National Archives and Records Administration, Washington, DC.

23. Sarah Catherine (Kate) Creath to Harriet Creath, 20 June 1870 and 12 Jan. 1872, Owen M. Creath Papers.

24. Sarah Catherine (Kate) Creath to Harriet Creath, 20 June 1870, Owen M. Creath Papers.

25. Owen Creath to Harriet Creath and children, 2 Mar. 1862, Owen M. Creath Papers; Chester E. Bryan, ed., *History of Madison County, Ohio* (Indianapolis: B. F. Bowen, 1915), 673, 819; Ellen Jane Ruff obituary, *Cincinnati Enquirer*, 14 Feb. 2016, www.legacy.com/obituaries/cincinnati/obituary.aspx?pid=177711289.

26. Larkin Kendrick to Mary Catherine Kendrick, 21 Jan. 1862, 28 Jan. 1863, PC.1921, Larkin S. Kendrick Papers, SANC.

27. Larkin Kendrick to Mary Catherine Kendrick, 28 Apr. [1863], 21 Aug. 1863, and Exemption from Service Notice for Larkin Kendrick, 22 Feb. 1865, Larkin S. Kendrick Papers. Injury is reconstructed from Larkin Kendrick to Mary Catherine Kendrick, 28 Jan. 1863, and T. D. Lattimore, "Thirty-Fourth Regiment," in *Histories of the Several Regiments and Battalions from North Carolina*, vol. 2, ed. Walter Clark (Goldsboro, NC: Nash Brothers, 1901), 581–590.

28. Larkin Kendrick to Mr. Hill and Mary Catherine Kendrick, 19 June 1872, Larkin S. Kendrick Papers.

29. Typescripts of Hettie Wallace to "My Dear Niece," 18 Dec. 1872, Ruth Ownbey to "Dear Cousin," 6 Apr. 1874, and John O. Wallace to "Cousin Kendrick," 7 Apr. 1874, Larkin S. Kendrick Papers.

30. Emeline Putnam and J. G. Hill to Larkin and Mary Catherine Kendrick, 28 June 1868, Larkin S. Kendrick Papers; J. Timothy Cole, *The Forest City Lynching of 1900: Populism, Racism, and White Supremacy in Rutherford County, North Carolina* (Jefferson, NC: McFarland, 2003), quotations on 125, 126; Mark L. Bradley, *Bluecoats and Tar Heels: Soldiers and Civilians in Reconstruction North Carolina* (Lexington: University Press of Kentucky, 2009), 237–246, quotation on 238. Also see Paul Yandle, "'Resistless Uprising'? Thomas Dixon's Uncle and Western North Carolinians as Klansmen and Statesmen," in *Reconstructing Appalachia: The Civil War's Aftermath*, ed. Andrew L. Slap (Lexington: University Press of Kentucky, 2010), 135–161; and Allen W. Trelease, *White Terror: The Ku Klux Klan Conspiracy and Southern Reconstruction* (New York: Harper & Row, 1971), 336–348.

31. Raymond A. Cook, *Thomas Dixon* (New York: Twayne, 1974), 23.

32. Larkin Kendrick to Mary Catherine Kendrick, 20 Jan. 1862, Larkin S. Kendrick Papers; Abraham Lincoln, "Address Delivered at the Dedication of the Ceme-

tery at Gettysburg," in *The Collected Works of Abraham Lincoln*, vol. 7, ed. Roy P. Basler (New Brunswick, NJ: Rutgers University Press, 1953), 23; Barack Obama, "Remarks by the President in Farewell Address," 10 Jan. 2017, https://obama whitehouse.archives.gov/the-press-office/2017/01/10/remarks-president -farewell-address.

Acknowledgments

This book would not have been possible without the many descendants of Civil War–era Americans who preserved their family letters and ultimately entrusted them to university and historical society libraries. I am grateful to them and to the archivists and librarians who have stewarded those letters and made them available to researchers like me, especially those at the Alabama Department of Archives and History; Bentley Historical Library, University of Michigan; Connecticut Historical Society; David M. Rubenstein Rare Book & Manuscript Library, Duke University; DePauw University Archives; Dolph Briscoe Center for American History, University of Texas at Austin; Farmington (Connecticut) Public Library; Huntington Library; Indiana Historical Society; Louis Round Wilson Special Collections Library, University of North Carolina at Chapel Hill; Maine Historical Society; Manuscripts and Archives, Yale University; Ohio History Center; Spencer County (Indiana) Public Library; State Archives of North Carolina; State Historical Society of Iowa; Stuart A. Rose Manuscript, Archives, and Rare Book Library, Emory University; Tennessee State Library and Archives; U.S. Army Heritage and Education Center; Watkinson Library, Trinity College; and W. S. Hoole Special Collections Library, University of Alabama.

I am indebted to fellow researchers who shared their knowledge and labors with me, most notably John Coski, for transcriptions of the former "Soldier Letters" collection of the Confederate Memorial Literary Society, which would have been otherwise inaccessible to me during its transfer to the Virginia Historical Society; Michael Ellis, for generously sharing transcriptions from the prodigious Corpus of American Civil War Letters he has spent years developing, and for his keen insights about those letters as well; Daryl Lovell, a descendant of Thornton Clark and historian of Spencer County, Indiana, for sharing parts of his private collection with me; and Hanson Meyer, another Clark descendant, for granting me access to his extensive family tree.

This book could not have been written without the generous support of the National Endowment for the Humanities, especially the Public Scholar Program. (Any views, findings, conclusions, or recommendations expressed in this book do not necessarily reflect those of the National Endowment for the Humanities.) My research was also supported by grants from the American Philosophical Society; the Summersell Center for the Study of the South at the University of Alabama; and the Willson Center for Humanities and Arts at the University of Georgia.

Much of this book was written while I was in residence at DePauw University as the Nancy Schaenen Visiting Scholar at the Janet Prindle Institute for Ethics. There, I benefited from discussions among the participants in the "Hearing the Inarticulate" summer seminar; the research assistance of Gillian Campbell, Megan Hadley, and Emma Mazurek; and the gracious support of the Prindle Institute staff, especially Andy Cullison and Linda Clute. I also am grateful for the collegiality of many DePauw faculty during my time there, especially Harry Brown and David Gellman.

I have benefited from many helpful questions, comments, and suggestions offered by fellow scholars and audience members at lectures and presentations based on the research for this book, including at the Harry Ransom Center at the University of Texas at Austin; Indiana University–Purdue University, Indianapolis; the University of Georgia; West Virginia University; and the Civil War Caucus of the Midwest Modern Language Association, whose members have provided an incomparable intellectual community for nearly a decade.

At Trinity College, the Dean of Faculty's office, the Trinity Institute for Interdisciplinary Studies, and the English Department have provided material support for this book. Dina Anselmi, Cheryl Greenberg, Melanie Stein, and Chloe Wheatley deserve special thanks for helping me balance my commitments to Trinity and to this book, as does Allison Read for shoring up my sense of balance in all things. My treasured colleagues in the English Department have encouraged my work throughout the past ten years. I am grateful to Christina Bolio and Margaret Grasso for assistance with everything under the sun and for making the department a place of both efficiency and good cheer.

I am profoundly fortunate to have a professional community with boundless capacity to inspire, encourage, challenge, and guide me. These collaborators, mentors, and friends have done much more to shape me as a thinker and writer than I can express by simply naming them here: Kathleen Diffley, Harvey Graff, Jay Grossman, Grey Gundaker, Cole Hutchison, Paul Lauter, Cody Marrs, Hilary Moss, Elizabeth Renker, Jane Schultz, Julia Stern, and Tim Sweet. To several such people who also devoted their time to reading and commenting on my manuscript, I owe a signal debt for helping make this book what it is: David Blight, Marcy Dinius, Ian Finseth, Scott Gac, Alan Hager, Joan Hedrick, Martha Hodes, Lou Masur, Lida Maxwell, David Rosen, Ron Spencer, and an anonymous reader for the press. Where the book has fallen short of what they, in their acuity, helped me envision, it is only because I fell short of realizing it.

It has been a privilege to work with Joyce Seltzer, without whose encouragement I might never have conceived this book. I also thank the many people who shepherded the book through the process of publication, especially Kathleen Drummy, Tamara Gaskell, Deborah Grahame-Smith, and Louise Robbins.

My wife, Alison Ehrmann Hager, took our kids to the MOOseum (brought to you by the Alabama Cattlemen's Association) in downtown Montgomery, and calmed them when they were terrified by an animatronic cow, so that I could read the letters of Thomas and Martha Warrick. My parents, Alan and Kathie Hager, gallivanted with them in the children's garden at the Huntington while I discovered Isaac and Sarah Mann. My mother-in-law, Lisa Contino, cooked Bolognese for them so that I could work through a few more of Thornton Clark's letters. (Out of such labors are books made.) To those children, Silvia and Josephine Hager—my Mary Creath, my Kate—and to their futures, I dedicate this book. But it is for my partners in preparing them for that future that I am thankful most of all. Especially Ali, with whom, whatever worries loom, I have unity, constancy, and peace.

Illustration Credits

14 Henry J. H. Thompson Papers, 1862–1865, RUB Bay 0037:09, box 1, c.1, folder 1 (letters 1862–63), David M. Rubenstein Rare Book & Manuscript Library, Duke University, Durham, NC.

20 Frederick Hooker Letters, MS 57315, folder 1, Connecticut Historical Society, Hartford.

32 Alonzo Reed Letters, 1864–1866, sec. A, box 110, items 1–21 c.1, David M. Rubenstein Rare Book & Manuscript Library, Duke University, Durham, NC.

81 Caleb Henry Phillips Collection, MSS 1672, box 6476, folder 29, W. S. Hoole Special Collections Library, University of Alabama, Tuscaloosa.

104 Letters from Isaac Mann to Susan Deaver Mann, 1862–1864, Isaac Mann Civil War letters (HM 21882–21908), Huntington Library, San Marino, CA.

111 Owen M. Creath Papers, 1857–1890, MSS 1532, folder 13, Ohio Historical Society, Columbus. Reproduction courtesy of the Ohio History Connection.

127 Owen M. Creath Papers, 1857–1890, MSS 1532, folder 19, Ohio Historical Society, Columbus. Reproduction courtesy of the Ohio History Connection.

173 Courtesy of Daryl Lovell.

189 George E. Worden Civil War Letters, Indiana Historical Society, Indianapolis.

199 John (Johannes) Lehman Correspondence, 1862, folder 8, Lehman Family Papers, Bentley Historical Library, University of Michigan, Ann Arbor.

220 Frederick Hooker Letters, MS 57315, folder 3, Connecticut Historical Society, Hartford.

234 PC.1825, Poteet-Dickson Letters, courtesy of the State Archives of North Carolina, Raleigh.

Index

Page numbers in *italics* refer to images.

Barrett, Cpl. Milton, 72

Barrow, Cpl. Henry, 43

"Battle Cry of Freedom" (Root), 64

"Battle Hymn of the Republic" (Howe), 63–64

Battles: Bull Run, 1, 106, 183; the Seven Days, 55, 66–67; Gettysburg, 57, 95, 181, 264; Shiloh, 66–67, 126–128, 206–207, 257–258; Chancellorsville, 73, 95, 212; Perryville, 82; Seven Pines, 94; Stones River, 97, 145, 149, 168; Antietam, 99, 197; Chickamauga, 166, 167–168, 171, 252; Fredericksburg, 176, 198, 225, 260, 309n43; Rappahannock Station, 177; the Crater, 184; the Wilderness, 203, 217, 245; Spotsylvania Courthouse, 217–219; Cold Harbor, 219, 221–222

Beauregard, Gen. P. G. T., 126, 231

Beecher, Charles, 147

Bermuda Hundred, Virginia, 231

Berry, Stephen, 269n3

Birth of a Nation, The, 263

Blacksmithing, 120, 124

Blackstone, William, 33

Blaisdell, Betsy: leaves blank space, 72; strain in letters of, 150–154, 156–164; urges Hiram to seek furlough, 213–214, 215; discourages desertion, 216; on capture of Richmond, 244; postwar life of, 254–255; opposes war, 304n52

Blaisdell, Pvt. Hiram: blank space left for, 72; strain in letters of, 150–154; comforts Betsy, 160–162; urged to seek furlough, 213–214, 215; on capture of Richmond, 244; postwar life of, 254–255; on freed slaves, 304n52

Blank space, 71–72, 287n24

Blount, Elizabeth, 178–179

Boardman, Pvt. Oliver, 297n46

Bonner, Robert, 272n16

Botume, Elizabeth Hyde, 30, 37

Bourne, William Oland, 248

Bradstreet, Anne, 195

Bragg, Gen. Braxton, 126, 166, 167

Brannan, Gen. John, 167–168

Brown, Albert F., 255, 256

Buell, Gen. Don Carlos, 126

Bulkley, Will H., 83–84, 86

Burnell, Pvt. Henry, 57

Burning letters, 43, 130–131, 132–133

Burns, Ken, 2

Burnside, Gen. Ambrose, 239

Business, by letter, 137–139

Butler, Ann, 108–109

Butler, Gen. Benjamin, 231

Butler, Pvt. William, 109

Cameron, Cpl. Bluford Alexander, 174

Camp Douglas, 154, 243, 244

Camp Joe Reynolds. *See* Camp Morton

Camp Morton, 68–71, 77–78, 168, 252

Camp Sumpter. *See* Andersonville prison camp

Canada: and draft-dodging, 151, 153; Confederate attack from, 154–159

Captured letters, 93–101

Channing, William Ellery, 90

Character: handwriting as symbol of, 44, 281n49; homesickness as sign of weak, 190

Chesnut, Mary, 95–96, 99

Chidlow, Brother, 86, 87, 91

Children: learning to write, 43, 46–47, 91, 109–110, 170; illness and death of, 51, 59–60, 62, 125–126, 146, 150, 210, 230; letters to and from, 76, 109–112, 114, 115–117, 170–171, 205–206

Christianity, 83–86, 183, 194–195, 207, 250

Civil War, The, 1–2

Civil War letters: volume of, 4–5; content of, 5–6, 74–76, 270n9, 285n13, 287–288n28; literary quality of, 7–8, 9–10, 28–29, 30, 271n12, 272n16; scholarship on, 8–9; and literacy education, 12–13, 26; as intimate exchange, 14–15; apparent hollowness of, 52–53; preservation of women's, 107–109, 295–296n31; of married versus unmarried men, 294n20; changes to, 295n31; censorship of, 305n9

Civil War literature: articulateness of, 3; Civil War letters as, 7–8, 9–10, 271n12, 272n16; defined, 272n17

Clansman, The, 263–264

Clark, Alice, 91, 170, 255–256

Clark, Annie, 253